FREE VIDEO  FREE VIDEO

SIFT Essential Test Tips Video from Trivium Test Prep!

Dear Customer,

Thank you for purchasing from Trivium Test Prep! We're honored to help you prepare for your SIFT exam.

To show our appreciation, we're offering a **FREE *SIFT Essential Test Tips* Video by Trivium Test Prep.*** Our video includes 35 test preparation strategies that will make you successful on the SIFT. All we ask is that you email us your feedback and describe your experience with our product. Amazing, awful, or just so-so: we want to hear what you have to say!

To receive your **FREE *SIFT Essential Test Tips* Video**, please email us at 5star@ triviumtestprep.com. Include "Free 5 Star" in the subject line and the following information in your email:

1. The title of the product you purchased.
2. Your rating from 1 – 5 (with 5 being the best).
3. Your feedback about the product, including how our materials helped you meet your goals and ways in which we can improve our products.
4. Your full name and shipping address so we can send your **FREE *SIFT Essential Test Tips* Video**.

If you have any questions or concerns please feel free to contact us directly at 5star@trivium-testprep.com.

Thank you!

- Trivium Test Prep Team

*To get access to the free video please email us at 5star@triviumtestprep.com, and please follow the instructions above.

SIFT Study Guide 2019–2020

SIFT Test Prep and Practice Test Questions for the U.S. Army's Selection Instrument for Flight Training Exam

Copyright © 2019 by Trivium Test Prep

ALL RIGHTS RESERVED. By purchase of this book, you have been licensed one copy for personal use only. No part of this work may be reproduced, redistributed, or used in any form or by any means without prior written permission of the publisher and copyright owner.

USAREC was not involved in the creation or production of this product, is not in any way affiliated with Trivium Test Prep, and does not sponsor or endorse this product. All test names (and their acronyms) are trademarks of their respective owners. This study guide is for general information and does not claim endorsement by any third party.

Printed in the United States of America.

TABLE OF CONTENTS

ONLINE RESOURCES   i

INTRODUCTION   iii

1 SIMPLE DRAWINGS   1

2 HIDDEN FIGURES   3

3 AVIATION INFORMATION   5
- The Physics of Flight   5
- Rotary-Wing Aircraft   15
- The Four Fundamental Flight Maneuvers   20
- Flight Instruments   24
- Airports and Flight Protocols   32
- Aviation History   36

4 SPATIAL APPERCEPTION   39
- Identifying Pitch   39
- Identifying Bank   41
- Identifying Heading   41

5 READING COMPREHENSION   43
- The Main Idea   43
- Supporting Details   47
- Text Structure   52
- Drawing Conclusions   54
- Understanding the Author   56
- Vocabulary in Context   63

6 MATH SKILLS   67
- Types of Numbers   67
- Positive and Negative Numbers   69
- Order of Operations   70
- Units of Measurement   72
- Decimals and Fractions   74
- Ratios   78
- Proportions   79
- Percentages   80
- Exponents and Radicals   82
- Algebraic Expressions   85
- Operations with Expressions   86
- Linear Equations   88
- Properties of Shapes   92
- Three-Dimensional Shapes   107

7 MECHANICAL COMPREHENSION   109
- Newton's Laws   109
- Forces   111
- Simple Machines   115

8 PRACTICE TEST   119
- Answer Key   175

SPC Werner-Gillu

ONLINE RESOURCES

To help you fully prepare for the SIFT, Trivium Test Prep includes online resources with the purchase of this study guide.

Practice Test

In addition to the practice test included in this book, we also offer an online exam. Since many exams today are computer-based, getting to practice your test-taking skills on the computer is a great way to prepare.

Flashcards

A convenient supplement to this study guide, Trivium's e-flashcards enable you to review important terms easily on your computer or smartphone.

Cheat Sheets

Review the core skills you need to master with easy-to-read Cheat Sheets. Topics covered include Numbers and Operations, Algebra, Geometry, Statistics and Probability, and Grammar.

From Stress to Success

Watch *From Stress to Success*, a brief but insightful YouTube video that offers the tips, tricks, and secrets experts use to score higher on the exam.

Reviews

Leave a review, send us helpful feedback, or sign up for Trivium's promotions—including free books!

To access these materials, please enter the following URL into your browser:

www.triviumtestprep.com/sift-online-resources

SPC Werner-Gille

SPC Werner-Gille

INTRODUCTION

Congratulations on choosing to take the Selection Instrument for Flight Training (SIFT) exam! By purchasing this book, you've taken an important step on your path to joining the military.

This guide will provide you with a detailed overview of the SIFT, so you know exactly what to expect on exam day. We'll take you through all the concepts covered on the exam and give you the opportunity to test your knowledge with practice questions. Even if it's been a while since you last took a major exam, don't worry; we'll make sure you're more than ready!

WHAT IS THE SIFT?

The SIFT exam is required for acceptance to the US Army Warrant Officer Flight Training (WOFT) program. The US Army Personnel Test Program Office replaced the Alternate Flight Aptitude Selection Test (AFAST) with the SIFT exam in 2013. Results and qualification standards are currently monitored and controlled by the US Army Aviation Branch and US Army Recruiting Command. Civilians who possess at least a high school diploma and current military members may attempt the SIFT and complete an application packet for consideration to the WOFT program.

The exam is designed to assess your knowledge and aptitude in mechanical concepts, aviation-related terminology, and basic flight rules and aerodynamic principles, in addition to your familiarity with helicopter components and functions.

Candidates may take the exam at Military Entrance Processing Stations (MEPS), US Army Education Centers, Reserve Officer Training Corps (ROTC) units, and select US Army personnel testing centers. Allow at least two and a half hours to complete the exam, which includes time for candidate verification and test registration, taking the exam, and an authorized break as designated by the test proctor.

COMPUTER ADAPTIVE TESTING

Computer adaptive testing (CAT) allows the test administrators to get a more complete view of your skills in less time and with fewer questions. These tests start with a question of average difficulty. If you answer this question correctly, the next question will be harder; if you answer it incorrectly, the next one will be easier. This continues as you go through the section, with questions getting harder or easier based on how well you perform. Once you've answered enough questions for the computer to determine your score, that section of the test will end.

Often you will be able to immediately see your score after taking a CAT exam. You will also probably answer fewer questions than if you'd taken a paper-and-pencil test, and the section will take less time. However, you will not be able to go back and check or change your answers.

On the SIFT, the Math Skills Test and the Mechanical Comprehension Test are CAT tests.

WHAT'S ON THE SIFT?

The SIFT is only presented in a web-based format consisting of seven subtests. The first five subtests contain fixed questions where candidates get a set number of questions. The last two subtests use CAT where the difficulty of questions is presented to the candidate based on the correctness of previous answers. The time allowed for the last two subtests may vary due to the CAT format.

Your testing strategy is very important, as in certain areas it may or may not be to your advantage to make an educated guess on unanswered questions if time is about to expire. This is explained in further detail later, where the subtests are individually described.

The following table summarizes the subtests, approximate number of questions, and time limit allowed for each subtest.

What's on the SIFT?

SUBTEST	APPROXIMATE NUMBER OF QUESTIONS	TIME LIMIT
Simple Drawings	100	2 minutes
Hidden Figures	50	5 minutes
Army Aviation Information Test	40	30 minutes
Spatial Apperception Test	25	10 minutes
Reading Comprehension Test	20	30 minutes
Math Skills Test	Varies	40 minutes
Mechanical Comprehension Test	Varies	15 minutes
Total	235 multiple-choice questions + CAT tests	2 hours, 12 minutes

Simple Drawings (SD): asks you to select the odd item or figure in a series of images. You must work rapidly through the questions because of the two-minute time limit. DO NOT guess on questions; incorrect answers are subtracted from your overall score.

Hidden Figures (HF): asks you to identify a hidden image in a complex picture of shapes and lines. DO NOT guess on questions; incorrect answers are subtracted from your overall score.

Army Aviation Information Test (AAIT): measures your knowledge of helicopter flight concepts, theory of flight controls, and aircraft components. Make an educated guess for ALL questions; incorrect answers will NOT be subtracted from your overall score.

Spatial Apperception Test (SAT): asks you to identify views as seen from the cockpit, and visualize the corresponding orientation of the aircraft in three-dimensional images. Make an educated guess for ALL questions—incorrect answers will not be subtracted from your overall score.

Reading Comprehension Test (RCT): assesses your level of reading comprehension by testing your understanding of the text in word passages. You must demonstrate the process of eliminating answers as there is only one correct answer possible. Make an educated guess for all questions; incorrect answers will not be subtracted from your overall score.

Math Skills Test (MST): a CAT-formatted subtest that assesses your ability to compute mathematical equations and word problems derived from basic algebraic principles, order of operations, and geometric figures. You may also be asked to solve logical puzzles.

Mechanical Comprehension Test (MCT): a CAT-formatted subtest that assesses your knowledge of physics concepts as related to flight, such as air pressure and force. You must also solve problems using scientific formulas. It is recommended that you DO NOT randomly guess at unknown questions.

HOW IS THE SIFT SCORED?

SIFT scores are calculated on a range from 20 to 80 with 40 being a minimum qualifying score for WOFT at the time of publishing this study guide. The current mean score for accepted candidates is 50 with a standard deviation of 10. The US Aviation Branch and US Recruiting Command may adjust the qualifying level based on accession requirements.

Subtests are scored using a compensatory method; the effects of attaining a low score on one subtest may be reduced by receiving a high score on another subtest. There is no published weighted average identifying the importance of scoring high in any one subtest versus another.

Results from taking the SIFT are available immediately after completing the exam. The test control officer (TCO) will provide you with a score letter. Make sure the score letter is signed by the TCO before leaving the testing location.

RETAKING THE SIFT

Candidates may take the SIFT exam twice in a lifetime. Once the initial exam is completed, you must wait at least 180 days to pass before attempting a retest. Once you pass the SIFT test with a qualifying score, you may not retake the exam to attain a higher score. Likewise, if you fail to attain a qualifying score after taking the SIFT twice, you are barred from taking the SIFT again.

HOW IS THE SIFT ADMINISTERED?

Recruiters schedule civilian candidates for the SIFT once the WOFT initial qualification requirements are met. Military members may contact their local Education Center on post to register for the SIFT. The actual test dates vary among testing locations. Candidates will be notified of available test dates when they register to take the test.

On the date of the test, you must bring valid photo identification and your Social Security card to verify your identity. Personal bags and electronic devices such as cell phones and calculators are not allowed in the testing room. The test proctor will provide pencils and scratch paper for you to use to solve problems.

Getting to Know the United States Army

Candidates attain the rank of warrant officer upon completion of WOFT. Graduating with the rank of WO1, warrant officers may progress through the ranks up to WO5 during their career. Upon completion of WOFT, pilots are assigned to a specific rotary-wing aircraft and receive additional flight training. Although flight candidates get the opportunity to request specific aircraft assignments, eventual assignment is based on the Army's needs. During this additional training, pilots receive in-depth academics and hands-on experience in a multitude of subjects specific to that aircraft's role and mission, such as advanced flight planning, tactics, and gunnery qualification as required. Currently, the US Army encompasses the use of rotary- and fixed-wing aircraft. Assignment to fixed-wing and specialized-mission aircraft are reserved for only experienced US Army aviators. WOFT graduates are assigned to one of the following four types of helicopters:

- utility—for troop transport and medical evacuations
- cargo—to transport larger number of personnel or haul equipment internally or externally of aircraft
- attack—to deliver precise lethal force upon enemy locations
- observation—to scout locations and provide surveillance for follow on aircraft or ground movements

The US Army stations pilots worldwide to conduct aviation missions ranging from unit training to participation in multinational military operations as needed to protect our nation's interests.

The Military Recruitment Process

As stated before, the SIFT is just one requirement toward being qualified for attendance to the US Army WOFT program. To begin the recruitment process, civilians who possess at least a high school diploma may contact their local recruiter through their high school counselor or college adviser, or they may visit their local military recruitment center.

The process of being accepted to the WOFT program is much more complex than joining the military as enlisted (going to basic training) or even applying for attendance at Officer Candidate School. Each step is designed to ensure highly qualified candidates possess the determination, dedication, and stamina required to successfully complete the WOFT program. The WOFT program is very intense and will test all your personal characteristics, as well as your physical and mental abilities.

Once you contact your local recruiter, he or she will meet with you at the recruiting office, your school, or your home. During this meeting, the recruiter will conduct an interview to initiate the recruitment process. This process begins with the recruiter determining if you meet the basic qualification requirements. Expect a review of your education level, financial record, background investigation, interests, criminal record or drug history, height and weight, age, and citizenship. Once basic qualifications have been established, the recruiter schedules you to take the required aptitude exams (to include the SIFT exam), a MEPS physical exam, a Class 1A flight physical, and a physical fitness exam. You will develop and submit a resume and receive multiple letters of recommendations as part of your application packet. You must be able to apply for and obtain an interim secret security clearance. After these standards, you will meet with your recruiter to discuss your testing scores and any medical issue that may preclude your participation in the WOFT program. The last major step is attending an interview by a local battalion board. Your recruiter and recommendations from current Army warrant officers will prepare you for this interview.

After you are accepted to the WOFT program, your recruiter can provide you with possible entry dates for your training.

Your recruiter can answer any concerns or questions you have along the way; however, do not expect him or her to ensure your application packet is complete. Take the initiative to research these requirements, gain knowledge from military aviation personnel, and know your deadlines to ensure you are putting your best foot forward.

ABOUT THIS GUIDE

This guide will help you master the most important test topics and also develop critical test-taking skills. We have built features into our books to prepare you for your tests and increase your score. Along with a detailed summary of the test's format, content, and scoring, we offer an in-depth overview of the content knowledge required to pass the test. In the review you'll find sidebars that provide interesting information, highlight key concepts, and review content so that you can solidify your understanding of the exam's concepts. You can also test your knowledge with sample questions throughout the text and practice questions that reflect the content and format of the SIFT. We're pleased you've chosen Trivium Test Prep to be a part of your military journey!

SIMPLE DRAWINGS

T he Simple Drawings test evaluates how quickly a candidate can identify differences between images or drawings. Each question will present five shapes marked A – E. Four of these shapes will be the same, and one will be different. The correct answer choice will be the shape that is different.

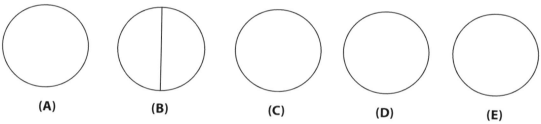

(A)   **(B)**   **(C)**   **(D)**   **(E)**

Figure 1.1. Example Problem

Candidates are given two minutes to answer one hundred questions, which equates to just over one second per question. Obviously, speed is the most important factor for doing well on Simple Drawings. The questions themselves are simple—the challenge is to answer them as quickly as possible. There is nothing to study or memorize for the Simple Drawings chapter. The best way to prepare is simply to practice as much as possible.

🔒————

Do not hesitate or spend too much time on a single question.

Examples

1.

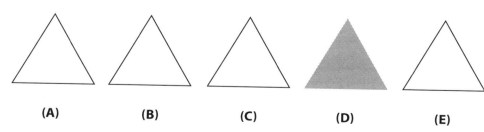

(A)   **(B)**   **(C)**   **(D)**   **(E)**

Answer:

(D)

2.

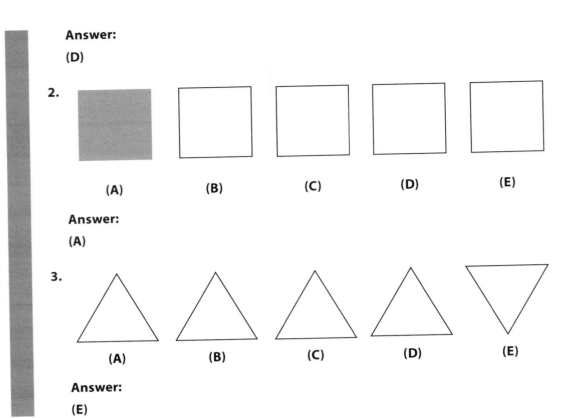

(A)　　　　(B)　　　　(C)　　　　(D)　　　　(E)

Answer:

(A)

3.

(A)　　　　(B)　　　　(C)　　　　(D)　　　　(E)

Answer:

(E)

HIDDEN FIGURES

The Hidden Figures chapter of the test requires candidates to identify a specific shape hidden within a more complex figure. Each question will present a figure composed of overlapping lines and shapes, and each set of five questions will be accompanied by an answer bank lettered A – E. The shapes in the answer bank may appear in one, multiple, or none of the question figures.

This chapter includes fifty questions to be answered in five minutes, meaning candidates will have about six seconds per question. As with all the spatial reasoning chapters on the exam, speed will be the most important factor for doing well on Hidden Figures.

Practice is the best way to improve on the Hidden Figures test. The more comfortable candidates are with the test format, the more questions can be answered. Here are a few strategies for answering questions quickly.

- Candidates should work methodically, looking at shape A, then examining each of the five question figures for that shape before moving on to shape B, and so on.

- Candidates should look for any unique angles or shapes within the answer choices, then look for the same angle or shape in the question figures.

- Some shapes in the answer choices may not show up in the questions, so candidates should move on quickly if a shape does not appear.

The hidden figure in each drawing will always have the same size and position as the shape in the answer choice.

Example

(A) (B) (C) (D) (E)

1.

2.

3.

4.

5.

Answers:

1. (B) **2.** (C) **3.** (E) **4.** (A) **5.** (D)

AVIATION INFORMATION

THE PHYSICS OF FLIGHT

A successful aircraft flight is the result of an understanding of the scientific theories and principles involved in moving 300 to 400 tons of machinery through the skies at speeds ranging from 100 to 750 miles per hour (mph). Newton's laws of motion, Newton's law of universal gravitation, and Bernoulli's principle, along with weight, balance, the factors that constitute the flight envelope, and the axes of an aircraft all play a part in aeronautics.

Newton's Laws of Motion

Isaac Newton's three laws of motion detail the fundamental mechanics of motion. The first law focuses on inertia, the second law defines when an accelerated motion is applied to a force, and the third law explains the relationship of motion between any two objects.

NEWTON'S FIRST LAW OF MOTION, also called the LAW OF INERTIA, states that an object at rest will stay at rest, and an object in motion will remain in motion at a constant velocity unless acted upon by an unbalanced force. The unbalanced force may be any force, such as gravity or friction. For example, a ball sitting on the floor will remain still unless a force is exerted upon it—a kick from a foot, a push from a hand, or a strong wind moving it.

Inertia is the tendency of an object to resist changes in velocity whether the object is in motion or motionless.

There are four types of friction:

- **SLIDING**, or **KINETIC**, **FRICTION** results when the surface of one object slides along the surface of another object. This is commonly seen when pushing a solid object, such as a plate or book along a tabletop.
- **FLUID FRICTION** is the resistance on an object when it is moved through either air (gas) or water (liquid). This is witnessed when a fish moves through water, a bird flies through air, or an airplane creates drag.
- **ROLLING FRICTION** is similar to sliding friction except rolling friction occurs when an object rolls—instead of slides—across a surface. This is observed when a bowling ball rolls down an alley. The ball, once pushed, moves at a

particular rate, or velocity, while also resisting that movement due to qualities of the surface on which it is rolling.

- **STATIC FRICTION** is what keeps an object at rest when that object is acted upon by an external force. A trash can initially remains in place due to static friction when an attempt is made to drag it across a floor.

As an example of the four frictions, if a car is traveling at 40 mph, the passengers and contents inside the car are also moving at a rate of 40 mph, until the driver applies the brakes to avoid a collision with a tree. If the passengers are not restrained by seat belts, the full effects of a collision pass from the vehicle to them as well as to the contents of the vehicle. The tires of the vehicle rolling along the road overcome rolling friction. The vehicle counteracts fluid friction from any oncoming wind. When the driver applies the brakes, the wheels may stop rolling but the car skids along the surface of the road, exemplifying sliding friction. At the moment of the car's impact with the tree, objects inside the vehicle overcome static friction as they scatter.

NEWTON'S SECOND LAW OF MOTION states that when a body is acted upon by a constant force, its resulting acceleration is inversely proportional to the mass of the body and directly proportional to the applied force.

The net force of an object is equal to the product of the mass of the object and the acceleration. The equation to determine the amount of force is $F = ma$. One unit of force (F) is defined as Newtons (N). Mass is weighed in kilograms (kg) and acceleration is measured in meters per second per second (m/s/s or m/s^2).

NEWTON'S THIRD LAW OF MOTION states that if two objects interact, the force exerted by the first object on the second object is equal in magnitude and opposite in direction to the force exerted by the second object on the first object.

For example, the force exerted by a tennis racket hitting a tennis ball is equal in magnitude and opposite the force exerted by the ball on the tennis racket. Likewise, during a launch of a rocket into space, the gases expelled under the rocket exert enough force to cause the rocket to lift off the launchpad in the opposite direction.

Example

Consider an object acted on by only two forces, as shown below. If the magnitudes of F_1 and F_2 are equal, which of the following statements is true?

(A) The velocity of the object must be zero.

(B) The velocity of the object must be constant.

(C) The velocity of the object must be increasing.

(D) The velocity of the object must be decreasing.

(E) The object must remain stationary.

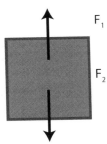

Answers:

(A) is incorrect. An object experiencing a net force of zero can be in motion.

(B) is correct. The velocity of an object experiencing a net force of zero will remain constant (meaning its acceleration is zero).

(C) is incorrect. The velocity of an object experiencing a net force of zero cannot change.

(D) is incorrect. The velocity of an object experiencing a net force of zero cannot change.

(E) is incorrect. An object experiencing a net force of zero can be in motion.

Newton's Law of Universal Gravitation

Isaac Newton's law of universal gravitation states that a particle attracts every other particle in the universe with a force that is directly proportional to the product of their masses and inversely proportional to the square of the distance between them. This law helps scientists understand the effects of gravity on aircraft during flight, because the gravitational force between two objects increases with mass and decreases with distance.

Equation: $F_g = G\dfrac{m_1 m_2}{d^2}$

F: unit of force (N) of gravity
G: gravitational constant value (e.g., $6.673 \times 10^{-11}\ \mathrm{m^3\,kg^{-1}\,s^{-2}}$)
m_1: mass of object 1
m_2: mass of object 2
d: distance in meters between the centers of both objects

Example

Consider two objects a distance *d* apart. According to Newton's law of universal gravitation, what happens to the force between the two objects if the distance (*d*) is increased by a factor of 4?

(A) The force decreases by a factor of 4.

(B) The force increases by a factor of 4.

(C) The force increases by a factor of 2.

(D) The force decreases by a factor of 16.

(E) The force decreases by a factor of 32.

Answer:

(D) is correct. In the equation for Newton's law of universal gravitation, , increasing *d* by a factor of 4 decreases the value of F_g by a factor of d^2, or 16.

Bernoulli's Principle

Mathematician and physicist Daniel Bernoulli devised the following principle in relation to hydrodynamics: within a horizontal flow of fluid, points of faster fluid speed will experience less pressure than points of slower fluid speed.

This principle is imperative when analyzing the flow of hydraulic fluids through an aircraft. An accurate pressure flow of fluids is essential to the intricate operation of braking and flight control systems.

Bernoulli's principle also applies to airflow during the basic phases of flight: takeoff, in-flight, and landing. The curvature of an airplane wing causes air to pass faster over the top of the wing (creating a lower pressure area) than under the wing (a higher pressure

Drag develops from friction and changes in air pressure, which cause an aircraft to slow down. Inputs to the flight controls affect weight, lift, thrust, and drag, resulting in the aircraft speeding up, slowing down, and/or gaining or losing altitude.

area). During takeoff, this produces the lift an airplane requires. During flight and when landing, the aircraft must compensate for and utilize all four forces of flight: WEIGHT (the force of gravity pushing the aircraft down), LIFT (the force required to raise the aircraft), THRUST (the force applied in order to move the aircraft forward), and DRAG (the force that slows the aircraft down in preparation for landing).

Example

Which statement is true about fluid pressure according to Bernoulli's principle?

(A) Fluids moving at a point in a horizontal pipe at a higher speed have lower pressure than fluids moving at a point at a slower speed.

(B) Fluids moving at a point in a horizontal pipe at a higher speed have higher pressure than fluids moving at a point at a slower speed.

(C) Fluids moving along a vertical pipe at a slower speed have higher pressure than fluids moving along at a higher speed.

(D) Horizontal and vertical pipe fluid pressure levels do not change.

(E) The fluid pressure at constricting points along a pipe does not differ from the fluid pressure at free-flowing areas of that pipe.

Answers:

(A) is correct. This statement is congruent with Bernoulli's principle.

(B) is incorrect. This statement is the opposite of Bernoulli's principle.

(C) is incorrect. Bernoulli's principle applies to the horizontal flow of fluid.

(D) is incorrect. Bernoulli's principle applies to the horizontal flow of fluid.

(E) is incorrect. This statement contradicts Bernoulli's principle.

Aircraft Weight and Balance

The calculation of an aircraft's weight and balance must be identified during preflight. It is important that the combination of passengers, baggage, usable and unusable fuel or fluids, and cargo are within established weight and balance limits. A predetermined *empty weight center of gravity (EWCG)* is provided by the aircraft's manufacturer along with a weight limit, which is specific to each aircraft.

The following are acronyms of other weight specifications:

- MANUFACTURER'S EMPTY WEIGHT (**MEW**) is the total weight of the aircraft as it was built. This includes systems and components required for the aircraft to operate. It does not include the weight of baggage, passengers, or either usable or unusable fuel or fluids.

Usable fuel is the total amount of fuel expected for taxi/ground movements, flight time, and reserve fuel requirements. **Unusable fuel** is the amount of fuel that cannot get to the engine.

- OPERATING EMPTY WEIGHT (**OEW**) is the MEW plus the weight of the crew, fluids, unusable fuel, and the equipment required for flight. It does not include baggage, passengers, or usable fuel.

- ALL-UP WEIGHT (**AUW**), or AIRCRAFT GROSS WEIGHT (**AGW**), is the total aircraft weight at any given moment during a flight. The

AUW decreases as fuel and fluids are consumed during the operation of the flight.

- **MAXIMUM LANDING WEIGHT (MLW)** is an aircraft's weight limit for landing. Exceeding this weight increases stress on the landing gear and may affect the distance required for a safe landing.

- **MAXIMUM ZERO FUEL WEIGHT (MZFW)** is the permissible weight of an aircraft with its contents and includes unusable fuel. The total MZFW excludes the weight of usable fuel on board and any consumable fluids.

- **MAXIMUM TAKEOFF WEIGHT (MTOW)** is an aircraft's weight limit for takeoff. Exceeding this limit increases the power required for takeoff, lengthens the runway distance needed for a successful lift off, and places excess stress on the aircraft structure.

- **MAXIMUM RAMP WEIGHT (MRW)** is the weight limit for an aircraft to taxi or be towed on the ground.

 Takeoff weight is determined by totaling the OEW, the cargo, the passengers, the baggage, and the taxi, flight, and reserve fuel requirements.

Example

Why is it important for an airplane not to exceed the MLW limit?

(A) All-up weight is calculated correctly.

(B) Most airplanes do not have to consider MLW.

(C) Undue stress may be placed on the landing gear system while landing.

(D) The airplane may not have enough fuel for the scheduled flight.

(E) The airplane can land on any runway length.

Answers:

(A) is incorrect. The all-up weight is the total weight of the airplane during all phases of flight, not just landing.

(B) is incorrect. Every pilot must consider MLW when assessing whether an aircraft's landing gear can support its weight and the runway is long enough for the aircraft's safe landing.

(C) is correct. By not exceeding the MLW, the pilot ensures that the landing gear will be able to support the weight of the aircraft and a longer than normal runway will not be required to land the plane.

(D) is incorrect. Although the MLW includes fuel on board, a pilot must ensure enough fuel is on board to reach his or her destination, or an alternate airfield if required.

(E) is incorrect. The MLW does not allow an airplane to land on any runway.

The Flight Envelope

The **FLIGHT ENVELOPE** encompasses the limits of speed, altitude, and angle of attack required by any aircraft to maintain a stable flight. An incorrect combination of these factors may result in a stall, during which the aircraft experiences a decrease in lift and a reduction in airspeed.

The **ANGLE OF ATTACK (AOA)** is the angle between the direction of the airflow against the wing and the **CHORD**, an imaginary reference line that extends from the leading edge to the trailing edge of the wing.

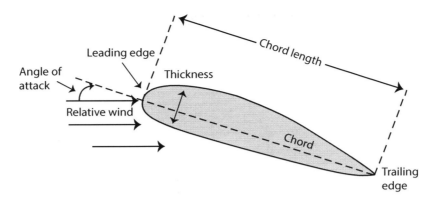

Figure 3.1. Identifying the AOA

An aircraft's airfoil section (wing) is designed for maximum lift and fuel efficiency. An aircraft wing is curved along its front, leading edge, which creates low pressure above and high pressure below as air passes by the wing. As air passes over the end of the wing, or over the end of a helicopter rotor blade, it changes direction, a deflection called DOWNWASH. This deflection of air downward helps produce lift. This is clearly visible when a helicopter hovers above water. The air deflected off the rotor blades accelerates downward, causing outward ripples in the water under the helicopter.

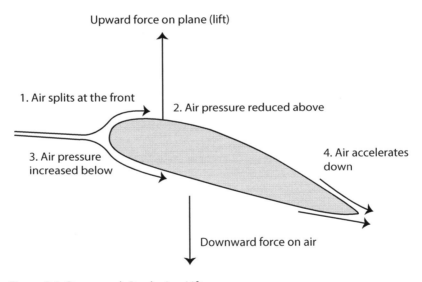

Figure 3.2. Downwash Producing Lift

The trailing edge of a wing has two control parts—ailerons and flaps—which extend outward and in opposite directions to aid the aircraft in rolling. The AILERONS are located from the midpoint of the trailing edge of the wing to the wing's tip. The FLAPS are located from the fuselage (main cabin body) to about the midpoint of the wing. Ailerons and flaps are in a closed position (flush against the wing's surface) during cruising altitude.

To land, the pilot first creates drag to slow the aircraft. SPOILERS are extended upward to help reduce airspeed. As the pilot approaches the runway, the wing flaps are progressively extended too. Once the aircraft is on the ground, raising the spoilers assists in slowing the airplane while the pilot also brakes. The following figure illustrates the positions of the flaps during takeoff, flight, and landing.

Best efficiency: for climbing, cruising, and descent

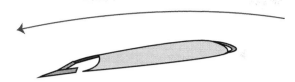

Increased wing area: for take off and initial climb

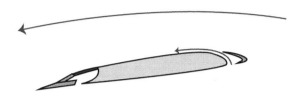

Maximum lift and high drag: approach and landing

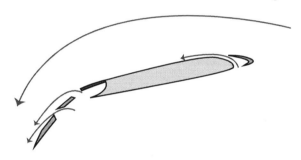

Maximum drag and reduced lift: for braking on runway

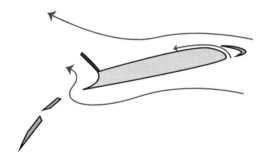

Figure 3.3. Wing Positions during Flight

Drag is air resistance experienced during flight:

- **PARASITE DRAG** is just that—any "parasite" on the structure of the aircraft: low air pressure in the tires, skin friction, or anything that increases turbulence on the aircraft. *Skin friction* refers to any rough spot on the skin of the aircraft structure. This, along with rivet heads that may project above the skin, causes resistance to the air current flowing across the wing.

- **PROFILE DRAG** is produced mainly by the shape of the aircraft. A smaller, slimmer aircraft reduces profile drag.
- **INDUCED DRAG** is when, at the back of the wing, air flowing rapidly across the top meets air flowing more slowly underneath, creating a vortex. This type of drag depends on the performance of the aircraft. When lift, airspeed, and AOA increase, induced drag automatically increases too.

Examples

1. What is an example of induced drag?

   (A) a decrease in airspeed

   (B) a decrease in AOA

   (C) a decrease in lift

   (D) an increase in AOA

   (E) the landing gear system set in the UP position

   Answers:

   (A) is incorrect. A decrease in airspeed does not result in a form of induced drag.

   (B) is incorrect. A decrease in the AOA also does not result in a form of induced drag.

   (C) is incorrect. A decrease in lift does not result in induced drag either.

   (D) is correct. An increase in AOA, lift, or airspeed will result in induced drag on an airplane.

   (E) is incorrect. A landing gear system in the UP position will not create induced drag.

2. When an airplane increases its lift, which statement is true about the air pressure flowing above and below its wings?

   (A) Air pressure is equal above and below the wings since the wings split the air evenly.

   (B) Air pressure is higher above the wings and lower below the wings.

   (C) Air pressure is lower above the wings and higher below the wings.

   (D) Air pressure causes the trailing edges of the wings to extend outward.

   (E) Both B and D are true.

   Answers:

   (A) is incorrect. Air pressure is not equal above and below the wings.

   (B) is incorrect. Air pressure is not higher above the wings, which would defeat the purpose of lift.

   (C) is correct. Air pressure is lower above the wings and higher below the wings, producing lift.

   (D) is incorrect. A pilot's input at the controls causes the wings to extend outward.

   (E) is incorrect. Both statements are incorrect.

The Axes of an Aircraft

Aircraft fly on a combination of three axes: longitudinal, lateral, and vertical. The LONGITUDINAL AXIS (roll) runs lengthwise from the nose (front) of the aircraft to the tail (rear) of the aircraft; the LATERAL AXIS (pitch) runs wingtip to wingtip; and the VERTICAL AXIS (yaw) runs perpendicular to the wings at the center of the aircraft.

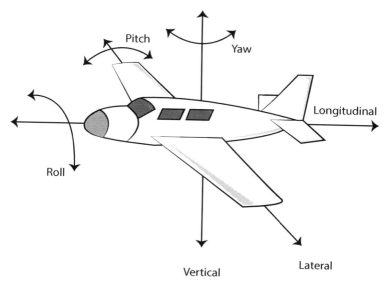

Figure 3.4. Aircraft Axes

Controlling the axes of the aircraft is necessary to keep the aircraft in TRIM, its desired position. ROLL along the aircraft's longitudinal axis is controlled by an adjustment of the ailerons, located at the trailing edges of the wings. PITCH—the lateral angle of ascent or descent—is controlled by the elevators, located in the rear portion of the horizontal tail assembly. YAW is controlled by the rudder, located in the rear portion of the vertical tail assembly; movement of the rudder causes the nose of the aircraft to move from side to side.

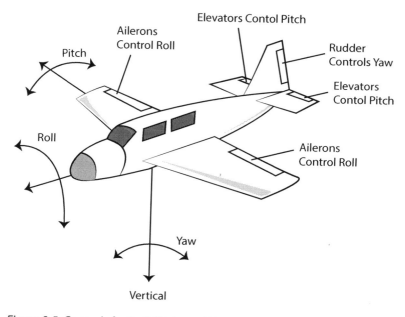

Figure 3.5. Controls for Roll, Pitch, and Yaw

Example

Which components increase the pitch of an airplane?

(A) the ailerons and elevators along the longitudinal axis

(B) the ailerons and rudder along the vertical axis

(C) the elevators along the lateral axis

(D) the elevators along the longitudinal axis

(E) the rudder along the longitudinal axis

Answers:

(A) is incorrect. The ailerons control roll along the longitudinal axis.

(B) is incorrect. Neither component nor the vertical axis affects the pitch of an airplane.

(C) is correct. The elevators may increase or decrease the pitch of an airplane along the lateral axis.

(D) is incorrect. The elevators affect the lateral axis, not the longitudinal axis.

(E) is incorrect. The rudder affects the yaw along the vertical axis.

The Atmosphere

Atmospheric pressure is an extreme concern for a pilot when flying. Air weighs approximately 14.7 pounds per square inch (psi), and flight controls are calibrated for a standard atmosphere. Humidity and low air density levels reduce an aircraft's capability for power, thrust, and lift. When the intake engines receive less air, the propellers are less efficient, and thin air applies less force on the wings, resulting in less than maximum lift.

Altitude, pressure, temperature, and humidity all affect the performance of an aircraft. The **PRESSURE ALTIMETER** in the cockpit is automatically calibrated for 29.92 inches of mercury (Hg). A pilot resets the pressure altitude indicator after departing an airfield to ensure the correct pressure altitude of the aircraft is displayed for the destination airfield (if it is different from the departure airfield). If this is not done, the aircraft may be at a lower altitude than what the altimeter displays.

All aircraft perform more efficiently in colder temperatures because the air is denser than when the air is warm. However, if the temperature drops too low, de-icing of the wings may be required during preflight procedures, extending the time required to complete preflight checks.

Example

How does air density affect the performance of an airplane?

(A) Low air density and humidity increase engine performance.

(B) High air density decreases engine performance.

(C) High air density increases engine performance.

(D) Low temperatures and low air density increase engine performance.

(E) Temperature and air density have no effect on engine performance.

Answers:

(A) is incorrect. Low air density and humidity decrease engine performance.

(B) is incorrect. High air density does not decrease engine performance.

(C) is correct. High air density increases engine performance.

(D) is incorrect. Low temperatures and low air density levels decrease engine performance.

(E) is incorrect. All aspects of the atmosphere affect the performance of airplane engines.

ROTARY-WING AIRCRAFT

Disclaimer: For the purposes of this section we will be discussing a helicopter with an underslung rotor system and skid-type landing gear. Popular versions of this type of aircraft include the Bell 206B3 (US Army TH-67) and the Bell 205 (US Army UH-1).

Rotary-Wing Aircraft Structure

The major components of a rotary-wing aircraft allow the aircraft to hover and fly directionally. Some of the most vital of these will be detailed in this section.

The **MAST** (also known as the **SHAFT**) is a long cylindrical component that extends vertically from the main rotor transmission up to the **MAIN ROTOR HUB**. The mast is responsible for the rotational drive force that turns the main rotor hub, where all components of the main rotor head are attached. These include the blade grips, the rotor blades, the pitch horn (or yoke), the stabilizer bar and weight (or flybar), and the teeter hinge (or trunnion).

The **BLADE GRIPS** connect the rotor blades to the rotor system. The primary responsibility of the blade grips is to allow the rotor blades to feather. *Feathering* is a term used to describe the change of the blades' angle relative to their rotation plane (also known as *angle of attack*).

ROTOR BLADES are most often made of metal, but as rotorcraft and composite technologies evolve, more rotor blades are being made of composites such as fiberglass or carbon fiber. The rotor blades give a rotary-wing aircraft lift. Shaped much like airplane wings, the airfoils of rotor blades, when spun along a rotational axis, ultimately create lift for the aircraft.

The **PITCH HORN** (or **YOKE**) extends perpendicular to the main rotor blades. It connects directly to the blade grips and stabilizer bar and receives control inputs from the pitch links. Its job is to collect control input from the pilot and translate that input into force, moving the blade grips. This force feathers the blades, or changes their angle of attack.

The **STABILIZER BAR AND WEIGHT** (or **FLYBAR**) help to maintain a constant plane of rotation for the rotor blades. The stabilizer bar is connected to the swashplate (described more fully later in this section) via a series of mechanical linkages, which combine with the stabilizer bar to dampen any over-control by the pilot as well as help the aircraft weather extreme wind gusts, thereby reducing pilot workload.

The **TEETER HINGE** (also known as the **TRUNNION**) connects the mast to the main rotor hub. The teeter hinge allows the rotor hub and blades to flap up or down depending on

The twisting movement of helicopter blade grips is due to a component installed inside them. Wire is wrapped several hundred times around two opposing spindles and then completely covered in a flexible polymer that forms a blade grip. As blade grips twist on their ball bearings, these internal wire tension-torsion (TT) straps work like large rubber bands to prevent centrifugal force from allowing the blades to be pulled from the rotor head. Without these straps the rotational forces exerted on the rotor blades would be so great they would fly off in opposite directions.

control input and aerodynamic forces. As one blade rises, the teeter hinge enables the opposite blade to fall in its plane of rotation, much like the up and down of a teeter-totter.

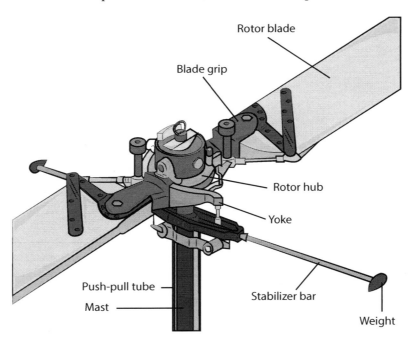

Figure 3.6. Main Rotor System Assembly

Below the mast and the main rotor hub's components is the main rotor transmission. Mounted to this transmission is the **SWASHPLATE**, without which directional control of a rotary-wing aircraft would not be possible. Although there are a number of helicopter rotor designs, from the single main rotor to the tandem rotor (like the CH-47 Chinook) to the coaxial rotor (like the Kamov KA-50), all these aircraft have a swashplate. The two primary components of the swashplate—the inner, or non-rotating, swashplate and the outer, or rotating, swashplate—form concentric rings, which rest on a type of bearing. This bearing allows the swashplate to tilt along a horizontal plane as well as move up and down. The mast runs through the center of the swashplate, and as the mast turns, driving the main rotor system, a **SCISSORS LINK** connected to the mast in turn drives the outer, rotating swashplate. The inner, non-rotating swashplate lifts and tilts, controlling the directional movement of the outer, rotating swashplate, which changes the pitch of the rotor blades.

PITCH LINKS, or **PUSH-PULL TUBES**, connect to both the rotating swashplate and the stabilizer bar, or directly to the pitch horn. Pitch links are the mechanical linkage that translates pilot input to control the blade's pitch.

The tail boom of most light rotary-wing aircraft has almost no internal support structure. On the Bell 206B3 Jet Ranger there is structural reinforcement where the tail boom couples with the fuselage and where the tail rotor gearbox couples with the tail boom, but the rest of the tail boom is hollow.

The **TAIL BOOM** is the structural component of the helicopter that supports the tail rotor and in some cases the directional fins.

In a helicopter design known as a NOTAR (no tail rotor), a **DUCTED FAN** is used in place of a traditional tail rotor to cancel out torque effect or the counter-rotating force applied to the airframe as a main rotor system turns. This ducted fan is usually connected to the engine, and as the fan rotates, it creates thrust similar to that of a rotating propeller. As this thrust is forced through a duct in the tail boom it is vented out the back of the aircraft at a 90-degree angle and is controlled by a louver that allows either more or less air to pass out of the thrust opening. It is this vectored thrust that gives a NOTAR rotary-wing aircraft directional control in the hover and cancels out torque effect.

COWLINGS are removable pieces of an aircraft's outer skin that protect important areas of the aircraft from aerodynamic and environmental forces. They also allow for inspection or maintenance of those areas.

SKIDS, a type of landing gear, allow a rotary-wing aircraft to land safely without damaging its undercarriage. Skids are often made of tubular steel and run parallel to the airframe.

Example

Which rotary-wing aircraft component allows the rotor hub and blades to flap?

(A) the teeter hinge

(B) the rotor hub

(C) the swashplate

(D) the skids

(E) the pitch horn

Answers:

(A) is correct. The teeter hinge allows the blades to flap up and down.

(B) is incorrect. The rotor hub is the center attachment point for the rotor head components.

(C) is incorrect. The swashplate is the component that allows for directional movement of the aircraft.

(D) is incorrect. The skids are used as landing gear on a rotary-wing aircraft.

(E) is incorrect. The pitch horn's job is to collect control input from the pilot and translate that input into movement of the blade grips.

The Physics of Rotary-Wing Aircraft

Hovering flight is the balance of the four aerodynamic forces—weight, lift, thrust, and drag—at a given period of time. In a rotary-wing aircraft during a hover, these forces are in opposition straight up and straight down. In order for the aircraft to hover, it has to overcome its weight via the generation of lift. If lift is greater than the aircraft's weight, then the helicopter rises from the ground.

A rotary-wing aircraft creates lift via the rotational movement of its airfoils. As its rotor blades turn, the slow-moving high-pressure air below the blades pushes up against the faster-moving low-pressure air above the blades. This upward force is known as the MAGNUS EFFECT.

Once the aircraft is airborne, it must produce enough lift and thrust to counteract the weight and drag of the aircraft and keep the aircraft in the air. As long as the helicopter maintains a balance between these forces, it will remain in a stabilized hover, suspended in a column of air created by the rotational movement of the rotor

✔ The Magnus effect was first described (though not named) by Isaac Newton in 1672. In fact, in 1742 a British mathematician named Benjamin Robins arguably described the Magnus effect, though only as it relates to the trajectory of a spinning musket ball. However, the force itself would not actually be *called* the Magnus effect until 1852, when German physicist Gustav Magnus officially "discovered" it.

blades. This column of air passing through the rotor blades is known as INDUCED FLOW, or downwash.

While the aircraft is in a stabilized hover, it is attempting to counteract another aerodynamic principle of vertical flight: translating tendency. TRANSLATING TENDENCY is the tendency of a rotary-wing aircraft to drift laterally due to tail rotor thrust. The tail rotor of a rotary-wing aircraft is used to counteract torque and to provide directional control of the aircraft. As the main rotor blades turn, the airframe wants to rotate opposite to that movement. The tail rotor creates the horizontal thrust necessary to counteract that rotational pull of the airframe, which results in the helicopter drifting laterally—its translating tendency.

GYROSCOPIC PRECESSION is another aerodynamic factor exhibited in rotary-wing aircraft. When a force is applied to a rotating rotor, the force will be felt 90 degrees later in the plane of rotation, just as it would in a gyroscope. For example, if force is applied at the six o'clock position of a counterclockwise spinning component, the force is felt or viewed at the three o'clock position.

As a rotary-wing aircraft moves forward, the next aerodynamic factor it will encounter is known as TRANSVERSE FLOW EFFECT. When the helicopter begins to accelerate, the induced flow created by the lifting action of the rotor blades drops to nearly zero in the front half of the rotor system and increases in the rear half of the rotor system. This drop in induced flow causes the angle of attack in the front half of the rotor system to increase, causing the blades to flap up. In contrast, as the induced flow increases in the rear half of the rotor system, the angle of attack decreases, causing the blades to flap down. Due to gyroscopic precession, the displacement of the flapping blades is not felt until 90 degrees later in the plane of rotation, which causes the rotary-wing aircraft to roll laterally.

TRANSLATIONAL LIFT is another factor that rotary-wing aircraft have to contend with. While a rotary-wing aircraft hovers, the induced flow created is nearly vertical. As this vertical column of air hits the ground, it extends outward in all directions and often is pulled back vertically to be recirculated through the aircraft's rotor system. This movement of air creates vortices at the ends of the rotor blades. It is these vortices that hinder the effectiveness of the rotor system, requiring more power for the aircraft to stay aloft.

To achieve an *effective translational lift (ETL)*, the efficiency of the main rotor system must be increased. When an aircraft moves either forward or laterally, it begins to outrun its rotor vortices and thereby creates greater efficiency in the rotor system. The efficiency is not directionally equal, though, since the rotor system does not outrun different vortices at the same time. As the forward half of the rotor system becomes more efficient, the blades flap up, creating more lift and causing the nose of the aircraft to pitch up and, due to gyroscopic precession, to roll laterally. Both transverse flow effect and translational lift can be countered by using the cyclic pitch control (detailed in the upcoming controls section), which can tip the aircraft's plane of rotation.

Lifting forces in the main rotor are not equal at all times either. DISSYMMETRY OF LIFT is an unequal lifting of forces created by the advancing and retreating blades. As a rotary-wing aircraft moves forward through the air, *relative wind* is created, which is the motion of air across an airfoil. As a counterclockwise rotating blade moves an aircraft forward, it encounters fast-moving air along the right-hand side of that aircraft. As it encounters this fast-moving air, more lift is created. Conversely, the leading edge of the airfoil on the left-hand side of the aircraft—the retreating blade—does not run into fast-moving air;

therefore lift decreases. Due to this difference in lift between the advancing and retreating halves of the rotor system, the aircraft is inclined to roll toward the left.

One of the things that makes a rotary-wing aircraft unique is its ability to autorotate. AUTOROTATION is a situation in which the rotor blades are driven by relative wind rather than by the aircraft's powerplant. For example, in the event of an engine failure a pilot can adjust his or her flight controls to allow the induced flow of air through the rotor system to reverse the aircraft's direction. As gravity pulls the aircraft back to the ground, this induced flow can travel vertically through the rotor system and continue to drive the blades in their plane of rotation. As long as the rotor system is turning, the pilot can maintain full directional control of the aircraft and steer it to a suitable landing area. The rotor system stores inertia, giving the pilot an opportunity to cushion the helicopter upon landing. This is a skilled maneuver and if not performed well can cause the rotor system to lose all rotational movement and, in turn, the last remaining vestiges of lift.

Example

Which direction will a rotary-wing aircraft roll due to the transverse flow effect?

(A) upside down

(B) vertically

(C) backward

(D) laterally

(E) inverted

Answers:

(A) is incorrect. The aircraft will not roll upside down.

(B) is incorrect. The aircraft will not roll vertically.

(C) is incorrect. The aircraft will not roll backward.

(D) is correct. The aircraft will roll laterally due to the transverse flow effect.

(E) is incorrect. The aircraft will not roll inverted.

Rotary-Wing Aircraft Controls

There are four primary controls of the rotary-wing aircraft. The CYCLIC CONTROL SYSTEM, mounted on the flight deck floor and centered between the pilot's legs, is utilized to adjust the aircraft's pitch and roll axes. A causal effect of the spinning motion of rotor blades is vertical thrust. As the blades spin, a column of air is created that the pilot can manipulate via the use of the helicopter's flight controls. When the cyclic control is pushed forward, the column of air supporting the rotary-wing aircraft is directed aft, creating a forward lift vector that moves the helicopter forward. This cyclic movement is able to change the direction of the lift vector up to 360 degrees around the aircraft, allowing a pilot to hover in one location.

The COLLECTIVE CONTROL, located to the left of the pilot's seat, is used to "collectively" change the pitch of the rotor blades. When the pilot raises the collective, the pitch angle of the blades increases simultaneously. As the pitch angle increases, so does the angle of attack of the blades; this in turn creates more lift. To perform a level climb the pilot simply pulls the collective up; to descend, he or she pushes it down.

Yaw control of the aircraft is adjusted by the use of the TAIL ROTOR PEDALS, or the DIRECTIONAL CONTROLS. Much like the collective control over the main rotor system, the tail rotor pedals change the pitch of the tail rotor blades, causing a larger or smaller horizontal lifting vector.

Many modern rotary-wing aircraft also have a self-governing THROTTLE CONTROL, meaning once the throttle is switched to a flight setting, engine performance is managed by a computer. Smaller as well as some older aircraft have a manual throttle control, which requires the pilot to increase and reduce the throttle to maintain optimal flying parameters. The throttle can be located in a variety of places within the aircraft, but the majority of throttle controls are found on the collective control in the form of an attached twisting grip, very similar to a collar. By twisting this grip, the throttle can be either increased or decreased.

Example

Which primary rotary-wing flight control increases the pitch angle of the blades simultaneously?

(A) the cyclic

(B) the directional controls

(C) the ducted fan

(D) the collective

(E) the throttle

Answers:

(A) is incorrect. The cyclic controls the pitch and roll axes of the aircraft.

(B) is incorrect. The directional controls manage the aircraft's yaw.

(C) is incorrect. The ducted fan is a component of the NOTAR aircraft design.

(D) is correct. The collective control changes the pitch of the blades simultaneously.

(E) is incorrect. The throttle manages the engine performance.

THE FOUR FUNDAMENTAL FLIGHT MANEUVERS

The four fundamentals of flight are STRAIGHT-AND-LEVEL FLIGHT, TURNS, CLIMBS, and DESCENTS.

Straight-and-Level Flight

The key to smooth flight is the handling of the flight controls by the pilot. The controls should be held with a light touch, not gripped strongly. Straight-and-level flight is achieved when the aircraft is in cruising mode and the four forces of flight—weight, lift, thrust, and drag—are in balance. Straight-and-level flight still requires a monitoring of the controls, but it does not necessarily require moving the controls when the aircraft is not set to autopilot. Avoiding rash inputs on the flight controls maintains a smooth flight.

When an aircraft banks, it tends to change altitude while in the turn. After the turn is complete, the altitude indicator (among the flight instruments discussed later) will confirm the aircraft's heading. The pilot must ensure the natural reference point of the horizon and the perpendicular positions of the wings to return to level flight.

Example

Which of the following is NOT considered necessary to achieve straight-and-level flight?

(A) monitoring the controls

(B) setting the aircraft in cruising mode

(C) moving the flight controls

(D) using a light touch

(E) avoiding rash inputs

Answers:

(A) is incorrect. Monitoring the controls assures a successful straight-and-level flight.

(B) is incorrect. A straight-and-level flight is achieved when the aircraft is in cruising mode.

(C) is correct. Moving the controls is not always necessary to maintain a straight-and-level flight.

(D) is incorrect. A light touch is essential to a straight-and-level flight.

(E) is incorrect. Rash inputs on the flight controls will not achieve a smooth flight.

Turns

When an aircraft is turned, its ailerons should be banked toward the direction of the turn. The degree of the bank angle determines how much input and adjustment a pilot must make to restore the airplane or helicopter to level flight. The lift force acts at the same angle as the angle of bank to tilt the aircraft away from the vertical. To return to level flight, the vertical lift component must equal the weight of the aircraft. When a pilot pulls back on the stick (or cyclic in helicopters), the total lift is greater than the total aircraft weight, counterbalancing the vertical lift component with the weight to maintain altitude. The horizontal lift component becomes unbalanced and causes the aircraft to accelerate inward to perform the turn.

To perform a turn, the following actions are required.

- The pilot first moves the stick (or cyclic): to the left for left turns or to the right for right turns.
- Enough power or pitching up is also added to counteract the loss of lift.
- The controls are neutralized to stop any increase in the bank angle and to maintain the desired bank angle.
- After the turn is accomplished, the ailerons are leveled to resume flight.

During a turn maneuver, a pilot must maintain visual reference with the horizon and keep alert to the aircraft limits of airspeed and altitude displayed on the flight instruments. Typically, altitude and airspeed decrease in a turn. The elevators are used to hold altitude, and the throttle is used to increase speed. As airspeed and altitude decrease, a stall and loss of lift on the wings may result. In this case, the pilot must lower the AOA by one of several means to apply power.

There are three types of turns: shallow, medium, and steep turns. A SHALLOW TURN consists of a bank of up to 20 degrees; after such a turn, the stability of an aircraft naturally returns it to level flight without pilot interference. The bank of a MEDIUM TURN is between 20 and 45 degrees; the pilot during this turn must input aileron pressure to return the aircraft to level flight. A STEEP TURN includes any bank greater than 45 degrees; after a steep turn the pilot must input opposite pressure on the controls to return the aircraft to level flight.

Example

What action must a pilot perform when flying out of a steep turn that is not usually required during a shallow or medium turn?

(A) apply drag by lowering the aileron on the rising wing

(B) decrease airspeed

(C) exceed aircraft limits to finish the turn as soon as possible

(D) ensure a smooth descent

(E) input opposite pressure on the controls

Answers:

(A) is incorrect. Additional drag during turns should not be applied. Airspeed and altitude decrease naturally due to the airflow around the wings.

(B) is incorrect. Aircraft airspeed decreases naturally. An additional loss of airspeed may result in a stall.

(C) is incorrect. An aircraft's limitations should never be exceeded.

(D) is incorrect. Altitude should be maintained during turns.

(E) is correct. An input of opposite pressure on the controls will return the aircraft to level flight.

Climbs

A CLIMB is when an aircraft flight path changes from a lower to a higher level in altitude. During this maneuver, a pilot must increase lift to overcome the aircraft's weight. Climbing without increasing thrust results in a decrease in airspeed. The corrective action is to input additional thrust without exceeding the aircraft's maximum power settings.

A NORMAL CLIMB—sometimes referred to as a CRUISE CLIMB—is performed within the aircraft manufacturer's standards; the aircraft increases airspeed, but it may not be operating at its optimum performance. A BEST RATE OF CLIMB (V_y) involves gaining the most altitude in a given amount of time using the most power available to reach cruising altitude. This climb is steeper than a normal climb and results in the greatest altitude gain over a set amount of time. It is used when an aircraft must take off or gain altitude quickly. A BEST ANGLE OF CLIMB (V_x) involves gaining the most altitude over a given distance. This climb is also used during takeoff but especially at airports where there are obstructions in the flight path. Navigating obstacles typically requires this climbing technique.

Example

Which statement is correct regarding the best rate of climb?

(A) The least amount of power should be applied.

(B) Obstructions in the flight path require a best rate of climb.

(C) The most altitude in a given amount of time can be obtained.

(D) The best rate of climb accomplishes the best climb angle over a given distance.

(E) A best rate of climb is also referred to as a *cruise climb*.

Answers:

(A) is incorrect. The best rate of climb requires the most amount of available power.

(B) is incorrect. Obstructions in the flight path require a best angle of climb.

(C) is correct. The best rate of climb results in the most altitude gain over a given amount of time.

(D) is incorrect. The best rate of climb is not the best angle of climb.

(E) is incorrect. A normal climb is referred to as a *cruise climb*.

Descents

The opposite of a climb in aviation is a DESCENT. When lift is decreased, induced drag is minimized, and the aircraft has a tendency to gain airspeed and thrust. Engine power levels must be reduced to maintain airspeed and avoid an excess speed situation.

A PARTIAL POWER DESCENT is the preferred way to decrease altitude. During this type of descent the aircraft should drop at a rate of 500 feet per minute (fpm). A DESCENT AT MINIMUM SAFE AIRSPEED (MSA) is a nose-high controlled descent used to clear obstacles on short approach to a short runway. The aircraft's angle during this descent is steeper than during a partial power descent. An EMERGENCY DESCENT occurs when the aircraft rapidly loses altitude. Emergency procedures dictate the power settings and control positions for all emergency descents.

A fixed-wing aircraft is by design able to GLIDE for a short distance, including during a descent with little or no engine power; gravity naturally takes over. The best glide speed allows for traveling the greatest distance while still airborne.

Example

What is the standard rate of descent for a partial power descent?

(A) 100 fpm

(B) 200 fpm

(C) 500 fpm

(D) 1,000 fpm

(E) 1,500 fpm

Answers:

(A) is incorrect. This is not the preferred rate of descent.

(B) is incorrect. This is not the preferred rate of descent.

(C) is correct. This is indeed the preferred rate of descent for a partial power descent.

(D) is incorrect. This is not the preferred rate of descent.

(E) is incorrect. This is not the preferred rate of descent.

FLIGHT INSTRUMENTS

A pilot uses outside visual reference cues against the horizon to maneuver a helicopter. When weather degrades to less than the minimum visual flight rules (VFR), flight instruments must be relied upon for guiding the helicopter along the flight path, providing altitude, heading, and airspeed. The altimeter, the airspeed indicator, and the vertical speed indicator are common pitot-static instruments. A pitot tube and static ports extend outside the aircraft's structure to collect the outside air and static pressure. The air passes through a pitot line to the instruments calibrated to measure the aircraft's altitude and speed.

Altimeter

An altimeter displays the altitude of a helicopter. It computes this by measuring the atmospheric pressure at the aircraft's current altitude and comparing this to a preset value. Air pressure decreases 1 inch of mercury for each 1,000 feet of altitude.

There are three types of altimeters: the three-pointer, the counter drum, and the encoding.

Of the three "hands" on a THREE-POINTER ALTIMETER, the longest, thinnest hand displays altitude in tens of thousands of feet; the shortest hand displays thousands of feet;

Figure 3.7. Three-Pointer Altimeter

and the medium-length hand displays hundreds of feet. The box on the right side of the altimeter displays the set ground atmospheric pressure. This setting may be adjusted using the knob at the bottom left of the instrument.

The COUNTER DRUM ALTIMETER digitally displays the altitude without needing manual figuring. Just as the three-pointer altimeter, it also displays the set ground atmospheric pressure.

Figure 3.8. Counter Drum Altimeter

The ENCODING ALTIMETER converts the altitude into a digital code, which is then relayed to ground control radar via a transponder.

Several types of altitudes may be displayed on an altimeter:

- INDICATED ALTITUDE is the altitude actually displayed on the altimeter.
- TRUE ALTITUDE is the height of the aircraft above mean sea level (MSL).

Figure 3.9. Encoding Altimeter

- **ABSOLUTE ALTITUDE** is the height of the aircraft above ground level (AGL).
- **PRESSURE ALTITUDE** is a pre-calibrated altitude with a standard atmosphere level setting of 29.92 inches of Hg. (This altitude is often used in flight planning calculations.)
- **DENSITY ALTITUDE** is pressure altitude modified for a nonstandard temperature.

Example

Air pressure decreases 1 inch of mercury for each _____ feet of altitude.

(A) 100

(B) 500

(C) 1,000

(D) 1,500

(E) 2,000

Answers:

(A) is incorrect. Changes in air pressure are not measured at 1 inch of mercury for each 100 feet of altitude.

(B) is incorrect. Changes in air pressure are not measured at 1 inch of mercury for each 500 feet of altitude.

(C) is correct. Air pressure indeed decreases 1 inch of mercury for each 1,000 feet of altitude.

(D) is incorrect. Changes in air pressure are not measured at 1 inch of mercury for each 1,500 feet of altitude.

(E) is incorrect. Changes in air pressure are not measured at 1 inch of mercury for each 2,000 feet of altitude.

Vertical Speed Indicator

A vertical speed indicator (VSI) displays the vertical speed of an aircraft, in 500-foot increments, measured in thousands of feet per minute, and indicates if the aircraft is climbing, descending, or in level flight, and it shows the rate of climb or descent. The instrument uses a diaphragm to compare the static pressure outside the aircraft to the static pressure surrounding the diaphragm inside the instrument. The difference in the pressures identifies a climb or a descent. When the aircraft is on the ground, the pilot may reset the indicator to zero with a *zeroing screw*.

Figure 3.10. Vertical Speed Indicator

The VSI does not display in real time; there is typically a six- to nine-second delay, or *lag*, in the reading. *Trend information* (a sudden climb or descent) shows initially, then the feet per minute rate is displayed.

CONTINUE

Example

An increase in the static pressure, as measured around the diaphragm inside the VSI, indicates an aircraft is in which of the following maneuvers?

(A) a bank

(B) a climb

(C) a descent

(D) a straight-and-level flight

(E) a yaw

Answers:

(A) is incorrect. A level bank would not cause a difference between the static pressure of the aircraft and the static pressure surrounding the diaphragm of the flight instrument.

(B) is correct. An increase in static pressure surrounding the diaphragm indicates the aircraft is in a climb.

(C) is incorrect. A descent would cause a decrease in the static pressure surrounding the diaphragm versus the static pressure of the aircraft.

(D) is incorrect. Straight-and-level flight does not cause a decrease in the static pressure surrounding the diaphragm versus the static pressure of the aircraft.

(E) is incorrect. A yaw also would not cause a decrease in the static pressure surrounding the diaphragm versus the static pressure of the aircraft.

Airspeed Indicator

The airspeed indicator is a differential pressure gauge that determines how fast the aircraft is moving by contrasting the ambient (inside) air pressure with the ram (outside) air pressure using the aircraft's pitot tube and static ports. A diaphragm in the indicator expands and contracts, causing the linkage to the indicator pointer to move. Airspeed is measured in knots, and each level of airspeed is color-coded:

- The WHITE ARC displays the flap operating speed. The lower limit of the white arc (V_{SO}) is the stalling speed with the flaps down. The upper limit (V_{FE}), where the white and green arcs meet, indicates the maximum speed at which the flaps can be extended.

- The GREEN ARC displays the aircraft's normal operating range, from the lowest limit (V_{S1}) to the highest limit(V_{NO}), also known as the *maximum structural cruising speed*.

Figure 3.11. Airspeed Indicator

- The RED RADIAL LINE represents the never-exceed speed (V_{NE}).

There are different types of airspeed: INDICATED AIRSPEED is what is displayed on the indicator instrument; CALIBRATED AIRSPEED is the indicated airspeed corrected for position error; **EQUIVALENT AIRSPEED** is the calibrated airspeed corrected for non-standard pressure; and **TRUE AIRSPEED** is the equivalent airspeed corrected for non-standard density.

Example

Which type of airspeed is displayed on the airspeed indicator?

(A) calibrated airspeed

(B) equivalent airspeed

(C) indicated airspeed

(D) pressure airspeed

(E) true airspeed

Answers:

(A) is incorrect. Calibrated is the airspeed on the indicator corrected for position error.

(B) is incorrect. Equivalent airspeed is the calibrated airspeed measurement corrected for non-standard pressure.

(C) is correct. Indicated airspeed is indeed what is displayed on the airspeed indicator instrument.

(D) is incorrect. This is not a type of airspeed.

(E) is incorrect. True airspeed is the equivalent airspeed corrected for non-standard density.

Turn and Slip Indicator

The turn and slip indicator combines a turn indicator pointer and a slip indicator ball (inclinometer) in the same housing to measure the yaw rotation of the aircraft. This instrument indicates if the pilot is making a coordinated left or right standard turn. The turn and slip indicator operates on a gyro in a vertical plane aligned with the longitudinal axis, and displays the bank of the aircraft along its vertical axis as well as the rate at which the aircraft turns. A 360-degree turn completed in 2 minutes, at 3 degrees per second, would be considered a standard turn.

The indicator also displays the direction of the turn the aircraft takes.

- In a **SLIPPING TURN**, there is more bank than needed and gravity is greater than the centrifugal force reaction on the slip indicator ball, thus the ball moves toward the inside of the turn.
- In a **SKIDDING TURN**, the centrifugal force reaction is greater than gravity on the slip indicator ball, and the ball moves toward the outside of the turn.
- In a **COORDINATED TURN**, centrifugal force and gravity react equally on the slip indicator ball, and the ball remains in the lowest part of the glass.

Example

What is the purpose of the turn and slip indicator?

(A) to display the aircraft's angle of descent

(B) to display the degree of a turn

(C) to indicate whether an increase of altitude is needed

(D) to indicate if the pilot is making a coordinated left or right standard turn

(E) to measure the rate of a climb

Answers:

(A) is incorrect. This indicator does not identify the angle of an aircraft's descent.

(B) is incorrect. This indicator does not identify the actual degree of a turn.

(C) is incorrect. This indicator does not display any need for an increase of altitude.

(D) is correct. The turn and slip indicator allows the pilot to confirm whether he or she is making a coordinated turn and if any adjustments are needed.

(E) is incorrect. This indicator does not identify the rate of a climb.

Attitude Indicator

The attitude indicator provides real-time and direct attitude information during changes in an aircraft's pitch (along the lateral axis) and when banking (along the longitudinal axis). It displays the relationship of the aircraft's orientation to an artificial horizon. Modern aircraft may have additional features included in the attitude indicator to assist with flight navigation.

The indicator's BANK SCALE represents the sky in blue and the ground/horizon in brown or black. The numbers are in degrees of attitude. The top hashes are degrees of bank, displayed in 30-degree increments. The POINTER at the 12 o'clock position of the indicator (an upside down triangle) is used to check the aircraft's position; it turns toward the direction the aircraft banks.

Figure 3.12 displays a straight-and-level flight in progress. If the aircraft is performing, for example, a *level left bank*, the indicator would show the miniature aircraft tilting to the left with the center of the aircraft wings remaining at the horizontal bar. A *climbing*

Figure 3.12. Attitude Indicator

right bank would be displayed with the aircraft's wings above the horizontal bar and the artificial horizon dipping to the left and rising on the right (thus the right wing would be closer to the ground). In a *level climb* or *dive* the wings would be displayed parallel along the horizontal bar, and the aircraft would be moving toward the blue portion of the indicator for a climb or the brown or black portion for a dive.

Example

The lateral axis of an aircraft controls what?

(A) a bank

(B) a level left bank

(C) pitch

(D) a shallow turn

(E) yaw

Answers:

(A) is incorrect. The longitudinal axis controls banking.

(B) is incorrect. The longitudinal axis controls all banks.

(C) is correct. The lateral axis controls the pitch of the aircraft.

(D) is incorrect. The longitudinal axis controls turns.

(E) is incorrect. The vertical axis controls yaw.

Magnetic Compass

The magnetic compass is a navigational instrument that displays the cardinal headings (north, south, east, and west) in 30-degree increments. Long vertical hash marks identify 10-degree increments, and short vertical hashes identify 5-degree increments. Due to nearby electromagnetic interference from metal structures and electrical components in an aircraft, COMPASS MAGNETIC DEVIATION exists. This deviation is allowable up to 10 degrees.

When the compass card is not level, the magnets dip downward toward Earth. This process, called MAGNETIC DIP, happens when the aircraft is in a bank toward the west or east or when it is accelerating or decelerating while on a west or east heading. Also, when on a west or east heading, any increase in airspeed during a turn causes the compass to reflect a false turn toward the north. A decrease in airspeed during the turn causes the compass to reflect a false turn toward the south.

Compass deviations are caused by electromagnetic influences on the magnets in the compass.

Also, it is common for the direction on magnetic compasses to lag when an aircraft makes a turn. For example, when turning left from a north heading, the compass turns right to 30 degrees and will reset itself once 270 degrees is reached. When turning from a south heading, the compass leads at the same rate of location at degrees latitude. If the aircraft was at 40 degrees latitude, the pilot would have to roll back approximately 40 degrees past the south reading.

A number of other variations and errors can occur with a compass. A compass dial aligns itself with the north and south MAGNETIC POLES, not with geographic true north and south. Pilots fly with the aid of sectional charts that use the geographic poles instead. The difference between true north or south and magnetic north or south is called MAGNETIC VARIATION.

East is least, west is best. Subtract the degree of variation if the variation is east of true north; add the degree of variation if the variation is west of true north.

To identify the variation (in degrees) between magnetic and geographic north, say, a pilot must convert true north (from the sectional charts) to magnetic north (from the aircraft's magnetic compass). If the magnetic variation is east of true north, the degree of variation is subtracted from the map's true heading. If the magnetic variation is west of true north, that degree of variation is added to the map's true heading. The line where the true north and magnetic north variation is zero degrees is called an AGONIC LINE. Lines where the variation is greater or less than zero degrees are called ISOGONIC LINES.

Compass deviations may be corrected by using an airfield's compass rose. These indications are recorded on a compass compensation card placed near the compass in the cockpit.

Example

If the variation between the magnetic north pole and the true north pole is greater than +12 degrees west, how does a pilot adjust for the compass heading?

(A) by adding 6 degrees to the compass heading displayed

(B) by adding 12 degrees to the compass heading displayed

(C) No adjustment is needed; the magnetic compass automatically adjusts for the degree of variation.

(D) by subtracting 6 degrees to the compass heading displayed

(E) by subtracting 12 degrees to the compass heading displayed

Answers:

(A) is incorrect. The entire degree variation, not half, is added.

(B) is correct. Convert to magnetic north by adding the 12-degree variation.

(C) is incorrect. The magnetic compass does not automatically adjust for variation.

(D) is incorrect. The magnetic variation is west of true north, so add the degree of variation.

(E) is incorrect. The magnetic variation is west of true north, so add the degree of variation.

Heading Indicator

The heading indicator is similar to a magnetic compass but functions with a gyroscope and is not subject to the magnetic deviations inherent in magnetic compasses. Direction in this indicator is defined by the aircraft's horizontal plane. When this plane does not match Earth's horizon, a gimbal error exists, called a **DRIFT**. This drift needs to be corrected every ten to fifteen minutes by confirming the heading using the magnetic compass.

Figure 3.13. Heading Indicator

Example

Using Figure 3.13, what is the closest degree heading of this aircraft?

(A) 25 degrees

(B) 26 degrees

(C) 80 degrees

(D) 250 degrees

(E) 260 degrees

Answers:

(A) is incorrect. Add a zero after the numeral increment. The heading is closer to 260 degrees.

(B) is incorrect. Add a zero after the numeral increment. The heading is closer to 260 degrees.

(C) is incorrect. Read the compass needle at the nose of the miniature aircraft on the dial for its heading, not at the tail of the aircraft.

(D) is incorrect. The compass needle is closer to 260 than 250.

(E) is correct. The aircraft is on a 260-degree heading.

Vertical Card Compass

A vertical card compass is a dry compass, not a float-type compass. As seen in Figure 3.14, it is etched out in 30-degree increments with 3 representing 30, 6 representing 60, etc., and there is no overshoot with delayed readings. The heading is read from the 12 o'clock position and the nose of the miniature aircraft on the instrument.

Figure 3.14. Vertical Card Compass

Example

Using Figure 3.14, what is the degree heading of this aircraft?

(A) 10 degrees

(B) 20 degrees

(C) 100 degrees

(D) 190 degrees

(E) 290 degrees

Answers:

(A) is correct. Add a zero after the numeral increment. The heading is 10 degrees.

(B) is incorrect. The heading is closer to 10 degrees than 20 degrees.

(C) is incorrect. A 100-degree heading would be an easterly heading.

(D) is incorrect. Do not read the compass from the tail of the miniature aircraft.

(E) is incorrect. A 290-degree heading would be a westerly heading.

AIRPORTS AND FLIGHT PROTOCOLS

Runway Design and Function

The Federal Aviation Administration (FAA) oversees airport designs and improvements for federal airports, and has established a twenty-year structural design life expectancy for runway pavements. Runway materials must hold up to the stresses placed on them from the weight and impact of aircraft, and foreign object damage (FOD). Runways must also avoid causing undue wear on aircraft tires and provide water runoff and protection from harsh weather conditions.

Currently runways must be 9 to 12 inches deep at regional airfields capable of servicing smaller aircraft. Hub airports frequented by jumbo jets require a 15- to 18-inch depth of pavement. Of the different runway designs, a FLEXIBLE PAVEMENT consists of hot-mix asphalt installed on a base course and subbase, if required. This type of pavement resists cracking (versus rigid pavements). A FULL-DEPTH ASPHALT PAVEMENT contains asphaltic cement as its main material. A RIGID PAVEMENT may use rubberized Portland cement as a subbase. All pavement styles consist of layers: a base course (stabilized), a subbase, and a subgrade, and it is important that loose, gritty material does not exist between the layers.

Runway lengths are dependent on several factors, including the type of aircraft expected to use the runway, the expected maximum takeoff weight (MTOW), the elevation of the airfield, and the maximum local air temperature.

The movement area of an airfield includes the aprons and areas for takeoff, landing, and taxiing. Runway markings are designed to guide an aircraft through a safe landing and takeoff. Runways are defined by their markings, and there are three types.

VISUAL RUNWAY MARKINGS are visible so a pilot can view them as the aircraft approaches the runway. These runways are commonly small airstrips.

A NONPRECISION INSTRUMENT RUNWAY is generally found in small- to medium-size airports and displays a centerline, a threshold mark, and designators, as well as a visual cue called an *aiming point*—a wide strip located on both sides of the runway and approximately 1,000 feet from the landing threshold. This signifies the runway contains navigation facilities for an instrument approach with only horizontal guidance.

A PRECISION INSTRUMENT RUNWAY, found in larger airports, displays all the same markings of a nonprecision instrument runway as well as a touchdown zone and side stripes. This type of runway also contains an *instrument landing system (ILS)* or *precision approach radar (PAR)*. An ILS approach receives radio responses that provide both vertical and horizontal guidance (if a pilot is too low or too high, or too far left or right, as the aircraft approaches). Additionally, a runway number identifies the approach direction as read from a magnetic azimuth and left, center, and right designations identify parallel runways.

Along with physical design, features such as approach lighting and instrumentation requirements limit the type of aircraft a runway may service. RUNWAY END IDENTIFICATION LIGHTS (REILs) are synchronized illuminated lights placed on each side of the runway threshold to help a pilot identify the approach end of a runway. Additionally, the lights at the end of the runway are red, and outward from the runway end they are green, to indicate the threshold. RUNWAY EDGE LIGHTS identify the edges of the runway. These are of variable intensity and white in color, although instrument runways have yellow edge lighting along the last 2,000 feet, or half the length of runway, whichever is less.

An **APPROACH LIGHT SYSTEM (ALS)** assists a pilot in transitioning from instrument flight to visual flight for landing. Some airports have the flashing lights blink sequentially to guide a pilot to the end of the runway under instrument landings. A **VISUAL APPROACH SLOPE INDICATOR (VASI)** will assist with descents during visual landings. Each indicator has a white light on the upper portion and a red light on the lower portion to identify to the pilot his or her position along the glide path to the runway.

Example

Which answer lists different types of marked runways?

(A) approach, instrument, and visual

(B) FOD, REIL, and VASI

(C) precision instrument, non-precision instrument, and visual

(D) REIL and visual

(E) VASI, precision non-instrumentation, and visual

Answers:

(A) is incorrect. Approach is not a type of marked runway.

(B) is incorrect. FOD is not a marked runway and REIL and VASI are lighting systems.

(C) is correct. These are the three types of marked runways.

(D) is incorrect. Visual is a type of marked runway; however, REIL is not.

(E) is incorrect. Visual is a type of marked runway; however, VASI and precision non-instrumentation are not.

Airspace

Controlled airspace is the area controlled and maintained by the FAA-regulated air traffic control (ATC) service. This service controls the movement of all aviation assets within its designated area.

Airspace is divided into six classes by the FAA. (Note that aircraft must have operable equipment and meet certain certification to operate in certain classes. Student and recreational pilots must also be certified to conduct flight operations in certain classes of airspace. Pilots are required to contact the ATC controller to obtain clearance, when necessary, prior to inadvertently entering any controlled airspace.)

- **CLASS A**—Airspace from 18,000 feet MSL to pressure altitude of 60,000 feet, 12 nautical miles (NM) off the coast of the United States, and international airspace beyond 12 NM that is within the navigational signal of ATC radar. All aircraft must operate under instrument flight rules (IFR) at this level.

- **CLASS B**—Airspace from ground level to 10,000 feet MSL surrounding the busiest airports capable of IFR operations and commercial passenger traffic. ATC clearance is required to enter and leave this airspace. Aircraft and pilots must be certified to operate in this airspace.

- **CLASS C**—Airspace from ground level to 4,000 feet above the airport elevation surrounding airports with an operational control tower and serviced by radar approach control, IFR operations, and commercial passenger traffic. Airspace extends from 5 NM radius (surface to 4,000 feet above airport elevation) to 10 NM radius from 1,200 to 4,000 feet. No pilot certification is required to operate in this airspace; however, clearance is required to enter and exit this airspace. A two-way radio and an operable radar beacon transponder with automatic altitude reporting equipment are required.

- **Class D**—Airspace from ground level to 2,500 feet above the airport elevation surrounding airports with an operational control tower. Notices to Airmen (NOTAM) identify any specific requirements for pilots to operate in this controlled airspace. A two-way radio is required to operate in this airspace.

- **Class E**—Any controlled airspace not included in class A through class D. Special VFR operations are permitted with prior clearance obtained by the controlling facility. Class E airspace is distinguished on sectional charts in blue or magenta, and white on low altitude en route charts. No specific pilot or equipment requirement exists.

- **Class G**—Uncontrolled airspace with visibility requirements of 1 mile during the day and 3 miles at night. This airspace is valid for altitudes 1,200 feet AGL to 10,000 feet MSL. Above 10,000 feet, 5 miles of visibility is required day or night. Class G airspace is identified on sectional maps by a faded, thick blue line.

For any airspace, required flight visibility is 3 statute miles, except in Class A and Class E. There are established elevations where aircraft must remain clear of clouds in the controlled airspace. These restrictions are typically 1,000 feet above the clouds, 500 feet below the clouds, and anywhere from 1,000 feet to 1 statute mile when horizontal with the clouds. Obstacles and urban development may preclude the ability to abide by these set restrictions, but a pilot must display good judgment in this case.

Requirements to establish radio communications with a pilot are different among the classes of airspace.

- **Classes A and B**—The ATC controller must verbally grant clearance. Acknowledgment of the aircraft call sign is not considered an established communication.

- **Classes C and D**—If the ATC controller acknowledges with the aircraft call sign, communication is considered established. This is true even if the ATC controller responds with the aircraft call sign and instructs the pilot to "standby."

Example

Which of the following statements is true about controlled airspace?

(A) An operable two-way radio is all that is required for communications in any airspace.

(B) ATC controllers must verbally grant clearance for entry and exit of Class A and Class B airspaces.

(C) Controllers of Class A through Class D airspaces may establish communications by acknowledging the pilot with the aircraft call sign.

(D) Flight visibility required for Class B airspace is 5 NM.

(E) Pilots must operate under IFR when passing through Class B airspace.

Answers:

(A) is incorrect. Class D is the only airspace that requires only an operable two-way radio.

(B) is correct. Clearance is required to enter and exit Class A and Class B airspaces.

(C) is incorrect. Airspace Classes A and B require the ATC controller to grant clearance—not merely by acknowledging with the aircraft call sign.

(D) is incorrect. Flight visibility for Class B is 3 statute miles.

(E) is incorrect. Pilots must operate under IFR when passing through Class A airspace.

Right-of-Way

All aircraft have an inherent duty to steer clear of other aircraft and hot-air balloons. Steering clear means that an aircraft may not pass over, under, or ahead of another aircraft unless it is well clear. The following six rules establish the right-of-way for certain situations:

1. An aircraft in distress always has the right-of-way over all other air traffic.

2. When two aircraft of the same category approach each other (except head-on) at generally the same altitude, the aircraft on the right has the right-of-way.

3. When approaching aircraft are of different categories, refer to the following list, presented in order of right-of-way:

   - Hot-air balloons
   - Gliders
   - Airships
   - Powered parachutes
   - Powered hang gliders and ultra-light aircraft
   - Airplanes
   - Rotorcraft

   An exception to this list is an aircraft towing or refueling another aircraft, which has the right-of-way over all other engine-driven aircraft.

4. When two aircraft approach head-on, the pilot of each aircraft should change course to the right.

5. An overtaking aircraft has the right-of-way, and the pilot of the aircraft being overtaken must shift course to the right to stay clear.

6. When landing, an aircraft on final approach or beginning to land has the right-of-way, as long as it does not force an already landed aircraft off the runway. When two aircraft are landing at the same time, the aircraft at a lower altitude has the right-of-way but cannot cut in front of the other aircraft to become the lower level aircraft.

CONTINUE →

Example

Which right-of-way statement is true?

(A) An aircraft being towed must yield to a rotorcraft when the two aircraft approach each other.

(B) Aircraft in distress have the right-of-way despite their category.

(C) A landing aircraft on short final approach may force a landed aircraft to move off the runway.

(D) Rotorcraft has the right-of-way over a glider when both are approaching at the same time.

(E) When two aircraft approach head-on, both descend to the left until they are clear of each other.

Answers:

(A) is incorrect. An aircraft in tow has the right-of-way over the rotorcraft (an engine-driven aircraft).

(B) is correct. Any aircraft in distress always has the right-of-way.

(C) is incorrect. An aircraft on short final approach may not force an already landed aircraft off the runway.

(D) is incorrect. A glider has the right-of-way over a rotorcraft when they approach at the same time.

(E) is incorrect. When two aircraft approach head-on, both descend to their right until they are clear of each other.

AVIATION HISTORY

Since 1900, the year of the first flight of a Zeppelin, aircraft technology and capabilities have evolved beyond expectations. The following timeline includes some of the milestones in aviation history.

July 2, 1900: The Zeppelin makes its first flight.

October 22, 1900: The Wright brothers make their first glider flight.

December 17, 1903: The Wright brothers complete the first powered, manned, heavier-than-air controlled flight (it lasted twelve seconds).

February 22, 1920: The first transcontinental mail service is established, from San Francisco to New York.

May 3, 1923: The first nonstop coast-to-coast airplane flight travels from New York to San Diego.

May 21, 1927: Charles A. Lindbergh accomplishes the first nonstop solo flight across the Atlantic Ocean.

June 29, 1927: The first trans-Pacific flight travels from California to Hawaii.

June 1, 1937: Amelia Earhart is lost en route to Howland Island from New Guinea.

June 28, 1939: Pan American Airways flies the first trans-Atlantic passenger service.

October 14, 1947: Captain Charles E. Yeager exceeds the sound barrier in a rocket.

May 5, 1961: Alan Shepard pilots the first US manned space flight.

February 20, 1962: John Glenn becomes the first American to orbit Earth.

December 27, 1968: Apollo 8 is the first human flight to orbit the moon.

September 3, 1971: The Concorde makes its first transatlantic crossing.

1978: The US Airline Deregulation Act ends government regulation of airline routes and rates.

October 24, 2003: The Concorde supersonic jet makes its last flight.

SPATIAL APPERCEPTION

The spatial apperception questions all have a picture that represents the view from a plane's cockpit. They depict land or water with the horizon at varying angles and locations in the picture. Answer choices include several pictures showing an aircraft flying at different pitch and roll settings heading inland, out to sea, or along the shoreline. The test taker must determine which choice correctly depicts how the plane is situated in the air according to the view from the cockpit.

The figure below is an example of a spatial apperception question with answer choices. The "question" shows the view from the cockpit of a plane in level flight with no bank that is headed out to sea. The correct answer depicts the corresponding plane.

> ⚠ In the figures, the darker color (usually black or dark gray) represents the water; the lighter color (usually white or light gray) represents the land.

The key to correctly answering these questions is to determine the pitch, bank, and heading of the aircraft.

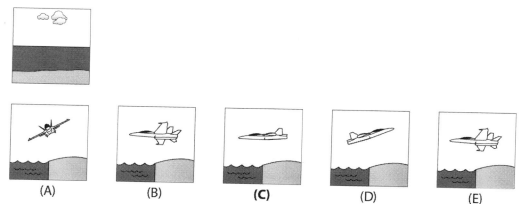

Figure 4.1. Example Problem

IDENTIFYING PITCH

Start by determining the pitch of the aircraft—whether the nose of the aircraft is up or down in relation to the horizon. This can be done by noting the position of the horizon in the picture. The horizon is the line where the water and land meet the sky.

If the horizon is in the middle of the picture vertically, the plane is level. If the horizon is above the middle of the image, the plane is descending (the nose is low). If the horizon is below the middle of the picture, the plane is climbing (the nose is high).

Figure 4.2. Pitch

If the horizon is tilted, the point of the horizon at the center of the picture can be used to determine the plane's status, taking into account the horizon's angle from left to right as well as its location relative to the sea and sky.

Figure 4.3. Identifying Pitch from a Tilted Horizon

The pitch of the airplane in the answers can be identified by referencing an imaginary line running from the nose to the tail of the plane.

If the line is level, the plane is flying straight and level. If the line is higher at the nose, the plane is climbing. The opposite is also true: if the line is lower at the nose, the plane is descending.

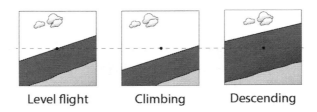

Figure 4.4. Identifying an Aircraft's Pitch

Pitch can be a little harder to determine if the plane is oriented directly in or out of the picture, but close examination will show if the nose is higher, lower, or even with the tail. In Figure 4.5, the plane is climbing.

Climbing

Figure 4.5. A
Climbing Aircraft

IDENTIFYING BANK

Bank is the position of the wings in relation to each other: one wing may be higher than the other, or they may be level. The direction of bank can be determined by referencing the tilt of the horizon. If the horizon is higher on the right in the question picture, the plane is turning right, and the answer will show the right wing low. Conversely, if the horizon is higher on the left, the plane is turning left, and the answer will show the left wing down (as in the figures below). In short, the wings are opposite of the horizon. A level horizon means there is no bank, and the wings will also be level.

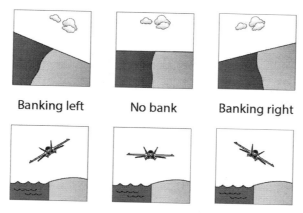

Figure 4.6. Identifying Bank

IDENTIFYING HEADING

Finally, identifying the aircraft heading, or the direction in which the nose is pointing, will reveal the correct answer. It is generally easiest to determine when the nose is pointing directly into land or out to sea. In these cases, the line between the land and the water will be level. If the aircraft is heading inland, the land will be on top; if it is heading out to sea, the sea will be on top.

Heading along the coast is also fairly simple to determine. In this case, the line between sea and land runs in the middle of the picture from left to right and closer to vertical. If the answer shows the tail of the plane, the land and water will be on the same sides in the answer as in the question. If the answer shows the nose of the plane, the land and water will be on the opposite sides in the answer.

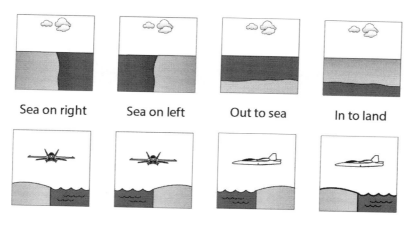

Figure 4.7. Identifying Heading

The third case is when the plane is flying at an angle out to sea or into land. In these cases, the line between land and water will be tilted. If it is tilted so water is above land, the plane is headed out to sea. If the line between land and coast is tilted so the land is above the sea, the plane is heading into land. The closer this line is to level, the closer the plane is to flying directly out to sea or into land.

READING COMPREHENSION

The Reading Comprehension section includes 20 short reading passages followed by questions about those passages. The passages will cover simple, easy-to-understand topics, and no outside knowledge will be needed to answer the questions. The sections below will introduce the types of questions that are included on the test and explain how to answer them.

THE MAIN IDEA

The **MAIN IDEA** of a text describes the author's main topic and general concept; it also generalizes the author's point of view about a subject. It is contained within and throughout the text. The reader can easily find the main idea by considering how the main topic is addressed throughout a passage. In the reading test, the expectation is not only to identify the main idea but also to differentiate it from a text's theme and to summarize the main idea clearly and concisely.

The main idea is closely connected to topic sentences and how they are supported in a text. Questions may deal with finding topic sentences, summarizing a text's ideas, or locating supporting details. The sections and practice examples that follow detail the distinctions between these aspects of text.

Identifying the Main Idea

To identify the main idea, first identify the topic. The difference between these two things is simple: the **TOPIC** is the overall subject matter of a passage; the main idea is what the author wants to say about that topic. The main idea covers the author's direct perspective about a topic, as distinct from the **THEME**, which is a generally true idea that the reader might derive from a text. Most of the time, fiction has a theme, whereas nonfiction has a main idea. This is the case because in a nonfiction text, the author speaks more directly to the audience about a topic—his or her perspective is more visible.

The author's perspective on the subject of the text and how he or she has framed the argument or story hints at the main idea. For example, if the author framed the story with a description, image, or short anecdote, this suggests a particular idea or point of view.

For example, the following passage conveys the topic as well as what the author wants to communicate about that topic.

> The "shark mania" of recent years can be largely pinned on the sensationalistic media surrounding the animals: from the release of *Jaws* in 1975 to the week of ultra-hyped shark feeding frenzies and "worst shark attacks" countdowns known as Shark Week, popular culture both demonizes and fetishizes sharks until the public cannot get enough. Swimmers and beachgoers may look nervously for the telltale fin skimming the surface, but the reality is that shark bites are extremely rare and they are almost never unprovoked. Sharks attack people at very predictable times and for very predictable reasons. Rough surf, poor visibility, or a swimmer sending visual and physical signals that mimic a shark's normal prey are just a few examples.

> Of course, some places are just more dangerous to swim. Shark attack "hot spots," such as the coasts of Florida, South Africa, and New Zealand try a variety of solutions to protect tourists and surfers. Some beaches employ "shark nets," meant to keep sharks away from the beach, though these are controversial because they frequently trap other forms of marine life as well. Other beaches use spotters in helicopters and boats to alert beach officials when there are sharks in the area. In addition, there is an array of products that claim to offer personal protection from sharks, ranging from wetsuits in different colors to devices that broadcast electrical signals in an attempt to confuse the sharks' sensory organs. At the end of the day, though, beaches like these remain dangerous, and swimmers must assume the risk every time they paddle out from shore.

The author of this passage has a clear topic: sharks and the relationship between humans and sharks. In order to identify the main idea of the passage, the reader must ask what the author wants to say about this topic, what the reader is meant to think or understand. The author makes sure to provide information about several different aspects of the relationship between sharks and humans, and points out that humans must respect sharks as dangerous marine animals, without sensationalizing the risk of attack. This conclusion results from looking at the various pieces of information the author includes as well as the similarities between them. The passage describes sensationalistic media, then talks about how officials and governments try to protect beaches, and ends with the observation that people must take personal responsibility. These details clarify what the author's main idea is. Summarizing that main idea by focusing on the connection between the different details helps the reader draw a conclusion.

Readers should identify the topic of a text and pay attention to how the details about it relate to one another. A passage may discuss, for example, topic similarities, characteristics, causes, and/ or effects.

Examples

The art of the twentieth and twenty-first centuries demonstrates several aspects of modern societal advancement. A primary example is the advent and ascendancy of technology: New technologies have developed new avenues for art making, and the globalization brought about by the Internet has both diversified the art world and brought it together simultaneously. Even as artists are able to engage in a global conversation about the categories and characteristics of art, creating a more uniform understanding, they can now express themselves in a diversity of ways for a diversity of audiences. The result has been a rapid change in how art is made and consumed.

1. This passage is primarily concerned with
    (A) the importance of art in the twenty-first century.
    (B) the use of art to communicate overarching ideals to diverse communities.
    (C) the importance of technology to art criticism.
    (D) the change in understanding and creation of art in the modern period.
    (E) artists' desires to diversify the media with which art is created.

    Answers:

    (A) is incorrect. The focus of the passage is what the art of the twentieth and twenty-first centuries demonstrates.

    (B) is incorrect. Although the passage mentions a diversity of audiences, it discusses the artists expressing themselves, not attempting to communicate overarching ideals.

    (C) is incorrect. The passage discusses how new technologies have "developed new avenues for art making," but nothing about criticism.

    (D) is correct. The art of the modern period reflects the new technologies and globalization possible through the Internet.

    (E) is incorrect. The passage mentions the diversity of ways artists express themselves, not the media specifically.

2. Which of the following best describes the main idea of the passage?
    (A) Modern advances in technology have diversified art making and connected artists to distant places and ideas.
    (B) Diversity in modern art is making it harder for art viewers to understand and talk about that art.
    (C) The use of technology to discuss art allows us to create standards for what art should be.
    (D) Art making before the invention of technology such as the Internet was disorganized and poorly understood.
    (E) Art making in the twenty-first century is dependent on the use of technology in order to meet current standards.

    Answers:

    (A) is correct. According to the text, technology and the Internet have "diversified the art world and brought it together simultaneously."

    (B) is incorrect. The passage explains that the global conversation about art has created a more uniform understanding.

    (C) is incorrect. The passage indicates that artists now engage in a global conversation about art, but this is one detail in the passage. The main idea of the passage concerns the advances in art in the twentieth and twenty-first centuries.

    (D) is incorrect. The invention of technology and the Internet have diversified art; however, that does not mean it was disorganized previously.

    (E) is incorrect. Technology is a means to an end; art is not dependent on it.

Topic and Summary Sentences

Identifying the main idea requires understanding the structure of a piece of writing. In a short passage of one or two paragraphs, the topic and summary sentences quickly relate what the paragraphs are about and what conclusions the author wants the reader to draw. These sentences function as bookends to a paragraph or passage, telling readers what to think and keeping the passage tied tightly together.

Generally, the **TOPIC SENTENCE** is the first, or very near the first, sentence in a paragraph. It is a general statement that introduces the topic, clearly and specifically directing the reader to access any previous experience with that topic.

A **summary** is a very brief restatement of the most important parts of an argument or text. Building a summary begins with the most important idea in a text. A longer summary also includes supporting details. The text of a summary should be much shorter than the original.

The **SUMMARY SENTENCE**, on the other hand, frequently—but not always!—comes at the end of a paragraph or passage, because it wraps up all the ideas presented. This sentence provides an understanding of what the author wants to say about the topic and what conclusions to draw about it. While a topic sentence acts as an introduction to a topic, allowing the reader to activate his or her own ideas and experiences, the summary statement asks the reader to accept the author's ideas about that topic. Because of this, a summary sentence helps the reader quickly identify a piece's main idea.

Examples

Altogether, Egypt is a land of tranquil monotony. The eye commonly travels either over a waste of waters, or over a green plain unbroken by elevations. The hills which inclose (sic) the Nile valley have level tops, and sides that are bare of trees, or shrubs, or flowers, or even mosses. The sky is generally cloudless. No fog or mist enwraps the distance in mystery; no rainstorm sweeps across the scene; no rainbow spans the empyrean; no shadows chase each other over the landscape. There is an entire absence of picturesque scenery. A single broad river, unbroken within the limits of Egypt even by a rapid, two flat strips of green plain at its side, two low lines of straight-topped hills beyond them, and a boundless open space where the river divides itself into half a dozen sluggish branches before reaching the sea, constitute Egypt, which is by nature a southern Holland—"weary, stale, flat and unprofitable."

—from *Ancient Egypt* by George Rawlinson

1. Which of the following best explains the general idea and focus indicated by the topic sentence?

   (A) Egypt is a boring place without much to do.

   (B) The land of Egypt is undisturbed; the reader will read on to find out what makes it so dull.

   (C) Egypt is a peaceful place; its people live with a sense of predictability.

   (D) The land of Egypt is quiet; the reader wants to know what is missing.

   (E) The reader is curious about how people survive in an area of worn-out uniformity.

   Answers:

   (A) is incorrect. The word *monotony* does suggest the idea of being bored; however, the focus is the land of Egypt, not what people have to do. In addition, tranquility is part of the general idea.

(B) is correct. This option indicates both the main idea and what the reader will focus on while reading.

(C) is incorrect. This option leaves out what the focus will be.

(D) is incorrect. This option leaves out the general idea of monotony.

(E) is incorrect. This option is inaccurate; the topic sentence does not suggest anything about survival.

2. Which of the following best states what the author wants the reader to understand after reading the summary sentence?

(A) There is not much to get excited about while visiting Egypt.

(B) Egypt is a poverty-stricken wasteland.

(C) The land of Egypt is worn out from overuse.

(D) The land of Egypt is quiet, but not worth visiting.

(E) The land of Egypt lacks anything fresh or inspiring.

Answers:

(A) is incorrect. The summary describes the place, not a visit to the place.

(B) is incorrect. The word *unprofitable* suggests that the land of Egypt is unrewarding, not poverty stricken.

(C) is incorrect. The reason the land is stale and weary may not be due to overuse. This summary describes; it does not explain the reasons the land is worn.

(D) is incorrect. The first part of the sentence is correct, but the summary sentence does not indicate that Egypt is not worth visiting.

(E) is correct. The words *weary*, *stale*, and *unprofitable* suggest a lack of freshness or anything that stimulates enthusiasm.

SUPPORTING DETAILS

Between a topic sentence and a summary sentence, the rest of a paragraph is built with SUPPORTING DETAILS. Supporting details come in many forms; the purpose of the passage dictates the type of details that will support the main idea. A persuasive passage may use facts and data or detail specific reasons for the author's opinion. An informative passage will primarily use facts about the topic to support the main idea. Even a narrative passage will have supporting details—specific things the author says to develop the story and characters.

The most important aspect of supporting details is exactly what the term states: They support the main idea. Examining the various supporting details and how they work with one another will solidify how the author views a topic and what the main idea of the passage is. Supporting details are key to understanding a passage.

Identifying Supporting Details

How can the reader identify the most important pieces of information in a passage? Supporting details build an argument and contain the concepts upon which the main idea rests. While supporting details will help the reader determine the main idea, it is actually easier to find the most important supporting details by first understanding the main idea; the pieces that make up the main argument then become clear.

SIGNAL WORDS—transitions and conjunctions—explain to the reader how one sentence or idea is connected to another. These words and phrases can be anywhere in a sentence, and it is important to understand what each signal word means. Signal words can add information, provide counterarguments, create organization in a passage, or draw conclusions. Some common signal words include *in particular, in addition, besides, contrastingly, therefore,* and *because.*

Examples

The war is inevitable—and let it come! I repeat it, sir, let it come! It is in vain, sir, to extenuate the matter. Gentlemen may cry, "Peace! Peace!"—but there is no peace. The war is actually begun! The next gale that sweeps from the north will bring to our ears the clash of resounding arms! Our brethren are already in the field! Why stand we here idle? What is it that gentlemen wish? What would they have? Is life so dear, or peace so sweet, as to be purchased at the price of chains and slavery? Forbid it, Almighty God! I know not what course others may take; but as for me, give me liberty or give me death!

—from "Give Me Liberty or Give Me Death"
speech by Patrick Henry

1. In the fourth sentence of the text, the word *but* signals

    (A) an example.

    (B) a consequence.

    (C) an exception.

    (D) a counterargument.

    (E) a reason

    Answers:

    (A) is incorrect. The author includes an example that the war has begun when he says "Our brethren are already in the field!" The word *but* does not signal this example.

    (B) is incorrect. The phrase "but there is no peace" is a fact, not a consequence.

    (C) is incorrect. In order to be an exception, the word *but* would have to be preceded by a general point or observation. In this case, *but* is preceded by a demand for peace.

    (D) is correct. The argument or claim that the country should be at peace precedes the word *but*. *But* counters the demand for peace with the argument that there is no peace; the war has begun.

    (E) is incorrect. *But* does not introduce a reason in this text; it introduces a contradictory point.

2. What argument does the author use to support his main point?

    (A) Life in slavery is not the goal of the country.

    (B) To die bravely is worthwhile.

    (C) Life without freedom is intolerable.

    (D) The cost of going to war is too great.

    (E) People cannot live in peace without going to war.

Answers:

(A) is incorrect. The main point is that the country has to go to war with England to be free. The author does not support his point with a discussion of the goals of the country.

(B) is incorrect. This does not relate to the main point of going to war.

(C) is correct. The author indicates that life is not so dear, nor peace so sweet, "as to be purchased at the price of chains and slavery."

(D) is incorrect. This is inaccurate. The author insists that the cost of not fighting for freedom is too great.

(E) is incorrect. Those who opposed going to war believed that Americans could find a way to live peacefully, without a war; the author's main point is the opposite.

Evaluating Supporting Details

Besides using supporting details to help understand a main idea, the reader must evaluate them for relevance and consistency. An author selects details to help organize a passage and support its main idea. Sometimes, the author's bias results in details left out that don't directly support the main idea or that support an opposite idea. The reader has to be able to notice not only what the author says but also what the author leaves out.

To understand how a supporting detail relates to the main idea, the purpose of the passage should be discerned: what the author is trying to communicate and what the author wants from the reader. Every passage has a specific goal, and each paragraph in a passage is meant to support that goal. For each supporting detail, the position in the text, the signal words, and the specific content work together to alert the reader to the relationship between the supporting ideas and the main idea.

Close reading involves noticing the striking features of a text. For example, does a point made in the text appeal to the reader's sense of justice? Does a description seem rather exaggerated or overstated? Do certain words—such as *agonizing*—seem emotive? Are rhetorical questions being used to lead the reader to a certain conclusion?

Though the author generally includes details that support the text's main idea, the reader must decide how those details relate to one another as well as find any gaps in the support of the author's argument. This is particularly important in a persuasive piece of writing, when an author may allow bias to show through. Discovering the author's bias and how the supporting details reveal that bias is also key to understanding a text.

Examples

In England in the 'fifties came the Crimean War, with the deep stirring of national feeling which accompanied it, and the passion of gratitude and admiration which was poured forth on Miss Florence Nightingale for her work on behalf of our wounded soldiers. It was universally felt that there was work for women, even in war—the work of cleansing, setting in order, breaking down red tape, and soothing the vast sum of human suffering which every war is bound to cause. Miss Nightingale's work in war was work that never had been done until women came forward to do it, and her message to her countrywomen was educate yourselves, prepare, make ready; never imagine that your task can be done by instinct, without training and preparation. Painstaking study, she insisted, was just as necessary as a preparation for women's work as for men's work; and she bestowed the whole of the monetary gift offered her by the gratitude of the nation to form training-schools for nurses at St. Thomas's and King's College Hospitals.

—from *Women's Suffrage: A Short History of a Great Movement*
by Millicent Garrett Fawcett

1. Which of the following best states the bias of the passage?

   (A) Society underestimates the capacity of women.

   (B) Generally, women are not prepared to make substantial contributions to society.

   (C) If women want power, they need to prove themselves.

   (D) One strong woman cannot represent all women.

   (E) The strength of women is their ability to take care of others.

   Answers:

   (A) is correct. The author is suggesting that the work Florence Nightingale did had not been done before women came forward. Up till that point, what a woman could do had not been recognized.

   (B) is incorrect. This fact may have been true at the time this text was written, but only because educational opportunities were not available to women, and women were not encouraged to develop their abilities. Including this fact reveals the bias that women should be granted opportunities to train and to contribute.

   (C) is incorrect. This option does not apply; Florence Nightingale did more than prove herself.

   (D) is incorrect. The fact that Florence Nightingale donated the money awarded her to the training of women indicates that other women were preparing themselves to contribute.

   (E) is incorrect. This may or may not be true. It does not matter what kind of strength women have; the bias is that the strength of women wasn't really known.

2. Which of the following best summarizes what the author left out of the passage?

   (A) Women can fight in wars.

   (B) Other women should be recognized.

   (C) Women need to stop wasting time giving speeches at conventions and start proving themselves.

   (D) Without the contributions of women, society suffers.

   (E) Women are the ones who get the important work done.

   Answers:

   (A) is incorrect. "It was universally felt that there was work for women, even in war" suggests that women had much to offer and didn't need to be sheltered; however, "there was work" does not mean the author thought women should engage in combat.

   (B) is incorrect. Since the passage is specifically about Florence Nightingale, nothing in it suggests the author included information about what other women did.

   (C) is incorrect. Information about women's suffrage conventions is unrelated to the topic of the paragraph.

(D) is correct. The author emphasizes that "Miss Nightingale's work in war was work that never had been done until women came forward to do it."

(E) is incorrect. The author shows the importance of Miss Nightingale's work, but that does not suggest it was the only important work being done.

Facts and Opinions

Authors use both facts and opinions as supporting details. While it is usually a simple task to identify the two, authors may mix facts with opinions or state an opinion as if it were a fact. The difference between the two is simple: A FACT is a piece of information that can be verified as true or false, and it retains the quality of truthfulness or falsity no matter who verifies it. An OPINION reflects a belief held by the author and may or may not be something each reader agrees with.

 To distinguish between fact and opinion, the reader should rely on what can be proven. Subjectivity is determined by asking if an observation varies according to the situation or the person observing.

Examples

I remember thinking how comfortable it was, this division of labor which made it unnecessary for me to study fogs, winds, tides, and navigation, in order to visit my friend who lived across an arm of the sea. It was good that men should be specialists, I mused. The peculiar knowledge of the pilot and captain sufficed for many thousands of people who knew no more of the sea and navigation than I knew. On the other hand, instead of having to devote my energy to the learning of a multitude of things, I concentrated it upon a few particular things, such as, for instance, the analysis of Poe's place in American literature—an essay of mine, by the way, in the current *Atlantic*. Coming aboard, as I passed through the cabin, I had noticed with greedy eyes a stout gentleman reading the *Atlantic*, which was open at my very essay. And there it was again, the division of labor, the special knowledge of the pilot and captain which permitted the stout gentleman to read my special knowledge on Poe while they carried him safely from Sausalito to San Francisco.

—from *The Sea-Wolf* by Jack London

1. Which of the following best summarizes an opinion stated by the narrator?

(A) Poe has a place in American literature.

(B) People have the time to read magazines like the *Atlantic* because there are other people to take care of other tasks.

(C) The narrator has no knowledge of the sea and navigation.

(D) Having specialized knowledge sets people apart and makes them superior.

(E) Division of labor is a beneficial practice.

Answers:

(A) is incorrect. This is a fact. The *significance* of Poe's place in American literature is an opinion.

(B) is incorrect. This is a fact. The reader is expected to agree with the point that if someone else had not been managing the boat, the people who wanted to get across the water would have had to do the work of getting themselves across.

(C) is incorrect. This is a fact. The narrator admits to "this division of labor which made it unnecessary for me to study fogs, winds, tides, and navigation."

(D) is incorrect. Although the narrator acknowledges that specialized knowledge exists, he does not indicate that he believes it creates superiority.

(E) is correct. The narrator provides several facts proving that he and the other passengers benefit from the specialized knowledge and labor of others.

2. Which of the following is an opinion expressed by the narrator that is NOT supported by facts within the passage?

   (A) People should live life focusing on and learning about only a few things.

   (B) Having general knowledge is good.

   (C) He has time to focus on writing about literature.

   (D) People depend on other people.

   (E) People can experience more freedom by depending on others.

   Answers:

   (A) is correct. When the narrator says "instead of having to devote my energy to the learning of a multitude of things, I concentrated it upon a few particular things," he conveys his view that he does not have to learn much. There are no facts to support the view that he has to learn only a few particular things in life.

   (B) is incorrect. The narrator does not express this opinion. He is speaking about specialized knowledge.

   (C) is incorrect. This is a fact that the narrator shares about his life.

   (D) is incorrect. The passage does offer facts to support this; both the narrator and the passenger reading depend on the pilot to navigate the boat safely.

   (E) is incorrect. This opinion is supported by the fact that the passenger has the freedom to sit back and read, and the narrator has the freedom to watch him read, while they both depend on the pilot.

TEXT STRUCTURE

The structure of a text determines how the reader understands the argument and how the various details interact to form the argument. There are many ways to arrange text, and various types of arrangements have distinct characteristics.

The organizing structure of a passage is defined by the order in which the author presents information and the transitions used to connect those pieces. Problem-and-solution and cause-and-effect structures use transitions that show causal relationships: *because, as a result, consequently, therefore.* These two types of structures may also use transitions that show contradiction. A problem-and-solution structure may provide alternative solutions; a cause-and-effect structure may explain alternative causes: *however, alternatively, although.*

> Authors often use repetition to reinforce an idea, including repeated words, phrases, or images.

Specific text structures include not only problem and solution and cause and effect, but also compare and contrast, descriptive, order of importance, and chronological. When analyzing a text, the reader should consider how text structure influences the author's meaning. Most important, the reader needs to be aware of how an author emphasizes an idea by the way he or she presents information. For instance, including a contrasting idea makes a central idea stand out, and including a series of concrete examples creates a force of facts to support an argument.

Examples

It was the green heart of the canyon, where the walls swerved back from the rigid plan and relieved their harshness of line by making a little sheltered nook and filling it to the brim with sweetness and roundness and softness. Here all things rested. Even the narrow stream ceased its turbulent down-rush long enough to form a quiet pool.... On one side, beginning at the very lip of the pool, was a tiny meadow, a cool, resilient surface of green that extended to the base of the frowning wall. Beyond the pool a gentle slope of earth ran up and up to meet the opposing wall. Fine grass covered the slope—grass that was spangled with flowers, with here and there patches of color, orange and purple and golden. Below, the canyon was shut in. There was no view. The walls leaned together abruptly and the canyon ended in a chaos of rocks, moss-covered and hidden by a green screen of vines and creepers and boughs of trees. Up the canyon rose far hills and peaks, the big foothills, pine-covered and remote. And far beyond, like clouds upon the border of the slay, towered minarets of white, where the Sierra's eternal snows flashed austerely the blazes of the sun.

—from "All Gold Canyon" by Jack London

1. The organizational structure of the passage is

(A) order of importance.

(B) cause and effect.

(C) problem and solution.

(D) descriptive.

(E) chronological.

Answers:

(A) is incorrect. A series of reasons is not presented from most to least or least to most important. The passage describes a restful nook in the canyon.

(B) is incorrect. The passage does not explain the origin of this nook or its effect on anything, although the reader understands from the details what makes the nook so restful.

(C) is incorrect. The description of the nook presents no problem, although time in the nook could be seen as a solution for many problems.

(D) is correct. The description of the nook begins with a general impression, moves from one side, to the area beyond the pool, to below the heart of the canyon, and finally to what is above the canyon.

(E) is incorrect. The description does not include a sequence of events in time.

2. How does the text structure emphasize the central idea of the passage?

(A) The logical reasons for needing to rest while hiking make the author's argument compelling.

(B) By explaining the activities within the canyon, the author convinces the reader that the canyon is safe.

(C) By describing the areas to the side, below, and above the canyon, the author is able to emphasize the softness at the heart of the canyon.

(D) The concrete examples included in the passage demonstrate the author's view that beauty is found in nature.

(E) The sensory details of the description make it easy for the reader to visualize and enjoy.

Answers:

(A) is incorrect. The passage does not indicate anything about a hike, although the valley is described as a restful place.

(B) is incorrect. The heart of the canyon is still, without activity; even the water stops rushing and forms a pool.

(C) is correct. The little restful nook is surrounded by the wall of the mountain, a "chaos of rocks," "boughs of trees," "far hills and peaks."

(D) is incorrect. The central idea of the passage is not finding beauty in nature but simply the restfulness of this nook.

(E) is incorrect. The passage does include sensory detail that's easy to visualize; however, this option does not indicate how the detail relates to the central idea.

DRAWING CONCLUSIONS

Reading text begins with making sense of the explicit meanings of information or a narrative. Understanding occurs as the reader draws conclusions and makes logical inferences. To draw a conclusion, the reader considers the details or facts. He or she then comes to a conclusion—the next logical point in the thought sequence. For example, in a Hemingway story, an old man sits alone in a café. A young waiter says that the café is closing, but the old man continues to drink. The waiter starts closing up, and the old man signals for a refill. Based on these details, the reader might conclude that the old man has not understood the young waiter's desire for him to leave.

When considering a character's motivations, the reader should ask what the character wants to achieve, what the character will get by accomplishing this, and what the character seems to value the most.

An inference is distinguished from a conclusion drawn. An INFERENCE is an assumption the reader makes based on details in the text as well as his or her own knowledge. It is more of an educated guess that extends the literal meaning. Inferences begin with the given details; however, the reader uses the facts to determine additional facts. What the reader already knows informs what is being suggested by the details of decisions or situations in the text. Returning to the example of the Hemingway story, the reader might infer that the old man is lonely, enjoys being in the café, and is reluctant to leave.

When reading fictional text, inferring character motivations is essential. The actions of the characters move the plot forward; a series of events is understood by making sense of why the characters did what they did. Hemingway includes contrasting details as the young waiter and an older waiter discuss the old man. The older waiter sympathizes with the old man; both men have no one at home and experience a sense of emptiness in life, which motivates them to seek the café.

Conclusions are drawn by thinking about how the author wants the reader to feel. A group of carefully selected facts can cause the reader to feel a certain way.

Another aspect of understanding text is connecting it to other texts. Readers may connect the Hemingway story about the old man in the café to other Hemingway stories about individuals struggling to deal with loss and loneliness in a dignified way. They can extend their initial connections to people they know or their personal experiences. When readers read a persuasive text, they often connect the arguments made to counterarguments and opposing evidence of which they are aware. They use these connections to infer meaning.

Examples

I believe it is difficult for those who publish their own memoirs to escape the imputation of vanity; nor is this the only disadvantage under which they labor: it is also their misfortune, that what is uncommon is rarely, if ever, believed, and what is obvious we are apt to turn from with disgust, and to charge the writer with impertinence. People generally think those memoirs only worthy to be read or remembered which abound in great or striking events, those, in short, which in a high degree excite either admiration or pity: all others they consign to contempt and oblivion. It is therefore, I confess, not a little hazardous in a private and obscure individual, and a stranger too, thus to solicit the indulgent attention of the public; especially when I own I offer here the history of neither a saint, a hero, nor a tyrant. I believe there are few events in my life, which have not happened to many: it is true the incidents of it are numerous; and, did I consider myself an European, I might say my sufferings were great: but when I compare my lot with that of most of my countrymen, I regard myself as a *particular favorite of Heaven*, and acknowledge the mercies of Providence in every occurrence of my life. If then the following narrative does not appear sufficiently interesting to engage general attention, let my motive be some excuse for its publication. I am not so foolishly vain as to expect from it either immortality or literary reputation. If it affords any satisfaction to my numerous friends, at whose request it has been written, or in the smallest degree promotes the interests of humanity, the ends for which it was undertaken will be fully attained, and every wish of my heart gratified. Let it therefore be remembered, that, in wishing to avoid censure, I do not aspire to praise.

—from *The Interesting Narrative of the Life of Olaudah Equiano, or Gustavus Vassa, The African* by Olaudah Equiano

1. Which of the following best explains the primary motivation of the narrator?

   (A) He wants his audience to know that he is not telling his story out of vanity.

   (B) He is hoping people will praise his courage.

   (C) He wants to give credit to God for protecting him.

   (D) He is honoring the wishes of his friends.

   (E) He is not seeking personal notoriety; he is hoping people will be influenced by his story and the human condition will improve.

Answers:

(A) is incorrect. That motive is how the passage begins, but it is not his primary motive.

(B) is incorrect. He says he does not aspire to praise, and he does not suggest that he was courageous.

(C) is incorrect. He does state that the "mercies of Providence" were always with him; however, that acknowledgement is not his primary motive.

(D) is incorrect. Although he says that he wrote it at the request of friends, the story is meant to improve humanity.

(E) is correct. In the passage "If it…in the smallest degree promotes the interests of humanity, the ends for which it was undertaken will be fully attained, and every wish of my heart gratified," the narrator's use of the word *humanity* could mean he wants to improve the human condition or he wants to increase human benevolence, or brotherly love.

2. Given the details of what the narrator says he is *not*, as well as what he claims his story is *not*, it can be inferred that his experience was

(A) a story that could lead to his success.

(B) an amazing story of survival and struggle that will be unfamiliar to many readers.

(C) an adventure that will thrill the audience.

(D) a narrow escape from suffering.

(E) an interesting story that is worthy of publication.

Answers:

(A) is incorrect. The narrator says that what is obvious in his story is what people "are apt to turn from with disgust, and to charge the writer with impertinence." The narrator is telling a story that his audience couldn't disagree with and might consider rude.

(B) is correct. By saying "what is uncommon is rarely, if ever, believed, and what is obvious we are apt to turn from with disgust," the narrator suggests that his experience wasn't common or ordinary and could cause disgust.

(C) is incorrect. The reader can infer that the experience was horrific; it will inspire disgust, not excitement.

(D) is incorrect. The narrator admits he suffered; he indicates that he narrowly escaped death. This is not an inference.

(E) is incorrect. By saying "If then the following narrative does not appear sufficiently interesting to engage general attention, let my motive be some excuse for its publication," the narrator makes clear that he does not think his narrative is interesting, but he believes his motive to help humanity makes it worthy of publication.

UNDERSTANDING THE AUTHOR

Many questions on the Reading Comprehension test will ask for an interpretation of an author's intentions and ideas. This requires an examination of the author's perspective and purpose as well as the way the author uses language to communicate these things.

In every passage, an author chooses words, structures, and content with specific purpose and intent. With this in mind, the reader can begin to comprehend why an author opts for particular words and structures and how these ultimately relate to the content.

The Author's Purpose

The author of a passage sets out with a specific goal in mind: to communicate a particular idea to an audience. The **AUTHOR'S PURPOSE** is determined by asking why the author wants the reader to understand the passage's main idea. There are four basic purposes to which an author can write: narrative, expository, technical, and persuasive. Within each of these general purposes, the author may direct the audience to take a clear action or respond in a certain way.

The purpose for which an author writes a passage is also connected to the structure of that text. In a **NARRATIVE**, the author seeks to tell a story, often to illustrate a theme or idea the reader needs to consider. In a narrative, the author uses characteristics of storytelling, such as chronological order, characters, and a defined setting, and these characteristics communicate the author's theme or main idea.

In an **EXPOSITORY** passage, on the other hand, the author simply seeks to explain an idea or topic to the reader. The main idea will probably be a factual statement or a direct assertion of a broadly held opinion. Expository writing can come in many forms, but one essential feature is a fair and balanced representation of a topic. The author may explore one detailed aspect or a broad range of characteristics, but he or she mainly seeks to prompt a decision from the reader.

Similarly, in **TECHNICAL** writing, the author's purpose is to explain specific processes, techniques, or equipment in order for the reader to use that process or equipment to obtain a desired result. Writing like this employs chronological or spatial structures, specialized vocabulary, and imperative or directive language.

In **PERSUASIVE** writing, though the reader is free to make decisions about the message and content, the author actively seeks to convince him or her to accept an opinion or belief. Much like expository writing, persuasive writing is presented in many organizational forms, but the author will use specific techniques, or **RHETORICAL STRATEGIES**, to build an argument. Readers can identify these strategies in order to clearly understand what an author wants them to believe, how the author's perspective and purpose may lead to bias, and whether the passage includes any logical fallacies.

Reading persuasive text requires an awareness of what the author believes about the topic.

Common rhetorical strategies include the appeals to ethos, logos, and pathos. An author uses these to build trust with the reader, explain the logical points of his or her argument, and convince the reader that his or her opinion is the best option.

An **ETHOS—ETHICAL—APPEAL** uses balanced, fair language and seeks to build a trusting relationship between the author and the reader. An author might explain his or her credentials, include the reader in an argument, or offer concessions to an opposing argument.

A **LOGOS—LOGICAL—APPEAL** builds on that trust by providing facts and support for the author's opinion, explaining the argument with clear connections and reasoning. At this point, the reader should beware of logical fallacies that connect unconnected ideas and build arguments on incorrect premises. With a logical appeal, an author strives to convince the reader to accept an opinion or belief by demonstrating that not only is it the most logical option but it also satisfies his or her emotional reaction to a topic.

Readers should consider how different audiences will react to a text. For example, how a slave owner's reactions to the narrative of Olaudah Equiano (on page 55) will differ from a slave trader's.

A **PATHOS—EMOTIONAL—APPEAL** does not depend on reasonable connections between ideas; rather, it seeks to remind the reader, through imagery, strong language, and personal connections, that the author's argument aligns with his or her best interests.

Many persuasive passages seek to use all three rhetorical strategies to best appeal to the reader.

Clues will help the reader determine many things about a passage, from the author's purpose to the passage's main idea, but understanding an author's purpose is essential to fully understanding the text.

Examples

Evident truth. Made so plain by our good Father in Heaven, that all *feel* and *understand* it, even down to brutes and creeping insects. The ant, who has toiled and dragged a crumb to his nest, will furiously defend the fruit of his labor, against whatever robber assails him. So plain, that the most dumb and stupid slave that ever toiled for a master, does constantly *know* that he is wronged. So plain that no one, high or low, ever does mistake it, except in a plainly *selfish* way; for although volume upon volume is written to prove slavery a very good thing, we never hear of the man who wishes to take the good of it, *by being a slave himself.*

Most governments have been based, practically, on the denial of the equal rights of men, as I have, in part, stated them; *ours* began, by *affirming* those rights. *They* said, some men are too *ignorant*, and *vicious*, to share in government. Possibly so, said we; and, by your system, you would always keep them ignorant and vicious. We proposed to give *all* a chance; and we expected the weak to grow stronger, the ignorant, wiser; and all better, and happier together.

We made the experiment; and the fruit is before us. Look at it. Think of it. Look at it, in its aggregate grandeur, of extent of country, and numbers of population, of ship, and steamboat.

—from Abraham Lincoln's speech fragment on slavery

1. The author's purpose is to
   (A) explain ideas.
   (B) narrate a story.
   (C) describe a situation.
   (D) persuade to accept an idea.
   (E) define a problem.

   Answers:

   (A) is incorrect. The injustice of slavery in America is made clear, but only to convince the audience that slavery cannot exist in America.

   (B) is incorrect. The author briefly mentions the narrative of America in terms of affirming the equal rights of all people, but he does not tell a story or relate the events that led to slavery.

   (C) is incorrect. The author does not describe the conditions of slaves or the many ways their human rights are denied.

   (D) is correct. The author provides logical reasons and evidence that slavery is wrong, that it violates the American belief in equal rights.

   (E) is incorrect. Although the author begins with a short definition of evident truth, he is simply laying the foundation for his persuasive argument that slavery violates the evident truth Americans believe.

2. To achieve his purpose, the author primarily uses
   (A) concrete analogies.
   (B) logical reasoning.
   (C) emotional appeals.
   (D) images.
   (E) figurative language.

Answers:

(A) is incorrect. The author mentions the ant's willingness to defend what is his but does not make an explicit and corresponding conclusion about the slave; instead, he says, "So plain, that the most dumb and stupid slave that ever toiled for a master, does constantly *know* that he is wronged." The implied parallel is between the ant's conviction about being wronged and the slave knowing he is wronged.

(B) is correct. The author uses logic when he points out that people who claim slavery is good never wish "to take the good of it, *by being a slave.*" The author also points out that the principle of our country is to give everyone, including the "ignorant," opportunity; then he challenges his listeners to look at the fruit of this principle, saying, "Look at it, in its aggregate grandeur, of extent of country, and numbers of population, of ship, and steamboat."

(C) is incorrect. The author relies on logic and evidence, and makes no emotional appeals about the suffering of slaves.

(D) is incorrect. The author does offer evidence of his point with an image of the grandeur of America, but his primary appeal is logic.

(E) is incorrect. Initially, the author uses hyperbole when he says, "Evident truth. Made so plain by our good Father in Heaven, that all *feel* and *understand it,* even down to brutes and creeping insects." However, the author's primary appeal is logos.

The Audience

The structure, purpose, main idea, and language of a text all converge on one target: the intended audience. An author makes decisions about every aspect of a piece of writing based on that audience, and readers can evaluate the writing through the lens of that audience. By considering the probable reactions of an intended audience, readers can determine many things: whether or not they are part of that intended audience; the author's purpose for using specific techniques or devices; the biases of the author and how they appear in the writing; and how the author uses rhetorical strategies. While readers evaluate each of these things separately, identifying and considering the intended audience adds depth to the understanding of a text and helps highlight details with more clarity.

When reading a persuasive text, students should maintain awareness of what the author believes about the topic.

Several aspects identify the text's intended audience. First, when the main idea of the passage is known, the reader considers who most likely cares about that idea, benefits from it, or needs to know about it. Many authors begin with the main idea and then determine the audience in part based on these concerns.

Then the reader considers language. The author tailors language to appeal to the intended audience, so the reader can narrow down a broad understanding of that audience. The figurative language John Steinbeck uses in his novel *The Grapes of Wrath* reveals the suffering of the migrant Americans who traveled to California to find work during the Great Depression of the 1930s. Steinbeck spoke concretely to the Americans who were discriminating against the migrants. Instead of finding work in the "land of milk and honey," migrants faced unbearable poverty and injustice. The metaphor that gives the novel its title is "and in the eyes of the people there is the failure; and in the eyes of the hungry there is a

A logical argument includes a claim, a reason that supports the claim, and an assumption that the reader makes based on accepted beliefs. All parts of the argument need to make sense to the reader, so authors often consider the beliefs of their audience as they construct their arguments.

growing wrath. In the souls of the people the grapes of wrath are filling and growing heavy, growing heavy for the vintage." Steinbeck, used the image of ripening grapes, familiar to those surrounded by vineyards, to condemn this harsh treatment, provide an education of the human heart, and inspire compassion in his audience. Readers who weren't directly involved in the exodus of people from Oklahoma to the West, could have little difficulty grasping the meaning of Steinbeck's language in the description: "66 is the path of a people in flight, refugees from dust and shrinking land, from the thunder of tractors and invasion, from the twisting winds that howl up out of Texas, from floods that bring no richness to the land and steal what little richness is there."

Examples

In the following text, consideration should be made for how an English political leader of 1729 might have reacted.

It is a melancholy object to those, who walk through this great town, or travel in the country, when they see the streets, the roads and cabin-doors crowded with beggars of the female sex, followed by three, four, or six children, all in rags, and importuning every passenger for an alms. These mothers instead of being able to work for their honest livelihood, are forced to employ all their time in strolling to beg sustenance for their helpless infants who, as they grow up, either turn thieves for want of work, or leave their dear native country, to fight for the Pretender in Spain, or sell themselves to the Barbados.

I shall now therefore humbly propose my own thoughts, which I hope will not be liable to the least objection.

I have been assured by a very knowing American of my acquaintance in London, that a young healthy child well nursed, is, at a year old, a most delicious nourishing and wholesome food, whether stewed, roasted, baked, or boiled; and I make no doubt that it will equally serve in a fricassee.

I do therefore humbly offer it to public consideration, that of the hundred and twenty thousand children, already computed, twenty thousand may be reserved for breed, whereof only one fourth part to be males; which is more than we allow to sheep, black cattle, or swine, and my reason is, that these children are seldom the fruits of marriage, a circumstance not much regarded by our savages, therefore, one male will be sufficient to serve four females. That the remaining hundred thousand may, at a year old, be offered in sale to the persons of quality and fortune, through the kingdom, always advising the mother to let them suck plentifully in the last month, so as to render them plump, and fat for a good table. A child will make two dishes at an entertainment for friends, and when the family dines alone, the fore or hind quarter will make a reasonable dish, and seasoned with a little pepper or salt, will be very good boiled on the fourth day, especially in winter.

—from *A Modest Proposal for Preventing the Children of Poor People in Ireland From Being a Burden on Their Parents or Country, and for Making Them Beneficial to the Public* By Jonathan Swift

1. Which of the following best states the central idea of the passage?

   (A) Irish mothers are not able to support their children.

   (B) The Irish people lived like savages.

   (C) The people of England are quality people of fortune.

   (D) The poverty of the Irish forces their children to become criminals.

   (E) The kingdom of England has exploited the weaker country of Ireland to the point that the Irish people cannot support their families.

Answers:

(A) is incorrect. This is a fact alluded to in the passage, not a central idea.

(B) is incorrect. Although the author does refer to the Irish as savages, the reader recognizes that the author is being outrageously satirical.

(C) is incorrect. The author does say "That the remaining hundred thousand may, at a year old, be offered in sale to the persons of quality and fortune, through the kingdom," referring to the English. However, this is not the central idea; the opposite is, given that this is satire.

(D) is incorrect. The author does mention children growing up to be thieves, but this is not the central idea.

(E) is correct. The author is hoping to use satire to shame England.

2. The author's use of phrases like "humbly propose," "liable to the least objection," "wholesome food" suggests which of the following purposes?

(A) to inform people about the attitudes of the English

(B) to use satire to reveal the inhumane treatment of the Irish by the English

(C) to persuade people to survive by any means

(D) to express his admiration of the Irish people

(E) to narrate the struggles of the English people

Answers:

(A) is incorrect. The author's subject is the poverty of the Irish, and his audience is the English who are responsible for the suffering of the Irish.

(B) is correct. The intended meaning of a satire sharply contradicts the literal meaning. Swift's proposal is not humble; it is meant to humble the arrogant. He expects the audience to be horrified. The children would make the worst imaginable food.

(C) is incorrect. The author is not serious. His intent is to shock his English audience.

(D) is incorrect. The author is expressing sympathy for the Irish.

(E) is incorrect. It is the Irish people who are struggling.

Tone and Mood

Two important aspects of the communication between author and audience occur subtly. The **TONE** of a passage describes the author's attitude toward the topic, distinct from the **MOOD**, which is the pervasive feeling or atmosphere in a passage that provokes specific emotions in the reader. The distinction between these two aspects lies once again in the audience: the mood influences the reader's emotional state in response to the piece, while the tone establishes a relationship between the audience and the author. Does the author intend to instruct the audience? Is the author more experienced than the audience, or does he or she wish to convey a friendly or equal relationship? In each of these cases, the author uses a different tone to reflect the desired level of communication.

To determine the author's tone, students should examine what overall feeling they are experiencing.

Primarily **DICTION**, or word choice, determines mood and tone in a passage. Many readers make the mistake of thinking about the ideas an author puts forth and using those alone to determine particularly tone; a much better practice is to separate specific words from the text and look for patterns in connotation and emotion. By considering categories of words used by the author, the reader can discover both the overall emotional atmosphere of a text and the attitude of the author toward the subject.

To decide the connotation of a word, the reader examines whether the word conveys a positive or negative association in the mind. Adjectives are often used to influence the feelings of the reader, such as in the phrase "an ambitious attempt to achieve."

Every word has not only a literal meaning but also a **CONNOTATIVE MEANING**, relying on the common emotions, associations, and experiences an audience might associate with that word. The following words are all synonyms: *dog, puppy, cur, mutt, canine, pet*. Two of these words—*dog* and *canine*—are neutral words, without strong associations or emotions. Two others—*pet* and *puppy*—have positive associations. The last two—*cur* and *mutt*—have negative associations. A passage that uses one pair of these words versus another pair activates the positive or negative reactions of the audience.

Examples

Day had broken cold and grey, exceedingly cold and grey, when the man turned aside from the main Yukon trail and climbed the high earth-bank, where a dim and little-travelled trail led eastward through the fat spruce timberland. It was a steep bank, and he paused for breath at the top, excusing the act to himself by looking at his watch. It was nine o'clock. There was no sun nor hint of sun, though there was not a cloud in the sky. It was a clear day, and yet there seemed an intangible *pall* over the face of things, a subtle gloom that made the day dark, and that was due to the absence of sun. This fact did not worry the man. He was used to the lack of sun. It had been days since he had seen the sun, and he knew that a few more days must pass before that cheerful orb, due south, would just peep above the sky-line and dip immediately from view.

—from "To Build a Fire" by Jack London

1. Which of the following best describes the mood of the passage?
   (A) exciting and adventurous
   (B) fierce and determined
   (C) bleak and forbidding
   (D) grim yet hopeful
   (E) intense yet filled with fear

Answers:

(A) is incorrect. The man is on some adventure as he turns off the main trail, but the context is one of gloom and darkness, not excitement.

(B) is incorrect. The cold, dark day is fierce, and the man may be determined; however, the overall mood of the entire passage is one of grim danger.

(C) is correct. The man is oblivious to the gloom and darkness of the day, which was "exceedingly cold and grey."

(D) is incorrect. The atmosphere is grim, and there is no indication the man is hopeful about anything. He is aware only of his breath and steps forward.

(E) is incorrect. The cold, grey scene of a lone man walking off the trail is intense, but "this fact did not worry the man."

2. The connotation of the words *intangible pall* is

(A) a death-like covering.

(B) a vague sense of familiarity.

(C) an intimation of communal strength.

(D) an understanding of the struggle ahead.

(E) a refreshing sense of possibility.

Answers:

(A) is correct. Within the context of the sentence "It was a clear day, and yet there seemed an intangible *pall* over the face of things, a subtle gloom that made the day dark," the words *gloom* and *dark* are suggestive of death; the words *over the face* suggest a covering.

(B) is incorrect. The word *intangible* can mean a vague sense, but there is nothing especially familiar about a clear day that is dark, with no sunlight.

(C) is incorrect. The word *intangible* suggests intimation; however, from the beginning, the author shows the man alone, and reports, "the man turned aside from the main Yukon trail."

(D) is incorrect. A struggle may be indicated by the darkness and gloom, but the man has no understanding of this possibility. The text refers to the darkness, saying, "This fact did not worry the man. He was used to the lack of sun."

(E) is incorrect. The man is hiking this trail for some possibility, but he is not refreshed; he is pausing to catch his "breath at the top, excusing the act to himself by looking at his watch."

VOCABULARY IN CONTEXT

Vocabulary in context questions ask about the meaning of specific words in the passage. The questions will ask which answer choice is most similar in meaning to the specified word, or which answer choice could be substituted for that word in the passage.

When confronted with unfamiliar words, the passage itself can help clarify their meaning. Often, identifying the tone or main idea of the passage can help eliminate answer choices. For example, if the tone of the passage is generally positive, try eliminating the answer choices with a negative connotation. Or, if the passage is about a particular occupation, rule out words unrelated to that topic.

Passages may also provide specific CONTEXT CLUES that can help determine the meaning of a word.

One type of context clue is a DEFINITION, or DESCRIPTION, CLUE. Sometimes, authors use a difficult word, then include *that is* or *which is* to signal that they are providing a definition. An author also may provide a synonym or restate the idea in more familiar words:

> *Teachers often prefer teaching students with intrinsic motivation; these students have an internal desire to learn.*

The meaning of *intrinsic* is restated as an *internal desire*.

Similarly, authors may include an EXAMPLE CLUE, providing an example phrase that clarifies the meaning of the word:

Teachers may view extrinsic rewards as efficacious; however, an individual student may not be interested in what the teacher offers. For example, a student who is diabetic may not feel any incentive to work when offered a sweet treat.

Efficacious is explained with an example that demonstrates how an extrinsic reward may not be effective.

Another commonly used context clue is the CONTRAST, or ANTONYM, CLUE. In this case, authors indicate that the unfamiliar word is the opposite of a familiar word:

In contrast to intrinsic motivation, extrinsic motivation is contingent on teachers offering rewards that are appealing.

The phrase "in contrast" tells the reader that *extrinsic* is the opposite of *intrinsic*.

Examples

1. One challenge of teaching is finding ways to incentivize, or to motivate, learning.

   Which of the following is the meaning of *incentivize* as used in the sentence?

   (A) encourage
   (B) determine
   (C) challenge
   (D) improve
   (E) dissuade

   Answers:

   (A) is correct. The word *incentivize* is defined immediately with the synonym *motivate*, or *encourage*.

   (B) is incorrect. *Determine* is not a synonym for *motivate*. In addition, the phrase "to determine learning" does not make sense in the sentence.

   (C) is incorrect. *Challenge* is not a synonym for motivate.

   (D) is incorrect. *Improve* is closely related to motivation, but it is not the best synonym provided.

   (E) is incorrect. *Dissuade* is an antonym for motivate.

2. If an extrinsic reward is extremely desirable, a student may become so apprehensive he or she cannot focus. The student may experience such intense pressure to perform that the reward undermines its intent.

   Which of the following is the meaning of *apprehensive* as used in the sentence?

   (A) uncertain
   (B) distracted
   (C) anxious
   (D) forgetful
   (E) resentful

   Answers:

   (A) is incorrect. Nothing in the sentence suggests the student is uncertain.

   (B) is incorrect. *Distracted* is related to the clue "focus" but does not address the clue "pressure to perform."

(C) is correct. The reader can infer that the pressure to perform is making the student anxious.

(D) is incorrect. Nothing in the sentence suggests the student is forgetful.

(E) is incorrect. The clue describes the student as feeling pressured but does not suggest the student is resentful.

6

MATH SKILLS

The Math Skills Test includes questions that cover concepts taught in high school-level math classes. Topics covered include percentages, proportions, properties of shapes, and algebraic expressions and equations. Because the Math Skills test is in the CAT format, the number of questions in this section will depend on individual candidate's performance.

TYPES OF NUMBERS

Numbers are placed in categories based on their properties.

- A **NATURAL NUMBER** is greater than 0 and has no decimal or fraction attached. These are also sometimes called counting numbers {1, 2, 3, 4, ...}.

- **WHOLE NUMBERS** are natural numbers and the number 0 {0, 1, 2, 3, 4, ...}.

- **INTEGERS** include positive and negative natural numbers and 0 {..., –4, –3, –2, –1, 0, 1, 2, 3, 4, ...}.

- A **RATIONAL NUMBER** can be represented as a fraction. Any decimal part must terminate or resolve into a repeating pattern. Examples include -12, $-\frac{4}{5}$, 0.36, $7.\overline{7}$, $26\frac{1}{2}$, etc.

- An **IRRATIONAL NUMBER** cannot be represented as a fraction. An irrational decimal number never ends and never resolves into a repeating pattern. Examples include $-\sqrt{7}$, π, and $0.34567989135...$

- A **REAL NUMBER** is a number that can be represented by a point on a number line. Real numbers include all the rational and irrational numbers.

- An **IMAGINARY NUMBER** includes the imaginary unit i, where $i = \sqrt{-1}$ Because $i^2 = -1$, imaginary numbers produce a negative value when squared. Examples of imaginary numbers include $-4i$, $0.75i$, $i\sqrt{2}$ and $\frac{8}{3}i$.

- A **COMPLEX NUMBER** is in the form $a + bi$, where a and b are real numbers. Examples of complex numbers include $3 + 2i$, $-4 + i$, $\sqrt{3} - i\sqrt[3]{5}$ and $\frac{5}{8} - \frac{7i}{8}$. All imaginary numbers are also complex.

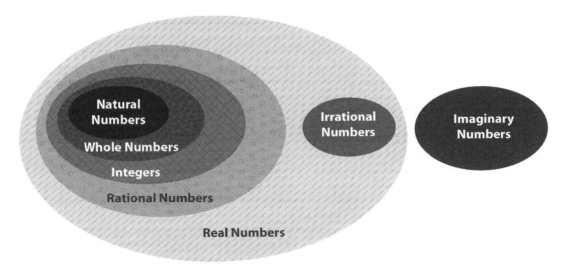

Figure 6.1. Types of Numbers

The **FACTORS** of a natural number are all the numbers that can multiply together to make the number. For example, the factors of 24 are 1, 2, 3, 4, 6, 8, 12, and 24. Every natural number is either prime or composite. A **PRIME NUMBER** is a number that is only divisible by itself and 1. (The number 1 is not considered prime.) Examples of prime numbers are 2, 3, 7, and 29. The number 2 is the only even prime number. A **COMPOSITE NUMBER** has more than two factors. For example, 6 is composite because its factors are 1, 6, 2, and 3. Every composite number can be written as a unique product of prime numbers, called the **PRIME FACTORIZATION** of the number. For example, the prime factorization of 90 is $90 = 2 \times 3^2 \times 5$. All integers are either even or odd. An even number is divisible by 2; an odd number is not.

> ⚠️ If a real number is a natural number (e.g., 50), then it is also a whole number, an integer, and a rational number.

Examples

1. Classify the following numbers as natural, whole, integer, rational, or irrational. (The numbers may have more than one classification.)

    (A) 72

    (B) $-\frac{2}{3}$

    (C) $\sqrt{5}$

    Answers:

    (A) The number is **natural**, **whole**, an **integer**, and **rational**.

    (B) The fraction is **rational**.

    (C) The number is **irrational**. (It cannot be written as a fraction, and written as a decimal is approximately 2.2360679...)

2. Determine the real and imaginary parts of the following complex numbers.

    (A) 20

    (B) $10 - i$

    (C) $15i$

Answers:

A complex number is in the form of $a + bi$, where a is the real part and bi is the imaginary part.

(A) $20 = 20 + 0i$ **The real part is 20, and there is no imaginary part.**

(B) $10 - i = 10 - 1i$ **The real part is 10, and $-1i$ is the imaginary part.**

(C) $15i = 0 + 15i$ **The real part is 0, and the imaginary part is 15i.**

POSITIVE AND NEGATIVE NUMBERS

POSITIVE NUMBERS are greater than 0, and **NEGATIVE NUMBERS** are less than 0. Both positive and negative numbers can be shown on a **NUMBER LINE**.

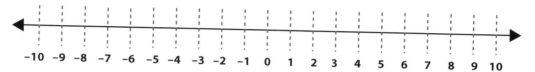

Figure 6.2. Number Line

The **ABSOLUTE VALUE** of a number is the distance the number is from 0. Since distance is always positive, the absolute value of a number is always positive. The absolute value of a is denoted $|a|$. For example, $|-2| = 2$ since -2 is two units away from 0.

Positive and negative numbers can be added, subtracted, multiplied, and divided. The sign of the resulting number is governed by a specific set of rules shown in the table below.

Table 6.1. Operations with Positive and Negative Numbers

ADDING REAL NUMBERS		**SUBTRACTING REAL NUMBERS***	
Positive + Positive = Positive	$7 + 8 = 15$	Negative – Positive = Negative	$-7 - 8 =$ $-7 + (-8) =$ -15
Negative + Negative = Negative	$-7 + (-8) =$ -15	Positive – Negative = Positive	$7 - (-8) =$ $7 + 8 = 15$

ADDING REAL NUMBERS		**SUBTRACTING REAL NUMBERS***	
Negative + Positive OR Positive + Negative = Keep the sign of the number with larger absolute value	$-7 + 8 = 1$ $7 + -8 = -1$	Negative – Negative = Keep the sign of the number with larger absolute value	$-7 - (-8) =$ $-7 + 8 = 1$ $-8 - (-7) = -8$ $+ 7 = -1$

MULTIPLYING REAL NUMBERS		**DIVIDING REAL NUMBERS**	
Positive × Positive = Positive	$8 \times 4 = 32$	Positive ÷ Positive = Positive	$8 \div 4 = 2$
Negative × Negative = Positive	$-8 \times (-4) = 32$	Negative ÷ Negative = Positive	$-8 \div (-4) = 2$
Positive × Negative OR Negative × Positive = Negative	$8 \times (-4) = -32$ $-8 \times 4 = -32$	Positive ÷ Negative OR Negative ÷ Positive = Negative	$8 \div (-4) = -2$ $-8 \div 4 = -2$

*Always change the subtraction to addition and change the sign of the second number; then use addition rules.

Examples

1. Add or subtract the following real numbers:

   (A) $-18 + 12$

   (B) $-3.64 + (-2.18)$

   (C) $9.37 - 4.25$

   (D) $86 - (-20)$

   Answers:

   (A) Since $|-18| > |12|$, the answer is negative: $|-18| - |12| = 6$. So the answer is **−6**.

   (B) Adding two negative numbers results in a negative number. Add the values: **−5.82**.

   (C) The first number is larger than the second, so the final answer is positive: **5.12**.

   (D) Change the subtraction to addition, change the sign of the second number, and then add: $86 - (-20) = 86 + (+20) = $ **106**.

2. Multiply or divide the following real numbers:

   (A) $\left(\frac{10}{3}\right)\left(-\frac{9}{5}\right)$

   (B) $\frac{-64}{-10}$

   (C) $(2.2)(3.3)$

   (D) $-52 \div 13$

   Answers:

   (A) Multiply the numerators, multiply the denominators, and simplify: $\frac{-90}{15} = $ **−6**.

   (B) A negative divided by a negative is a positive number: **6.4**.

   (C) Multiplying positive numbers gives a positive answer: **7.26**.

   (D) Dividing a negative by a positive number gives a negative answer: **−4**.

ORDER OF OPERATIONS

The ORDER OF OPERATIONS is simply the order in which operations are performed. **PEMDAS** is a common way to remember the order of operations:

1.	**P**arentheses	4.	**D**ivision
2.	**E**xponents	5.	**A**ddition
3.	**M**ultiplication	6.	**S**ubtraction

Multiplication and division, and addition and subtraction, are performed together from left to right. So, performing multiple operations on a set of numbers is a four-step process:

1. P: Calculate expressions inside parentheses, brackets, braces, etc.

2. E: Calculate exponents and square roots.

3. MD: Calculate any remaining multiplication and division in order from left to right.

4. AS: Calculate any remaining addition and subtraction in order from left to right.

Always work from left to right within each step when simplifying expressions.

Examples

1. Simplify: $2(21 - 14) + 6 \div (-2) \times 3 - 10$

Answer:

$2(21 - 14) + 6 \div (-2) \times 3 - 10$	
$= 2(7) + 6 \div (-2) \times 3 - 10$	Calculate expressions inside parentheses.
$= 14 + 6 \div (-2) \times 3 - 10$ $= 14 + (-3) \times 3 - 10$ $= 14 + (-9) - 10$	There are no exponents or radicals, so perform multiplication and division from left to right.
$= 5 - 10$ $= \mathbf{-5}$	Perform addition and subtraction from left to right.

2. Simplify: $-(3)^2 + 4(5) + (5 - 6)^2 - 8$

Answer:

$-(3)^2 + 4(5) + (5 - 6)^2 - 8$	
$= -(3)^2 + 4(5) + (-1)^2 - 8$	Calculate expressions inside parentheses.
$= -9 + 4(5) + 1 - 8$	Simplify exponents and radicals.
$= -9 + 20 + 1 - 8$	Perform multiplication and division from left to right.
$= 11 + 1 - 8$ $= 12 - 8$ $= \mathbf{4}$	Perform addition and subtraction from left to right.

3. Simplify: $\dfrac{(7 - 9)^3 + 8(10 - 12)}{4^2 - 5^2}$

Answer:

$\dfrac{(7 - 9)^3 + 8(10 - 12)}{4^2 - 5^2}$	
$= \dfrac{(-2)^3 + 8(-2)}{4^2 - 5^2}$	Calculate expressions inside parentheses.
$= \dfrac{-8 + (-16)}{16 - 25}$	Simplify exponents and radicals.
$= \dfrac{-24}{-9}$	Perform addition and subtraction from left to right.
$= \dfrac{\mathbf{8}}{\mathbf{3}}$	Simplify.

UNITS OF MEASUREMENT

The standard units for the metric and American systems are shown below, along with the prefixes used to express metric units.

Table 6.2. Units and Conversion Factors

DIMENSION	AMERICAN	SI
length	inch/foot/yard/mile	meter
mass	ounce/pound/ton	gram
volume	cup/pint/quart/gallon	liter
force	pound-force	newton
pressure	pound-force per square inch	pascal
work and energy	cal/British thermal unit	joule
temperature	Fahrenheit	kelvin
charge	faraday	coulomb

Table 6.3. Metric Prefixes

PREFIX	SYMBOL	MULTIPLICATION FACTOR
tera	T	1,000,000,000,000
giga	G	1,000,000,000
mega	M	1,000,000
kilo	k	1,000
hecto	h	100
deca	da	10
base unit	--	--
deci	d	0.1
centi	c	0.01
milli	m	0.001
micro	μ	0.0000001
nano	n	0.0000000001
pico	p	0.0000000000001

A mnemonic device to help remember the metric system is *King Henry Drinks Under Dark Chocolate Moon* (KHDUDCM).

Units can be converted within a single system or between systems. When converting from one unit to another unit, a conversion factor (a numeric multiplier used to convert a value with a unit to another unit) is used. The process of converting between units using a conversion factor is sometimes known as dimensional analysis.

Table 6.4. Conversion Factors

1 in. = 2.54 cm	1 lb. = 0.454 kg
1 yd. = 0.914 m	1 cal = 4.19 J
1 mi. = 1.61 km	$1\,^\circ F = \frac{5}{9}\,(^\circ F - 32\,^\circ C)$
1 gal. = 3.785 L	$1\,cm^3 = 1\,mL$
1 oz. = 28.35 g	1 hr = 3600 s

Examples

1. Convert the following measurements in the metric system.

   (A) 4.25 kilometers to meters

   (B) 8 m² to mm²

Answers:

(A) $4.25\ km\left(\frac{1000\ m}{1\ km}\right) =$ **4250 m**

(B) $\frac{8\ m^2}{1} \times \frac{1000\ mm}{1\ m} \times \frac{1000\ mm}{1\ m} =$ **8,000,000 mm²**

Since the units are square units (m²), multiply by the conversion factor twice, so that both meters cancel.

2. Convert the following measurements in the American system.

   (A) 12 feet to inches

   (B) 7 yd² to ft²

Answers:

(A) $12\ ft\left(\frac{12\ in}{1\ ft}\right) =$ **144 in**

(B) $7\ yd^2\left(\frac{3ft}{1yd}\right)\left(\frac{3ft}{1yd}\right) =$ **63 ft²**

Since the units are square units (yd²), multiply by the conversion factor twice.

3. Convert the following measurements in the metric system to the American system.

   (A) 23 meters to feet

   (B) 10 m² to yd²

Answers:

(A) $23\ m\left(\frac{3.28\ ft}{1\ m}\right) =$ **75.44 ft**

(B) $\frac{10\ m^2}{1} \times \frac{1.094\ yd}{1\ m} \times \frac{1.094\ yd}{1\ m} =$ **11.97 yd²**

4. Convert the following measurements in the American system to the metric system.

   (A) 8 in³ to milliliters

   (B) 16 kilograms to pounds

Answers:

(A) $8 \text{ in}^3 \left(\frac{16.39 \text{ ml}}{1 \text{ in}^3} \right) = \textbf{131.12 mL}$

(B) $16 \text{ kg} \left(\frac{2.2 \text{ lb}}{1 \text{ kg}} \right) = \textbf{35.2 lb}$

DECIMALS AND FRACTIONS

Decimals

A DECIMAL is a number that contains a decimal point. A decimal number is an alternative way of writing a fraction. The place value for a decimal includes TENTHS (one place after the decimal), HUNDREDTHS (two places after the decimal), THOUSANDTHS (three places after the decimal), etc.

Table 6.5. Place Values

1,000,000	10^6	millions
100,000	10^5	hundred thousands
10,000	10^4	ten thousands
1,000	10^3	thousands
100	10^2	hundreds
10	10^1	tens
1	10^0	ones
.		decimal
$\frac{1}{10}$	10^{-1}	tenths
$\frac{1}{100}$	10^{-2}	hundredths
$\frac{1}{1000}$	10^{-3}	thousandths

Decimals can be added, subtracted, multiplied, and divided:

- To add or subtract decimals, line up the decimal point and perform the operation, keeping the decimal point in the same place in the answer.

- To multiply decimals, first multiply the numbers without the decimal points. Then, sum the number of decimal places to the right of the decimal point in the original numbers and place the decimal point in the answer so that there are that many places to the right of the decimal.

$$4.2 \leftarrow \text{quotient}$$
$$2.5 \overline{)10.5} \leftarrow \text{dividend}$$
$$\uparrow$$
$$\text{divisor}$$

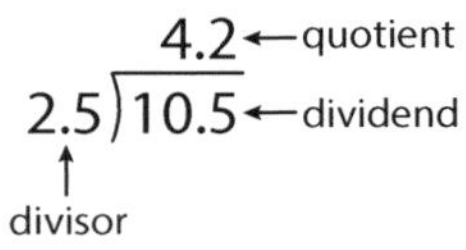

Figure 6.3. Division Terms

- When dividing decimals move the decimal point to the right in order to make the divisor a whole number and move the decimal the same number of places in the dividend. Divide the numbers without regard to the decimal. Then, place the decimal point of the quotient directly above the decimal point of the dividend.

Examples

1. Simplify: 24.38 + 16.51 − 29.87

Answer:

24.38 + 16.51 − 29.87	
24.38 + 16.51 = 40.89	Align the decimals and apply the order of operations left to right.
40.89 − 29.87 = **11.02**	

2. Simplify: (10.4)(18.2)

Answer:

(10.4)(18.2)	
104 × 182 = 18,928	Multiply the numbers ignoring the decimals.
18,928 → 189.28	The original problem includes two decimal places (one in each number), so move the decimal point in the answer so that there are two places after the decimal point.

Estimating is a good way to check the answer: $10.4 \approx 10$, $18.2 \approx 18$, and $10 \times 18 = 180$.

3. Simplify: 80 ÷ 2.5

Answer:

80 ÷ 2.5	
80 → 800 2.5 → 25	Move both decimals one place to the right (multiply by 10) so that the divisor is a whole number.
800 ÷ 25 = 32	Divide normally.

Fractions

A **FRACTION** is a number that can be written in the form $\frac{a}{b}$, where b is not equal to 0. The a part of the fraction is the **NUMERATOR** (top number) and the b part of the fraction is the **DENOMINATOR** (bottom number).

If the denominator of a fraction is greater than the numerator, the value of the fraction is less than 1 and it is called a **PROPER FRACTION** (for example, $\frac{3}{5}$ is a proper fraction). In an **IMPROPER FRACTION**, the denominator is less than the numerator and the value of the fraction is greater than 1 ($\frac{8}{3}$ is an improper fraction). An improper fraction can be written as a **MIXED NUMBER**, which has a whole number part and a proper fraction part. Improper fractions can be converted to mixed numbers by dividing the numerator by the denominator, which gives the whole number part, and the remainder becomes the numerator of the proper fraction part. (For example, the improper fraction $\frac{25}{9}$ is equal to mixed number $2\frac{7}{9}$ because 9 divides into 25 two times, with a remainder of 7.)

Conversely, mixed numbers can be converted to improper fractions. To do so, determine the numerator of the improper fraction by multiplying the denominator by the whole number, and then adding the numerator. The final number is written as the (now larger) numerator over the original denominator.

To convert mixed numbers to improper fractions:
$$a\frac{m}{n} = \frac{n \times a + m}{n}$$

Fractions with the same denominator can be added or subtracted by simply adding or subtracting the numerators; the denominator will remain unchanged. To add or subtract fractions with different denominators, find the **LEAST COMMON DENOMINATOR (LCD)** of all the fractions. The LCD is the smallest number exactly divisible by each denominator. (For example, the least common denominator of the numbers 2, 3, and 8 is 24.) Once the LCD has been found, each fraction should be written in an equivalent form with the LCD as the denominator.

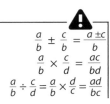

$$\frac{a}{b} \pm \frac{c}{b} = \frac{a \pm c}{b}$$
$$\frac{a}{b} \times \frac{c}{d} = \frac{ac}{bd}$$
$$\frac{a}{b} \div \frac{c}{d} = \frac{a}{b} \times \frac{d}{c} = \frac{ad}{bc}$$

To multiply fractions, the numerators are multiplied together and denominators are multiplied together. If there are any mixed numbers, they should first be changed to improper fractions. Then, the numerators are multiplied together and the denominators are multiplied together. The fraction can then be reduced if necessary. To divide fractions, multiply the first fraction by the reciprocal of the second.

Any common denominator can be used to add or subtract fractions. The quickest way to find a common denominator of a set of values is simply to multiply all the values together. The result might not be the least common denominator, but it will allow the problem to be worked.

Examples

1. Simplify: $2\frac{3}{5} + 3\frac{1}{4} - 1\frac{1}{2}$

Answer:

$2\frac{3}{5} + 3\frac{1}{4} - 1\frac{1}{2}$	
$= 2\frac{12}{20} + 3\frac{5}{20} - 1\frac{10}{20}$	Change each fraction so it has a denominator of 20, which is the LCD of 5, 4, and 2.
$2 + 3 - 1 = 4$ $\frac{12}{20} + \frac{5}{20} - \frac{10}{20} = \frac{7}{20}$	Add and subtract the whole numbers together and the fractions together.
$4\frac{7}{20}$	Combine to get the final answer (a mixed number).

2. Simplify: $\frac{7}{8} \times 3\frac{1}{3}$

Answer:

$\frac{7}{8} \times 3\frac{1}{3}$

$3\frac{1}{3} = \frac{10}{3}$	Change the mixed number to an improper fraction.
$\frac{7}{8}\left(\frac{10}{3}\right) = \frac{7 \times 10}{8 \times 3}$ $= \frac{70}{24}$	Multiply the numerators together and the denominators together.
$= \frac{35}{12}$ $= 2\frac{11}{12}$	Reduce the fraction.

3. Simplify: $4\frac{1}{2} \div \frac{2}{3}$

Answer:

$4\frac{1}{2} \div \frac{2}{3}$	
$4\frac{1}{2} = \frac{9}{2}$	Change the mixed number to an improper fraction.
$\frac{9}{2} \div \frac{2}{3}$ $= \frac{9}{2} \times \frac{3}{2}$ $= \frac{27}{4}$	Multiply the first fraction by the reciprocal of the second fraction.
$= 6\frac{3}{4}$	Simplify.

Converting Between Fractions and Decimals

A fraction is converted to a decimal by using long division until there is no remainder and no pattern of repeating numbers occurs.

A decimal is converted to a fraction using the following steps:

- Place the decimal value as the numerator in a fraction with a denominator of 1.
- Multiply the fraction by $\frac{10}{10}$ for every digit in the decimal value, so that there is no longer a decimal in the numerator.
- Reduce the fraction.

Examples

1. Write the fraction $\frac{7}{8}$ as a decimal.

Answer:

$\begin{array}{r} 0.875 \\ 8\overline{)7000} \\ \underline{-64}\downarrow \\ 60 \\ \underline{-56}\downarrow \\ 40 \end{array}$	Divide the denominator into the numerator using long division.

2. Write the fraction $\frac{5}{11}$ as a decimal.

Answer:

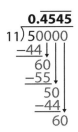

Dividing using long division yields a repeating decimal.

3. Write the decimal 0.125 as a fraction.

Answer:

0.125

$= \dfrac{0.125}{1}$

$\dfrac{0.125}{1} \times \dfrac{10}{10} \times \dfrac{10}{10} \times \dfrac{10}{10} = \dfrac{125}{1000}$

$= \dfrac{1}{8}$

Create a fraction with 0.125 as the numerator and 1 as the denominator.

Multiply by $\dfrac{10}{10}$ three times (one for each numeral after the decimal).

Simplify.

Alternatively, recognize that 0.125 is read "one hundred twenty-five thousandths" and can therefore be written in fraction form as $\dfrac{125}{1000}$.

RATIOS

A **RATIO** is a comparison of two numbers and can be represented as $\frac{a}{b}$, $a{:}b$, or a to b. The two numbers represent a constant relationship, not a specific value: for every a number of items in the first group, there will be b number of items in the second. For example, if the ratio of blue to red candies in a bag is 3:5, the bag will contain 3 blue candies for every 5 red candies. So, the bag might contain 3 blue candies and 5 red candies, or it might contain 30 blue candies and 50 red candies, or 36 blue candies and 60 red candies. All of these values are representative of the ratio 3:5 (which is the ratio in its lowest, or simplest, terms).

To find the "whole" when working with ratios, simply add the values in the ratio. For example, if the ratio of boys to girls in a class is 2:3, the "whole" is five: 2 out of every 5 students are boys, and 3 out of every 5 students are girls.

Examples

1. There are 10 boys and 12 girls in a first-grade class. What is the ratio of boys to the total number of students? What is the ratio of girls to boys?

Answer:

number of boys: 10
number of girls: 12
number of students: 22

Identify the variables.

number of boys : number of students $= 10 : 22$ $= \dfrac{10}{22}$ $= \dfrac{5}{11}$	Write out and simplify the ratio of boys to total students.
number of girls : number of boys $= 12 : 10$ $= \dfrac{12}{10}$ $= \dfrac{6}{5}$	Write out and simplify the ratio of girls to boys.

2. A family spends $600 a month on rent, $400 on utilities, $750 on groceries, and $550 on miscellaneous expenses. What is the ratio of the family's rent to their total expenses?

Answer:

rent $= 600$ utilities $= 400$ groceries $= 750$ miscellaneous $= 550$ total expenses $= 600 + 400 + 750 + 550$ $= 2300$	Identify the variables.
rent : total expenses $= 600 : 2300$ $= \dfrac{600}{2300}$ $= \dfrac{6}{23}$	Write out and simplify the ratio of rent to total expenses.

PROPORTIONS

A **PROPORTION** is an equation which states that two ratios are equal. A proportion is given in the form $\dfrac{a}{b} = \dfrac{c}{d}$, where the a and d terms are the extremes and the b and c terms are the means. A proportion is solved using cross-multiplication ($ad = bc$) to create an equation with no fractional components. A proportion must have the same units in both numerators and both denominators.

Examples

1. Solve the proportion for x: $\dfrac{3x-5}{2} = \dfrac{x-8}{3}$.

Answer:

$\dfrac{(3x-5)}{2} = \dfrac{(x-8)}{3}$	
$3(3x-5) = 2(x-8)$	Cross-multiply.

$$9x - 15 = 2x - 16$$
$$7x - 15 = -16$$
$$7x = -1$$
$$x = -\frac{1}{7}$$

Solve the equation for x.

2. A map is drawn such that 2.5 inches on the map equates to an actual distance of 40 miles. If the distance measured on the map between two cities is 17.25 inches, what is the actual distance between them in miles?

Answer:

$\frac{2.5}{40} = \frac{17.25}{x}$	Write a proportion where x equals the actual distance and each ratio is written as inches : miles.
$2.5x = 690$ $x = 276$ The two cities are **276 miles apart**.	Cross-multiply and divide to solve for x.

3. A factory knows that 4 out of 1000 parts made will be defective. If in a month there are 125,000 parts made, how many of these parts will be defective?

Answer:

$\frac{4}{1000} = \frac{x}{125{,}000}$	Write a proportion where x is the number of defective parts made and both ratios are written as defective : total.
$1000x = 500{,}000$ $x = 500$ There are **500 defective parts** for the month.	Cross-multiply and divide to solve for x.

PERCENTAGES

A PERCENT (or percentage) means per hundred and is expressed with a percent symbol (%). For example, 54% means 54 out of every 100. A percent can be converted to a decimal by removing the % symbol and moving the decimal point two places to the left, while a decimal can be converted to a percent by moving the decimal point two places to the right and attaching the % sign. A percent can be converted to a fraction by writing the percent as a fraction with 100 as the denominator and reducing. A fraction can be converted to a percent by performing the indicated division, multiplying the result by 100, and attaching the % sign.

The equation for finding percentages has three variables: the part, the whole, and the percent (which is expressed in the equation as a decimal). The equation, as shown below, can be rearranged to solve for any of these variables.

- part = whole × percent
- percent = $\frac{\text{part}}{\text{whole}}$
- whole = $\frac{\text{part}}{\text{percent}}$

This set of equations can be used to solve percent word problems. All that's needed is to identify the part, whole, and/or percent, and then to plug those values into the appropriate equation and solve.

Examples

1. Change the following values to the indicated form:

   (A) 18% to a fraction

   (B) $\frac{3}{5}$ to a percent

   (C) 1.125 to a percent

   (D) 84% to a decimal

   Answers:

   (A) The percent is written as a fraction over 100 and reduced: $\frac{18}{100} = \frac{9}{50}$.

   (B) Dividing 5 by 3 gives the value 0.6, which is then multiplied by 100: **60%**.

   (C) The decimal point is moved two places to the right: $1.125 \times 100 = \textbf{112.5\%}$.

   D. The decimal point is moved two places to the left: $84 \div 100 = \textbf{0.84}$.

2. In a school of 650 students, 54% of the students are boys. How many students are girls?

   Answer:

Percent of students who are girls = 100% − 54% = 46% percent = 46% = 0.46 whole = 650 students part = ?	Identify the variables.
part = whole × percent = 0.46 × 650 = 299 **There are 299 girls.**	Plug the variables into the appropriate equation.

Percent Change

Percent change problems involve a change from an original amount. Often percent change problems appear as word problems that include discounts, growth, or markups. In order to solve percent change problems, it's necessary to identify the percent change (as a decimal), the amount of change, and the original amount. (Keep in mind that one of these will be the value being solved for.) These values can then be plugged into the equations below:

Key terms associated with percent change problems include discount, sales tax, and markup.

- amount of change = original amount × percent change
- percent change = $\dfrac{\text{amount of change}}{\text{original amount}}$
- original amount = $\dfrac{\text{amount of change}}{\text{percent change}}$

Examples

1. An HDTV that originally cost $1,500 is on sale for 45% off. What is the sale price for the item?

Answer:

original amount =$1,500 percent change = 45% = 0.45 amount of change = ?	Identify the variables.
amount of change = original amount × percent change = 1500 × 0.45 = 675	Plug the variables into the appropriate equation.
1500 − 675 = 825 **The final price is $825.**	To find the new price, subtract the amount of change from the original price.

2. A house was bought in 2000 for $100,000 and sold in 2015 for $120,000. What was the percent growth in the value of the house from 2000 to 2015?

Answer:

original amount = $100,000 amount of change = 120,000 − 100,000 = 20,000 percent change = ?	Identify the variables.
percent change = $\dfrac{\text{amount of change}}{\text{original amount}}$ $= \dfrac{20,000}{100,000}$ = 0.20	Plug the variables into the appropriate equation.
0.20 × 100 = **20%**	To find the percent growth, multiply by 100.

EXPONENTS AND RADICALS

Exponents

An expression in the form b^n is in an exponential notation where b is the BASE and n is an EXPONENT. To perform the operation, multiply the base by itself the number of times indicated by the exponent. For example, 2^3 is equal to $2 \times 2 \times 2$ or 8.

Table 6.6. Operations with Exponents

RULE	EXAMPLE	EXPLANATION
$a^0 = 1$	$5^0 = 1$	Any base (except 0) to the 0 power is 1.
$a^{-n} = \dfrac{1}{a^n}$	$5^3 = \dfrac{1}{5^3}$	A negative exponent becomes positive when moved from numerator to denominator (or vice versa).
$a^m a^n = a^{m+n}$	$5^3 5^4 = 5^{3+4} = 5^7$	Add the exponents to multiply two powers with the same base.

RULE	EXAMPLE	EXPLANATION
$(a^m)^n = a^{mn}$	$(5^3)^4 = 5^{3(4)} = 5^{12}$	Multiply the exponents to raise a power to a power.
$\frac{a^m}{a^n} = a^{m-n}$	$\frac{5^4}{5^3} = 5^{4-3} = 5^1$	Subtract the exponents to divide two powers with the same base.
$(ab)^n = a^n b^n$	$(5 \times 6)^3 = 5^3 6^3$	Apply the exponent to each base to raise a product to a power.
$\left(\frac{a}{b}\right)^n = \frac{a^n}{b^n}$	$\left(\frac{5}{6}\right)^3 = \frac{5^3}{6^3}$	Apply the exponent to each base to raise a quotient to a power.
$\left(\frac{a}{b}\right)^{-n} = \left(\frac{b}{a}\right)^n$	$\left(\frac{5}{6}\right)^{-3} = \left(\frac{6}{5}\right)^3$	Invert the fraction and change the sign of the exponent to raise a fraction to a negative power.
$\frac{a^m}{b^n} = \frac{b^{-n}}{a^{-m}}$	$\frac{5^3}{6^4} = \frac{6^{-4}}{5^{-3}}$	Change the sign of the exponent when moving a number from the numerator to denominator (or vice versa).

Examples

1. Simplify: $\frac{(10^2)^3}{(10^2)^{-2}}$

Answer:

$\frac{(10^2)^3}{(10^2)^{-2}}$	
$= \frac{10^6}{10^{-4}}$	Multiply the exponents raised to a power.
$= 10^{6-(-4)}$	Subtract the exponent in the denominator from the one in the numerator.
$= 10^{10}$ $= \mathbf{10{,}000{,}000{,}000}$	Simplify.

2. Simplify: $\frac{(x^{-2}y^2)^2}{x^3 y}$

Answer:

$\frac{(x^{-2}y^2)^2}{x^3 y}$	
$= \frac{x^{-4}y^4}{x^3 y}$	Multiply the exponents raised to a power.
$= x^{-4-3}y^{4-1}$ $= x^{-7}y^3$	Subtract the exponent in the denominator from the one in the numerator.
$= \frac{y^3}{x^7}$	Move negative exponents to the denominator.

Radicals

RADICALS are expressed as $\sqrt[b]{a}$, where b is called the INDEX and a is the RADICAND. A radical is used to indicate the inverse operation of an exponent: finding the base which can be raised to b to yield a. For example, $\sqrt[3]{125}$ is equal to 5 because $5 \times 5 \times 5$ equals 125. The same operation can be expressed using a fraction exponent, so $\sqrt[b]{a} = \dfrac{1}{a^b}$. Note that when no value is indicated for b, it is assumed to be 2 (square root).

When b is even and a is positive, $\sqrt[b]{a}$ is defined to be the positive real value n such that $n^b = a$ (example: $\sqrt{16} = 4$ only, and not -4, even though $(-4)(-4) = 16$). If b is even and a is negative, $\sqrt[b]{a}$ will be a complex number (example: $\sqrt{-9} = 3i$). Finally if b is odd, $\sqrt[b]{a}$ will always be a real number regardless of the sign of a. If a is negative, $\sqrt[b]{a}$ will be negative since a number to an odd power is negative (example: $\sqrt[5]{-32} = -2$ since $(-2)^5 = -32$).

$\sqrt[n]{x}$ is referred to as the *n*th root of x.

- $n = 2$ is the square root
- $n = 3$ is the cube root
- $n = 4$ is the fourth root
- $n = 5$ is the fifth root

The following table of operations with radicals holds for all cases EXCEPT the case where b is even and a is negative (the complex case).

Table 6.7. Operations with Radicals

RULE	EXAMPLE	EXPLANATION
$\sqrt[b]{ac} = \sqrt[b]{a}\sqrt[b]{c}$	$\sqrt[3]{81} = \sqrt[3]{27}\sqrt[3]{3} = 3\sqrt[3]{3}$	The values under the radical sign can be separated into values that multiply to the original value.
$\sqrt[b]{\dfrac{a}{c}} = \dfrac{\sqrt[b]{a}}{\sqrt[b]{c}}$	$\sqrt{\dfrac{4}{81}} = \dfrac{\sqrt{4}}{\sqrt{81}} = \dfrac{2}{9}$	The *b*-root of the numerator and denominator can be calculated when there is a fraction under a radical sign.
$\sqrt[b]{a^c} = (\sqrt[b]{a})^c = a^{\frac{c}{b}}$	$\sqrt[3]{6^2} = (\sqrt[3]{6})^2 = 6^{\frac{2}{3}}$	The *b*-root can be written as a fractional exponent. If there is a power under the radical sign, it will be the numerator of the fraction.
$\dfrac{c}{\sqrt[b]{a}} \times \dfrac{\sqrt[b]{a}}{\sqrt[b]{a}} = \dfrac{c\sqrt[b]{a}}{a}$	$\dfrac{5}{\sqrt{2}}\dfrac{\sqrt{2}}{\sqrt{2}} = \dfrac{5\sqrt{2}}{2}$	To rationalize the denominator, multiply the numerator and denominator by the radical in the denominator until the radical has been canceled out.
$\dfrac{c}{b - \sqrt{a}} \times \dfrac{b + \sqrt{a}}{b + \sqrt{a}}$ $= \dfrac{c(b + \sqrt{a})}{b^2 - a}$	$\dfrac{4}{3 - \sqrt{2}}\dfrac{3 + \sqrt{2}}{3 + \sqrt{2}}$ $= \dfrac{4(3 + \sqrt{2})}{9 - 2} = \dfrac{12 + 4\sqrt{2}}{7}$	To rationalize the denominator, the numerator and denominator are multiplied by the conjugate of the denominator.

Examples

1. Simplify: $\sqrt{48}$

   Answer:

$\sqrt{48}$	
$= \sqrt{16 \times 3}$	Determine the largest square number that is a factor of the radicand (48) and write the radicand as a product using that square number as a factor.

$$= \sqrt{16}\,\sqrt{3}$$
$$= 4\sqrt{3}$$

| | Apply the rules of radicals to simplify. |

2. Simplify: $\dfrac{6}{\sqrt{8}}$

Answer:

$\dfrac{6}{\sqrt{8}}$	
$= \dfrac{6}{\sqrt{4}\,\sqrt{2}}$ $= \dfrac{6}{2\sqrt{2}}$	Apply the rules of radicals to simplify.
$= \dfrac{6}{2\sqrt{2}}\left(\dfrac{\sqrt{2}}{\sqrt{2}}\right)$ $= \dfrac{3\sqrt{2}}{2}$	Multiply by $\dfrac{\sqrt{2}}{\sqrt{2}}$ to rationalize the denominator.

ALGEBRAIC EXPRESSIONS

The foundation of algebra is the **VARIABLE**, an unknown number represented by a symbol (usually a letter such as x or a). Variables can be preceded by a **COEFFICIENT**, which is a constant (i.e., a real number) in front of the variable, such as $4x$ or $-2a$. An **ALGEBRAIC EXPRESSION** is any sum, difference, product, or quotient of variables and numbers (for example $3x^2$, $2x + 7y - 1$, and $\frac{5}{x}$ are algebraic expressions). **TERMS** are any quantities that are added or subtracted (for example, the terms of the expression $x^2 - 3x + 5$ are x^2, $3x$, and 5). A **POLYNOMIAL EXPRESSION** is an algebraic expression where all the exponents on the variables are whole numbers. A polynomial with only two terms is known as a **BINOMIAL**, and one with three terms is a **TRINOMIAL**. A **MONOMIAL** has only one term.

EVALUATING EXPRESSIONS is another way of saying "find the numeric value of an expression if the variable is equal to a certain number." To evaluate the expression, simply plug the given value(s) for the variable(s) into the equation and simplify. Remember to use the order of operations when simplifying:

1.	**P**arentheses	4.	**D**ivision
2.	**E**xponents	5.	**A**ddition
3.	**M**ultiplication	6.	**S**ubtraction

Example

If $m = 4$, find the value of the following expression:

$5(m - 2)^3 + 3m^2 - \dfrac{m}{4} - 1$

Answer:

$5(m - 2)^3 + 3m^2 - \dfrac{m}{4} - 1$	
$= 5(4 - 2)^3 + 3(4)^2 - \dfrac{4}{4} - 1$	Plug the value 4 in for m in the expression.
$= 5(2)^3 + 3(4)^2 - \dfrac{4}{4} - 1$	Calculate all the expressions inside the parentheses.

$= 5(8) + 3(16) - \frac{4}{4} - 1$	Simplify all exponents.
$= 40 + 48 - 1 - 1$	Perform multiplication and division from left to right.
$= 86$	Perform addition and subtraction from left to right.

OPERATIONS WITH EXPRESSIONS

Adding and Subtracting

Expressions can be added or subtracted by simply adding and subtracting LIKE TERMS, which are terms with the same variable part (the variables must be the same, with the same exponents on each variable). For example, in the expressions $2x + 3xy - 2z$ and $6y + 2xy$, the like terms are $3xy$ and $2xy$. Adding the two expressions yields the new expression $2x + 5xy - 2z + 6y$. Note that the other terms did not change; they cannot be combined because they have different variables.

Example

If $a = 12x + 7xy - 9y$ and $b = 8x - 9xz + 7z$, what is $a + b$?

Answer:

$a + b = (12x + 8x) + 7xy - 9y - 9xz + 7z =$
$20x + 7xy - 9y - 9xz + 7z$

The only like terms in both expressions are $12x$ and $8x$, so these two terms will be added, and all other terms will remain the same.

Distributing and Factoring

Distributing and factoring can be seen as two sides of the same coin. **DISTRIBUTION** multiplies each term in the first factor by each term in the second factor to get rid of parentheses. **FACTORING** reverses this process, taking a polynomial in standard form and writing it as a product of two or more factors.

Operations with polynomials can always be checked by evaluating equivalent expressions for the same value.

When distributing a monomial through a polynomial, the expression outside the parentheses is multiplied by each term inside the parentheses. Using the rules of exponents, coefficients are multiplied and exponents are added.

When simplifying two polynomials, each term in the first polynomial must multiply each term in the second polynomial. A binomial (two terms) multiplied by a binomial, will require 2 × 2 or 4 multiplications. For the binomial × binomial case, this process is sometimes called **FOIL**, which stands for first, outside, inside, and last. These terms refer to the placement of each term of the expression: multiply the first term in each expression, then the outside terms, then the inside terms, and finally the last terms. A binomial (two terms) multiplied by a trinomial (three terms), will require 2 × 3 or 6 products to simplify. The first

Distribute

$3x(7xy - z^3)$ $\longrightarrow$ $21x^2y - 3xz^3$

Factor

Figure 6.4. Distribution and Factoring

term in the first polynomial multiplies each of the three terms in the second polynomial, then the second term in the first polynomial multiplies each of the three terms in the second polynomial. A trinomial (three terms) by a trinomial will require 3 × 3 or 9 products, and so on.

Factoring is the reverse of distributing: the first step is always to remove ("undistribute") the GCF of all the terms, if there is a GCF (besides 1). The GCF is the product of any constants and/or variables that <u>every</u> term shares. (For example, the GCF of $12x^3$, $15x^2$ and $6xy^2$ is $3x$ because $3x$ evenly divides all three terms.) This shared factor can be taken out of each term and moved to the outside of the parentheses, leaving behind a polynomial where each term is the original term divided by the GCF. (The remaining terms for the terms in the example would be $4x^2$, $5x$, and $2y^2$.) It may be possible to factor the polynomial in the parentheses further, depending on the problem.

Example

1. Expand the following expression: $5x(x^2 - 2c + 10)$

   Answer:

$5x(x^2 - 2c + 10)$	
$(5x)(x^2) = 5x^3$ $(5x)(-2c) = -10xc$ $(5x)(10) = 50x$	Distribute and multiply the term outside the parentheses to all three terms inside the parentheses.
$= 5x^3 - 10xc + 50x$	

2. Expand the following expression: $(x^2 - 5)(2x - x^3)$

   Answer:

$(x^2 - 5)(2x - x^3)$	
$(x^2)(2x) = 2x^3$ $(x^2)(-x^3) = -x^5$ $(-5)(2x) = -10x$ $(-5)(-x^3) = 5x^3$	Apply FOIL: first, outside, inside, and last.
$= 2x^3 - x^5 - 10x + 5x^3$	Combine like terms and put them in order.
$= -x^5 + 7x^3 - 10x$	

3. Factor the expression $16z^2 + 48z$

   Answer:

$16z^2 + 48z$ $= 16z(z + 3)$	Both terms have a z, and 16 is a common factor of both 16 and 48. So the greatest common factor is $16z$. Factor out the GCF.

4. Factor the expression $6m^3 + 12m^3n - 9m^2$

CONTINUE

Answer:

$6m^3 + 12m^3n - 9m^2$

$= \mathbf{3m^2(2m + 4mn - 3)}$

All the terms share the factor m^2, and 3 is the greatest common factor of 6, 12, and 9. So, the GCF is $3m^2$.

LINEAR EQUATIONS

An **EQUATION** states that two expressions are equal to each other. Polynomial equations are categorized by the highest power of the variables they contain: the highest power of any exponent of a linear equation is 1, a quadratic equation has a variable raised to the second power, a cubic equation has a variable raised to the third power, and so on.

Solving Linear Equations

Solving an equation means finding the value or values of the variable that make the equation true. To solve a linear equation, it is necessary to manipulate the terms so that the variable being solved for appears alone on one side of the equal sign while everything else in the equation is on the other side.

The way to solve linear equations is to "undo" all the operations that connect numbers to the variable of interest. Follow these steps:

On multiple choice tests, it is often easier to plug the possible values into the equation and determine which solution makes the equation true than to solve the equation.

1. Eliminate fractions by multiplying each side by the least common multiple of any denominators.

2. Distribute to eliminate parentheses, braces, and brackets.

3. Combine like terms.

4. Use addition or subtraction to collect all terms containing the variable of interest to one side, and all terms not containing the variable to the other side.

5. Use multiplication or division to remove coefficients from the variable of interest.

Sometimes there are no numeric values in the equation or there are a mix of numerous variables and constants. The goal is to solve the equation for one of the variables in terms of the other variables. In this case, the answer will be an expression involving numbers and letters instead of a numeric value.

Examples

1. Solve for x: $\dfrac{100(x + 5)}{20} = 1$

Answer:

$\dfrac{100(x + 5)}{20} = 1$	
$(20)\left(\dfrac{100(x + 5)}{20}\right) = (1)(20)$ $100(x + 5) = 20$	Multiply both sides by 20 to cancel out the denominator.
$100x + 500 = 20$	Distribute 100 through the parentheses.

$100x = -480$	"Undo" the +500 by subtracting 500 on both sides of the equation to isolate the variable term.
$x = \frac{-480}{100}$	"Undo" the multiplication by 100 by dividing by 100 on both sides to solve for x.
$x = -4.8$	

2. Solve for x: $2(x + 2)^2 - 2x^2 + 10 = 42$

Answer:

$2(x + 2)^2 - 2x^2 + 10 = 42$	
$2(x + 2)(x + 2) - 2x^2 + 10 = 42$	Eliminate the exponents on the left side.
$2(x^2 + 4x + 4) - 2x^2 + 10 = 42$	Apply FOIL.
$2x^2 + 8x + 8 - 2x^2 + 10 = 42$	Distribute the 2.
$8x + 18 = 42$	Combine like terms on the left-hand side.
$8x = 24$	Isolate the variable. "Undo" +18 by subtracting 18 on both sides.
$x = 3$	"Undo" multiplication by 8 by dividing both sides by 8.

3. Solve the equation for D: $\frac{A(3B + 2D)}{2N} = 5M - 6$

Answer:

$\frac{A(3B + 2D)}{2N} = 5M - 6$	
$3AB + 2AD = 10MN - 12N$	Multiply both sides by 2N to clear the fraction, and distribute the A through the parentheses.
$2AD = 10MN - 12N - 3AB$	Isolate the term with the D in it by moving 3AB to the other side of the equation.
$D = \frac{(10MN - 12N - 3AB)}{2A}$	Divide both sides by 2A to get D alone on the right-hand side.

Graphs of Linear Equations

The most common way to write a linear equation is **SLOPE-INTERCEPT FORM**, $y = mx + b$. In this equation, m is the slope, which describes how steep the line is, and b is the y-intercept. Slope is often described as "rise over run" because it is calculated as the difference in y-values (rise) over the difference in x-values (run). The slope of the line is also the rate of change of the dependent variable y with respect to the independent variable x. The y-intercept is the point where the line crosses the y-axis, or where x equals zero.

To graph a linear equation, identify the y-intercept and place that point on the y-axis. If the slope is not written as a fraction,

 Use the phrase "Begin, Move" to remember that b is the y-intercept (where to begin) and m is the slope (how the line moves).

make it a fraction by writing it over 1 $\left(\frac{m}{1}\right)$. Then use the slope to count up (or down, if negative) the "rise" part of the slope and over the "run" part of the slope to find a second point. These points can then be connected to draw the line.

To find the equation of a line, identify the y-intercept, if possible, on the graph and use two easily identifiable points to find the slope. If the y-intercept is not easily identified, identify the slope by choosing easily identifiable points; then choose one point on the graph, plug the point and the slope values into the equation, and solve for the missing value b.

slope-intercept form:
$y = mx + b$
slope: $m = \frac{y_2 - y_1}{x_2 - x_1}$

- standard form: $Ax + By = C$
- $m = -\frac{A}{B}$
- x-intercept $= \frac{C}{A}$
- y-intercept $= \frac{C}{B}$

Another way to express a linear equation is standard form: $Ax + By = C$. In order to graph equations in this form, it is often easiest to convert them to point-slope form. Alternately, it is easy to find the x- or y-intercept from this form, and once these two points are known, a line can be drawn through them. To find the x-intercept, simply make $y = 0$ and solve for x. Similarly, to find the y-intercept, make $x = 0$ and solve for y.

Examples

1. What is the slope of the line whose equation is $6x - 2y - 8 = 0$?

Answer:

$6x - 2y - 8 = 0$	
$-2y = -6x + 8$ $y = \frac{-6x + 8}{-2}$ $y = 3x - 4$	Rearrange the equation into slope-intercept form by solving the equation for y.
$m = 3$	The slope is 3, the value attached to x.

2. What is the equation of the following line?

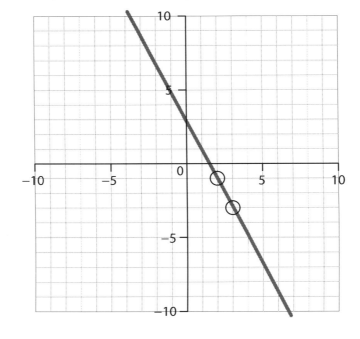

Answer:

$b = 3$	The *y*-intercept can be identified on the graph as $(0, 3)$.
$m = \dfrac{(-3) - (-1)}{3 - 2} = \dfrac{-2}{1} = -2$	To find the slope, choose any two points and plug the values into the slope equation. The two points chosen here are $(2, -1)$ and $(3, -3)$.
$y = -2x + 3$	Replace *m* with -2 and *b* with 3 in $y = mx + b$.

3. Write the equation of the line which passes through the points $(-2, 5)$ and $(-5, 3)$.

Answer:

$(-2, 5)$ and $(-5, 3)$	
$m = \dfrac{3 - 5}{(-5) - (-2)}$ $= \dfrac{-2}{-3}$ $= \dfrac{2}{3}$	Calculate the slope.
$5 = \dfrac{2}{3}(-2) + b$ $5 = \dfrac{-4}{3} + b$ $b = \dfrac{19}{3}$	To find *b*, plug into the equation $y = mx + b$ the slope for *m* and a set of points for *x* and *y*.
$y = \dfrac{2}{3}x + \dfrac{19}{3}$	Replace *m* and *b* to find the equation of the line.

4. What is the equation of the following graph?

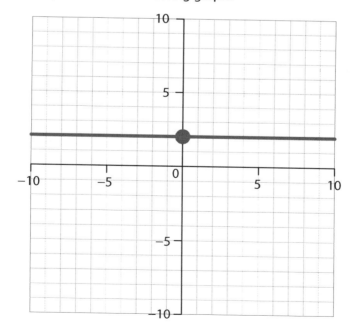

CONTINUE

$y = 0x + 2$, or $y = 2$

The line has a rise of 0 and a run of 1, so the slope is $\frac{0}{1} = 0$. There is no x-intercept. The y-intercept is $(0, 2)$, meaning that the b-value in the slope-intercept form is 2.

PROPERTIES OF SHAPES

Basic Definitions

The basic figures from which many other geometric shapes are built are points, lines, and planes. A POINT is a location in a plane. It has no size or shape, but is represented by a dot. It is labeled using a capital letter.

A LINE is a one-dimensional collection of points that extends infinitely in both directions. At least two points are needed to define a line, and any points that lie on the same line are COLINEAR. Lines are represented by two points, such as A and B, and the line symbol: ($\overleftrightarrow{AB}$). Two lines on the same plane will intersect unless they are PARALLEL, meaning they have the same slope. Lines that intersect at a 90-degree angle are PERPENDICULAR.

A LINE SEGMENT has two endpoints and a finite length. The length of a segment, called the measure of the segment, is the distance from A to B. A line segment is a subset of a line, and is also denoted with two points, but with a segment symbol: ($\overline{AB}$). The MIDPOINT of a line segment is the point at which the segment is divided into two equal parts. A line, segment, or plane that passes through the midpoint of a segment is called a BISECTOR of the segment, since it cuts the segment into two equal segments.

A RAY has one endpoint and extends indefinitely in one direction. It is defined by its endpoint, followed by any other point on the ray: $\overrightarrow{AB}$. It is important that the first letter represents the endpoint. A ray is sometimes called a half line.

Table 6.8. Basic Geometric Figures

TERM	DIMENSIONS	GRAPHIC	SYMBOL
point	zero	●	$\cdot A$
line segment	one	A ——— B	$\overline{AB}$
ray	one	A —— B →	$\overrightarrow{AB}$
line	one	←——→	$\overleftrightarrow{AB}$
plane	two	▱	Plane M

A PLANE is a flat sheet that extends indefinitely in two directions (like an infinite sheet of paper). A plane is a two-dimensional (2D) figure. A plane can always be defined through any three noncollinear points in three-dimensional (3D) space. A plane is named using any three points that are in the plane (for example, plane **ABC**). Any points lying in the same plane are said to be **COPLANAR**. When two planes intersect, the intersection is a line.

Example

1) Which points and lines are not contained in plane *M* in the diagram below?

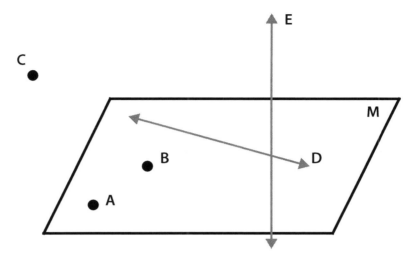

Answer:

Points *A* and *B* and line *D* are all on plane *M*. Point *C* is above the plane, and line *E* cuts through the plane and thus does not lie on plane *M*. The point at which line *E* intersects plane *M* is on plane *M* but the line as a whole is not.

Angles

ANGLES are formed when two rays share a common endpoint. They are named using three letters, with the vertex point in the middle (for example $\angle ABC$, where *B* is the vertex). They can also be labeled with a number or named by their vertex alone (if it is clear to do so). Angles are also classified based on their angle measure. A **right angle** has a measure of exactly 90°. **Acute angles** have measures that are less than 90°, and **obtuse angles** have measures that are greater than 90°.

Any two angles that add to make 90° are called **COMPLEMENTARY ANGLES**. A 30° angle would be complementary to a 60° angle. **SUPPLEMENTARY ANGLES** add up to 180°. A supplementary angle to a 60° angle would be a 120° angle; likewise, 60° is the **SUPPLEMENT** of 120°. Angles that are next to each other and share a common ray are called **ADJACENT ANGLES**. Angles that are adjacent and supplementary are called a **LINEAR PAIR** of angles. Their nonshared rays form a line (thus the *linear* pair). Note that angles that are supplementary do not need to be adjacent; their measures simply need to add to 180°.

 Angles can be measured in degrees or radians. Use the conversion factor 1 rad = 57.3 degrees to convert between them.

VERTICAL ANGLES are formed when two lines intersect. Four angles will be formed; the vertex of each angle is at the intersection point of the lines. The vertical angles across from each other will be equal in measure. The angles adjacent to each other will be linear pairs and therefore supplementary.

A ray, line, or segment that divides an angle into two equal angles is called an ANGLE BISECTOR.

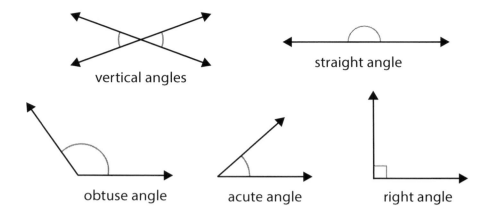

Figure 6.5. Types of Angles

Examples

1. If angles *M* and *N* are supplementary and ∠*M* is 30° less than twice ∠*N*, what is the degree measurement of each angle?

Answer:

∠*M* + ∠*N* = 180° ∠*M* = 2∠*N* − 30°	Set up a system of equations.
∠*M* + ∠*N* = 180° (2∠*N* − 30°) + ∠*N* = 180° 3∠*N* − 30° = 180° 3∠*N* = 210° **∠*N* = 70°**	Use substitution to solve for ∠*N*.
∠*M* + ∠*N* = 180° ∠*M* + 70° = 180° **∠*M* = 110°**	Solve for ∠*M* using the original equation.

2. How many linear pairs of angles are there in the following figure?

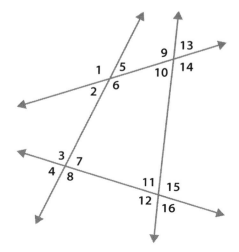

Answers:

Any two adjacent angles that are supplementary are linear pairs, so there are 16 linear pairs in the figure (∠1 and ∠5, ∠2 and ∠6, ∠5 and ∠6, ∠2 and ∠1, and so on).

Circles

A **CIRCLE** is the set of all the points in a plane that are the same distance from a fixed point called the **CENTER**. The distance from the center to any point on the circle is the **RADIUS** of the circle. The distance around the circle (the perimeter) is called the **CIRCUMFERENCE**.

The ratio of a circle's circumference to its diameter is a constant value called pi (π), an irrational number which is commonly rounded to 3.14. The formula to find a circle's circumference is $C = 2\pi r$. The formula to find the enclosed area of a circle is $A = \pi r^2$.

Circles have a number of unique parts and properties:

Trying to square a circle means attempting to create a square that has the same area as a circle. Because the area of a circle depends on π, which is an irrational number, this task is impossible. The phrase is often used to describe trying to do something that can't be done.

- The **DIAMETER** is the largest measurement across a circle. It passes through the circle's center, extending from one side of the circle to the other. The measure of the diameter is twice the measure of the radius.

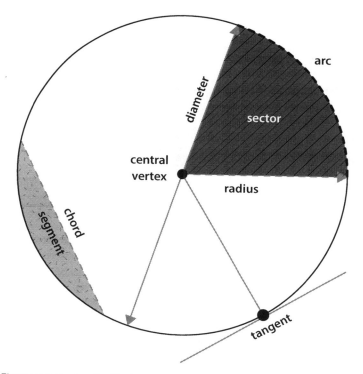

Figure 6.6. Parts of a Circle

- A line that cuts across a circle and touches it twice is called a **SECANT** line. The part of a secant line that lies within a circle is called a **CHORD**. Two chords within a circle are of equal length if they are are the same distance from the center.

- A line that touches a circle or any curve at one point is **TANGENT** to the circle or the curve. These lines are always exterior to the circle. A line tangent to a circle and a radius drawn to the point of tangency meet at a right angle (90°).

- An **ARC** is any portion of a circle between two points on the circle. The **MEASURE** of an arc is in degrees, whereas the **LENGTH OF THE ARC** will be in linear measurement (such as centimeters or inches). A **MINOR ARC** is the small arc between the two points (it measures less than 180°), whereas a **MAJOR ARC** is the large arc between the two points (it measures greater than 180°).

- An angle with its vertex at the center of a circle is called a **CENTRAL ANGLE**. For a central angle, the measure of the arc intercepted by the sides of the angle (in degrees) is the same as the measure of the angle.

- A **SECTOR** is the part of a circle *and* its interior that is inside the rays of a central angle (its shape is like a slice of pie).

	Area of Sector	Length of an Arc
Degrees	$A = \dfrac{\theta}{360°} \times \pi r^2$	$s = \dfrac{\theta}{360°} \times 2\pi r$
Radians	$A = \dfrac{1}{2}\pi r^2 \theta$	$s = r\theta$

- An **INSCRIBED ANGLE** has a vertex on the circle and is formed by two chords that share that vertex point. The angle measure of an inscribed angle is one-half the angle measure of the central angle with the same endpoints on the circle.

- A **CIRCUMSCRIBED ANGLE** has rays tangent to the circle. The angle lies outside of the circle.

- Any angle outside the circle, whether formed by two tangent lines, two secant lines, or a tangent line and a secant line, is equal to half the difference of the intercepted arcs.

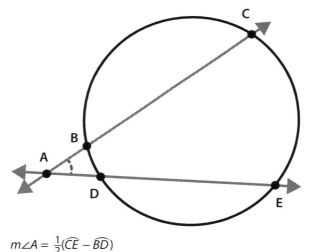

$m\angle A = \frac{1}{2}(\overset{\frown}{CE} - \overset{\frown}{BD})$

Figure 6.7. Angles Outside a Circle

- Angles are formed within a circle when two chords intersect in the circle. The measure of the smaller angle formed is half the sum of the two smaller arc measures (in degrees). Likewise, the larger angle is half the sum of the two larger arc measures.

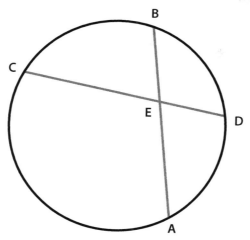

$$m\angle E = \tfrac{1}{2}(\widehat{AC} + \widehat{BD})$$

Figure 6.8. Intersecting Chords

- If a chord intersects a line tangent to the circle, the angle formed by this intersection measures one half the measurement of the intercepted arc (in degrees).

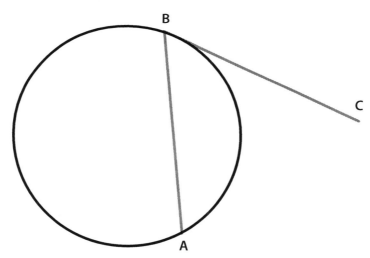

$$m\angle ABC = \tfrac{1}{2}m\widehat{AB}$$

Figure 6.9. Intersecting Chord and Tangent

CONTINUE

Examples

1. Find the area of the sector *NHS* of the circle below with center at *H*:

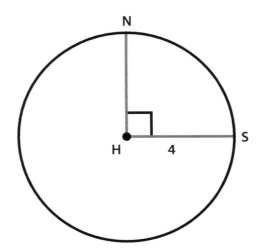

Answer:

$r = 4$ $\angle NHS = 90°$	Identify the important parts of the circle.
$A = \dfrac{\theta}{360°} \times \pi r^2$ $= \dfrac{90}{360} \times \pi(4)^2$	Plug these values into the formula for the area of a sector.
$= \dfrac{1}{4} \times 16\pi$ $= \mathbf{4\pi}$	Plug these values into the formula for the area of a sector (continued).

2. In the circle below with center *O*, the minor arc *ACB* measures 5 feet. What is the measurement of *m∠AOB*?

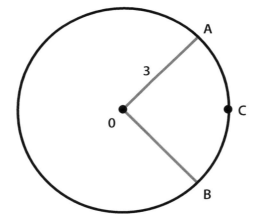

Answer:

$r = 3$ length of $\overset{\frown}{ACB} = 5$	Identify the important parts of the circle.

$$s = \frac{\theta}{360°} \times 2\pi r$$

$$5 = \frac{\theta}{360} \times 2\pi(3)$$

$$\frac{5}{6\pi} = \frac{\theta}{360}$$

$$\theta = 95.5°$$

$m\angle AOB = 95.5°$

Plug these values into the formula for the length of an arc and solve for θ.

Triangles

Much of geometry is concerned with triangles as they are commonly used shapes. A good understanding of triangles allows decomposition of other shapes (specifically polygons) into triangles for study.

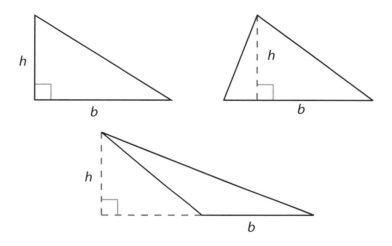

Figure 6.10. Finding the Base and Height of Triangles

Triangles have three sides, and the three interior angles always sum to 180°. The formula for the area of a triangle is $A = \frac{1}{2} bh$ or one-half the product of the base and height (or altitude) of the triangle.

Some important segments in a triangle include the angle bisector, the altitude, and the median. The **ANGLE BISECTOR** extends from the side opposite an angle to bisect that angle. The **ALTITUDE** is the shortest distance from a vertex of the triangle to the line containing the base side opposite that vertex. It is perpendicular to that line and can occur on the outside of the triangle. The **MEDIAN** extends from an angle to bisect the opposite side.

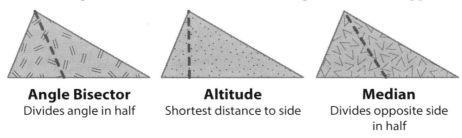

Angle Bisector
Divides angle in half

Altitude
Shortest distance to side

Median
Divides opposite side
in half

Figure 6.11. Important Segments in a Triangle

Triangles have two "centers." The CENTROID is where a triangle's three medians meet. The ORTHOCENTER is formed by the intersection of a triangle's three altitudes.

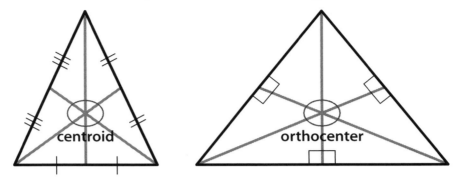

Figure 6.12. Centroid and Orthocenter of a Triangle

Triangles can be classified in two ways: by sides and by angles.

A SCALENE TRIANGLE has no equal sides or angles. An ISOSCELES TRIANGLE has two equal sides and two equal angles, often called BASE ANGLES. In an EQUILATERAL TRIANGLE, all three sides are equal as are all three angles. Moreover, because the sum of the angles of a triangle is always 180°, each angle of an equilateral triangle must be 60°.

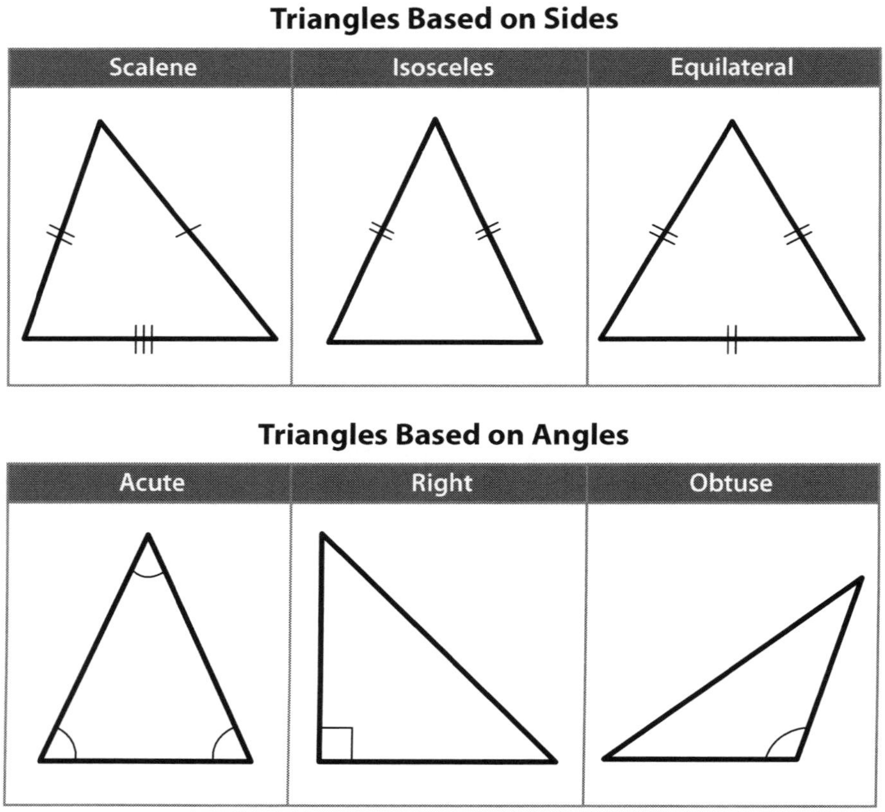

Triangles Based on Sides

Scalene	Isosceles	Equilateral

Triangles Based on Angles

Acute	Right	Obtuse

Figure 6.13. Types of Triangles

A RIGHT TRIANGLE has one right angle (90°) and two acute angles. An ACUTE TRIANGLE has three acute angles (all angles are less than 90°). An OBTUSE TRIANGLE has one obtuse angle (more than 90°) and two acute angles.

For any triangle, the side opposite the largest angle will have the longest length, while the side opposite the smallest angle will have the shortest length. The **TRIANGLE INEQUALITY THEOREM** states that the sum of any two sides of a triangle must be greater than the third side. If this inequality does not hold, then a triangle cannot be formed. A consequence of this theorem is the **THIRD-SIDE RULE**: if b and c are two sides of a triangle, then the measure of the third side a must be between the sum of the other two sides and the difference of the other two sides: $c - b < a < c + b$.

Trigonometric functions can be employed to find missing sides and angles of a triangle.

Solving for missing angles or sides of a triangle is a common type of triangle problem. Often a right triangle will come up on its own or within another triangle. The relationship among a right triangle's sides is known as the **PYTHAGOREAN THEOREM**: $a^2 + b^2 = c^2$, where c is the hypotenuse and is across from the 90° angle. Right triangles with angle measurements of 90° – 45° – 45° and 90° – 60° – 30° are known as "special" right triangles and have specific relationships between their sides and angles.

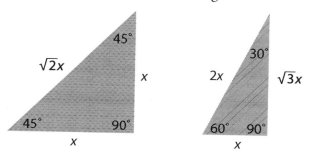

Figure 6.14. Special Right Triangles

Examples

1. Examine and classify each of the following triangles:

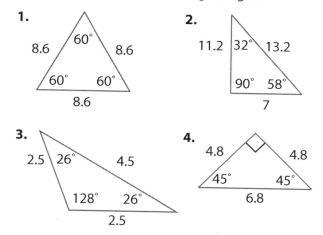

Answers:

Triangle 1 is an equilateral triangle (all 3 sides are equal, and all 3 angles are equal)

Triangle 2 is a scalene, right triangle (all 3 sides are different, and there is a 90° angle)

Triangle 3 is an isosceles triangle (there are 2 equal sides and, consequently, 2 equal angles)

Triangle 4 is a right, isosceles triangle (there are 2 equal sides and a 90° angle)

2. Given the diagram, if $XZ = 100$, $WZ = 80$, and $XU = 70$, then $WY = ?$

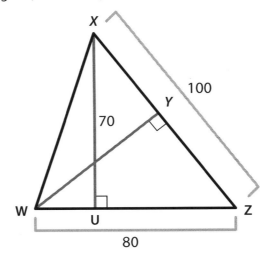

Answer:

$WZ = b_1 = 80$
$XU = h_1 = 70$
$XZ = b_2 = 100$
$WY = h_2 = ?$

$A = \frac{1}{2}bh$

$A_1 = \frac{1}{2}(80)(70) = 2800$

$A_2 = \frac{1}{2}(100)(h_2)$

The given values can be used to write two equation for the area of $\triangle WXZ$ with two sets of bases and heights.

$2800 = \frac{1}{2}(100)(h_2)$

$h_2 = 56$

$WY = 56$

Set the two equations equal to each other and solve for WY.

3. What are the minimum and maximum values of x to the nearest hundredth?

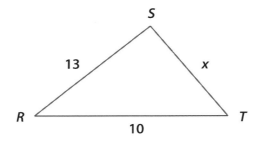

Answers:

The sum of two sides is 23 and their difference is 3. To connect the two other sides and enclose a space, x must be less than the sum and greater than the difference (that is, $3 < x < 23$). Therefore, **x's minimum value to the nearest hundredth is 3.01 and its maximum value is 22.99.**

Quadrilaterals

All closed, four-sided shapes are **QUADRILATERALS**. The sum of all internal angles in a quadrilateral is always 360°. (Think of drawing a diagonal to create two triangles. Since each triangle contains 180°, two triangles, and therefore the quadrilateral, must contain 360°.) The **AREA OF ANY QUADRILATERAL** is $A = bh$, where b is the base and h is the height (or altitude).

A **PARALLELOGRAM** is a quadrilateral with two pairs of parallel sides. A rectangle is a parallelogram with two pairs of equal sides and four right angles. A **KITE** also has two pairs of equal sides, but its equal sides are consecutive. Both a **SQUARE** and a **RHOMBUS** have four equal sides. A square has four right angles, while a rhombus has a pair of acute opposite angles and a pair of obtuse opposite angles. A **TRAPEZOID** has exactly one pair of parallel sides.

 All squares are rectangles and all rectangles are parallelograms; however, not all parallelograms are rectangles and not all rectangles are squares.

Table 6.9. Properties of Parallelograms

TERM	SHAPE	PROPERTIES
Parallelogram		Opposite sides are parallel. Consecutive angles are supplementary. Opposite angles are equal. Opposite sides are equal. Diagonals bisect each other.
Rectangle		All parallelogram properties hold. Diagonals are congruent *and* bisect each other. All angles are right angles.
Square		All rectangle properties hold. All four sides are equal. Diagonals bisect angles. Diagonals intersect at right angles and bisect each other.
Kite		One pair of opposite angles is equal. Two pairs of consecutive sides are equal. Diagonals meet at right angles.
Rhombus		All four sides are equal. Diagonals bisect angles. Diagonals intersect at right angles and bisect each other.
Trapezoid		One pair of sides is parallel. Bases have different lengths. Isosceles trapezoids have a pair of equal sides (and base angles).

CONTINUE

Examples

1. In parallelogram *ABCD*, the measure of angle *m* is is $m° = 260°$. What is the measure of *n°*?

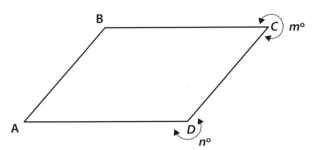

Answers:

$260° + m\angle C = 360°$ $m\angle C = 100°$	Find $\angle C$ using the fact that the sum of $\angle C$ and *m* is 360°.
$m\angle C + m\angle D = 180°$ $100° + m\angle D = 180°$ $m\angle D = 80°$	Solve for $\angle D$ using the fact that consecutive interior angles in a quadrilateral are supplementary.
$m\angle D + n = 360°$ **$n = 280°$**	Solve for *n* by subtracting $m\angle D$ from 360°.

2. A rectangular section of a football field has dimensions of *x* and *y* and an area of 1000 square feet. Three additional lines drawn vertically divide the section into four smaller rectangular areas as seen in the diagram below. If all the lines shown need to be painted, calculate the total number of linear feet, in terms of *x*, to be painted.

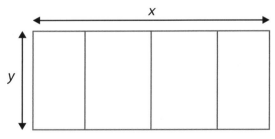

Answer:

$A = 1000 = xy$ $L = 2x + 5y$	Find equations for the area of the field and length of the lines to be painted (*L*) in terms of *x* and *y*.
$y = \frac{1000}{x}$ $L = 2x + 5y$ $L = 2x + 5\left(\frac{1000}{x}\right)$ **$L = 2x + \frac{5000}{x}$**	Substitute to find *L* in terms of *x*.

Polygons

Any closed shape made up of three or more line segments is a polygon. In addition to triangles and quadrilaterals, **OCTAGONS** and **HEXAGONS** are two common polygons.

The two polygons depicted below are REGULAR POLYGONS, meaning that they are equilateral (all sides having equal lengths) and equiangular (all angles having equal measurements). Angles inside a polygon are INTERIOR ANGLES, whereas those formed by one side of the polygon and a line extending outside the polygon are EXTERIOR ANGLES.

 Breaking an irregular polygon down into triangles and quadrilaterals helps in finding its area.

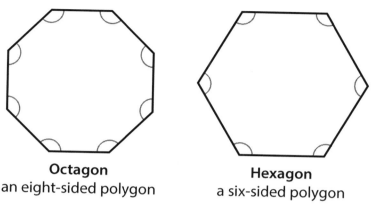

Octagon
an eight-sided polygon

Hexagon
a six-sided polygon

Figure 6.15. Common Polygons

The sum of all the exterior angles of a polygon is always 360°. Dividing 360° by the number of a polygon's sides finds the measure of the polygon's exterior angles.

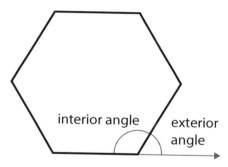

interior angle   exterior angle

Figure 6.16. Interior and Exterior Angles

To determine the sum of a polygon's interior angles, choose one vertex and draw diagonals from that vertex to each of the other vertices, decomposing the polygon into multiple triangles. For example, an octagon has six triangles within it, and therefore the sum of the interior angles is 6 × 180° = 1080°. In general, the formula for finding the sum of the angles in a polygon is *sum of angles* = $(n - 2) \times 180°$, where n is the number of sides of the polygon.

To find the measure of a single interior angle, simply divide the sum of the interior angles by the number of angles (which is the same as the number of sides). So, in the octagon example, each angle is $\frac{1080}{8}$ = 135°.

In general, the formula to find the measure of a regular polygon's interior angles is: *interior angle* = $\frac{(n - 2)}{n} \times 180°$ where n is the number of sides of the polygon.

To find the area of a polygon, it is helpful to know the perimeter of the polygon (p), and the **APOTHEM** (a). The apothem is the shortest (perpendicular) distance from the polygon's center to one of the sides of the polygon. The formula for the area is: $area = \frac{ap}{2}$.

Finally, there is no universal way to find the perimeter of a polygon (when the side length is not given). Often, breaking the polygon down into triangles and adding the base of each triangle all the way around the polygon is the easiest way to calculate the perimeter.

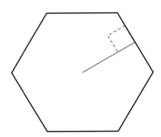

Figure 6.17. Apothem in a Hexagon

Examples

1. The circle and hexagon below both share center point T. The hexagon is entirely inscribed in the circle. The circle's radius is 5. What is the area of the shaded area?

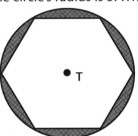

Answer:

$A_C = \pi r^2$ $= \pi(5)^2$ $= 25\pi$	The area of the shaded region will be the area of the circle minus the area of the hexagon. Use the radius to find the area of the circle.
$a = 2.5\sqrt{3}$ $A_H = \frac{ap}{2}$ $= \frac{(2.5\sqrt{3})(30)}{2}$ $= 64.95$	To find the area of the hexagon, draw a right triangle from the vertex, and use special right triangles to find the hexagon's apothem. Then, use the apothem to calculate the area.
$= A_C - A_H$ $= 25\pi - 64.95$ $\approx \mathbf{13.59}$	Subtract the area of the hexagon from the circle to find the area of the shaded region.

2. What is the measure of an exterior angle and an interior angle of a regular 400-gon?

Answer:

The sum of the exterior angles is 360°. Dividing this sum by 400 gives $\frac{360°}{400} = \mathbf{0.9°}$. Since an interior angle is supplementary to an exterior angle, all the interior angles have measure $180 - 0.9 = \mathbf{179.1°}$. Alternately, using the formula for calculating the interior angle gives the same result:

$$interior\ angle = \frac{400 - 2}{400} \times 180° = 179.1°$$

THREE-DIMENSIONAL SHAPES

THREE-DIMENSIONAL SHAPES have depth in addition to width and length. VOLUME is expressed as the number of cubic units any shape can hold—that is, what it takes to fill it up. SURFACE AREA is the sum of the areas of the two-dimensional figures that are found on its surface. Some three-dimensional shapes also have a unique property called a slant height (ℓ), which is the distance from the base to the apex along a lateral face.

Table 6.10. Three-Dimensional Shapes and Formulas

TERM	SHAPE	FORMULA	
Prism		$V = Bh$ $SA = 2lw + 2wh + 2lh$ $d^2 = a^2 + b^2 + c^2$	B = area of base h = height l = length w = width d = longest diagonal
Cube	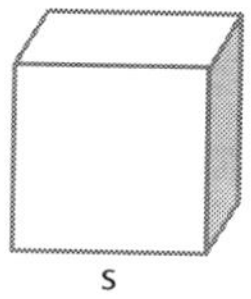	$V = s^3$ $SA = 6s^2$	s = cube edge
Sphere	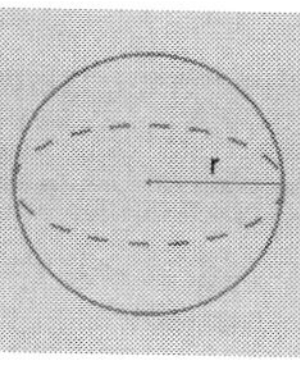	$V = \frac{4}{3}\pi r^3$ $SA = 4\pi r^2$	r = radius
Cylinder	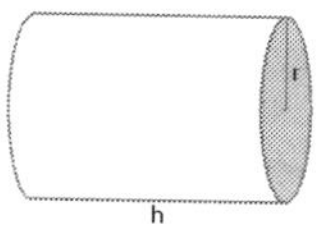	$V = Bh = \pi r^2 h$ $SA = 2\pi r^2 + 2\pi rh$	B = area of base h = height r = radius
Cone	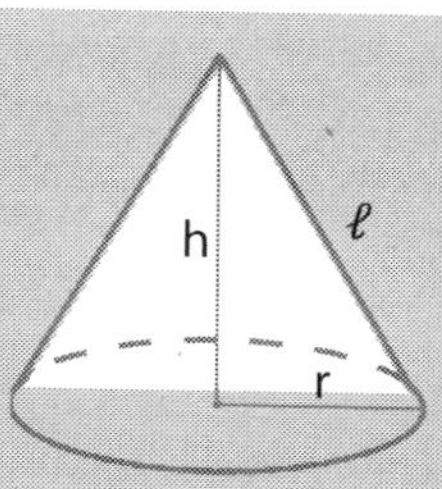	$V = \frac{1}{3}\pi r^2 h$	r = radius h = height

Table 6.10. Three-Dimensional Shapes and Formulas (continued)

TERM	SHAPE	FORMULA	
Pyramid	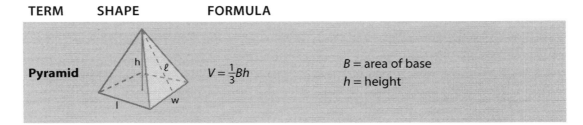	$V = \frac{1}{3}Bh$	B = area of base h = height

Finding the surface area of a three-dimensional solid can be made easier by using a **net**. This two-dimensional "flattened" version of a three-dimensional shape shows the component parts that comprise the surface of the solid.

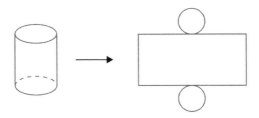

Figure 6.18. Net of a Cylinder

Examples

1. A sphere has a radius z. If that radius is increased by t, by how much is the surface area increased? Write the answer in terms of z and t.

   Answer:

$SA_1 = 4\pi z^2$	Write the equation for the area of the original sphere.
$SA_2 = 4\pi(z + t)^2$ $= 4\pi(z^2 + 2zt + t^2)$ $= 4\pi z^2 + 8\pi zt + 4\pi t^2$	Write the equation for the area of the new sphere.
$A_2 - A_1 = 4\pi z^2 + 8\pi zt + 4\pi t^2 - 4\pi z^2$ $\mathbf{= 4\pi t^2 + 8\pi zt}$	To find the difference between the two, subtract the original from the increased surface area.

2. A cube with volume 27 cubic meters is inscribed within a sphere such that all of the cube's vertices touch the sphere. What is the length of the sphere's radius?

   Answer:

   Since the cube's volume is 27, each side length is equal to $\sqrt[3]{27} = 3$. The long diagonal distance from one of the cube's vertices to its opposite vertex will provide the sphere's diameter:

   $$d = \sqrt{3^2 + 3^2 + 3^2} = \sqrt{27} = 5.2$$

   Half of this length is the radius, which is **2.6 meters**.

7

MECHANICAL COMPREHENSION

The Mechanical Comprehension section of the SIFT tests candidates' understanding of the basic principles of physics and how those principles are applied to real-world situations. The questions on this test do not require the use of equations or calculators—instead, candidates will answer questions about the physical relationship between objects and about the movement of those objects under specific circumstances. This subtest uses the CAT format, so the number of questions on this subtest will depend on candidates' performance.

NEWTON'S LAWS

A fundamental concept of mechanics is INERTIA, which states that an object has a tendency to maintain its state of motion. An object at rest will stay at rest, and an object moving at constant velocity will continue to move at that velocity, unless something pushes or pulls on it. This push or pull is called a FORCE. The newton (N) is the SI unit for force (1 newton is 1 kg m/s²).

MASS is a fundamental property of matter and is a measure of the inertia of an object. The kilogram (kg) is the SI unit for mass. An object with a larger mass will resist a change in motion more than an object with a smaller mass will. For example, it is harder to throw an elephant than it is to throw a baseball (the elephant has much more mass than a baseball).

In 1687, Isaac Newton published three laws of motion that describe the behavior of force and mass. Newton's first law is also called the law of inertia. It states that an object will maintain its current state of motion unless acted on by an outside force.

Newton's second law is an equation,

$$F = ma$$

where F is the sum of the forces on an object (also called the net force), m is the mass of the object, and a is the acceleration. The law states that the net force on an object will lead

A **system** is a collection of particles or objects that is isolated from its surroundings. All forces within a system are called internal forces, and forces outside the system are called external forces.

to an acceleration. Also, if an object has an acceleration, there must be a force that is causing it. Extending the previous example, if the same amount of force is applied to an elephant and a baseball, the baseball will have a much larger acceleration than the elephant (and so it is easier to throw).

Newton's second law, $F = ma$, can be used to remember all three laws.

If there is no outside force ($F = 0$), the object will not accelerate and thus will stay at rest or at a constant velocity (Newton's first law).

If an object is resting on the floor, it is not moving, and $a = 0$. To maintain this equilibrium, the weight of the object must be matched by the force pushing up from the floor (Newton's third law).

An object in EQUILIBRIUM is either at rest or is moving at constant velocity; in other words, the object has no acceleration, or $a = 0$. Using Newton's second law, an object is in equilibrium if the net force on the object is 0, or $F = 0$ (this is called the equilibrium condition).

Newton's third law states that for every action (force), there will be an equal and opposite reaction (force). For instance, if a person is standing on the floor, there is a force of gravity pulling him toward the earth. However, he is not accelerating toward the earth; he is simply standing at rest on the floor (in equilibrium). So, the floor must provide a force that is equal in magnitude and in the opposite direction to the force of gravity.

Another example is a person kicking a wall. While it may seem like kicking a wall would only damage the wall, the force applied to the wall from the person's foot is identical to the force applied to the person's foot from the wall.

Examples

1. When a car moving forward stops abruptly, which of the following describes what happens to the driver if she is wearing a seat belt?

   (A) The driver's body will continue to move forward due to inertia, and the seat belt will apply the required force to keep her in her seat.

   (B) The driver is inside the car, so she will stop with the car whether or not she is wearing a seat belt.

   (C) The driver will be pushed against the seat when the car stops; the seat belt has no effect.

   (D) Due to inertia, the driver's body wants to be at rest, so she will stop automatically once the car stops moving.

   (E) The driver's body will slow down because inertia is passed from the seat belt in the car to the driver.

   Answers:

   (A) is correct. The driver's body will continue moving forward due to inertia. A force is required to slow the driver down (Newton's first law).

   (B) is incorrect. Being inside the car does not matter; a force is required to slow the driver down.

   (C) is incorrect. The driver will be pushed against the seat only if the car is moving in reverse and comes to an abrupt stop.

   (D) is incorrect. Inertia states that an object will remain at rest or at constant velocity.

   (E) is incorrect. Inertia is not passed between objects; it is a property of matter stating that objects have a tendency to remain at rest or at constant velocity.

2. Which example describes an object in equilibrium?

(A) a parachutist after he jumps from an airplane

(B) an airplane taking off

(C) a person sitting still in a chair

(D) a soccer ball when it is kicked

(E) a baseball in a glove during a catch

Answers:

(A) is incorrect. The parachutist will accelerate toward the earth.

(B) is incorrect. The airplane is accelerating to take off.

(C) is correct. The person is not accelerating.

(D) is incorrect. During a kick, the soccer ball is accelerating.

(E) is incorrect. The ball is decelerating (slowing down) as it is caught in a glove.

FORCES

There are four **FUNDAMENTAL FORCES** that form the basis for all other forces. The **GRAVITATIONAL** force is the force that pulls mass together. It is an attractive force and is what holds stars and planets together as spheres and keeps them in orbit. It also keeps humans on the surface of the earth. The **WEAK** force is beyond the scope of this text, but it plays a role in nuclear reactions (like those in stars). The **ELECTROMAGNETIC** force is the force between electric charges. It is repulsive when the charges are the same sign (positive-positive or negative-negative) and is attractive when the charges are the opposite sign (positive-negative). This force holds the positive nuclei and negative electrons of atoms together. Finally, the **NUCLEAR** (or strong) force is so named because it holds together the nucleus in an atom. The nuclear force has a larger magnitude than the electromagnetic force that pushes protons (positive charges) away from each other in the nucleus.

Non-fundamental forces are defined as forces that can be derived from the four fundamental forces. These forces include weight, tension, friction, the normal force, and the buoyant force. The gravitational force felt by an object on the surface of the earth is called the object's **WEIGHT** (F_w). **TENSION** (F_T or T) is found in ropes pulling or holding up an object, and **FRICTION** (F_f) is created by two objects moving against each other. The **NORMAL**

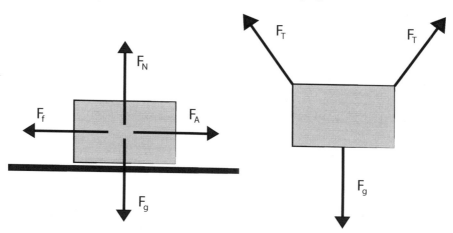

Figure 7.1. Free-Body Diagrams

FORCE (F_N or N) occurs when an object is resting on another object. The normal force is always equal and opposite to the force pushing onto the surface. The **BUOYANT** force (F_B) is the upward force experienced by floating objects. Finally, an **APPLIED FORCE** (F_A) is any force applied to an object by another object.

When working with forces, it is helpful to draw a **FREE-BODY DIAGRAM**, which shows all the forces acting on an object. Because forces are vectors, it is important to consider the direction of the force when drawing a diagram.

Example

Which of the following forces causes oppositely charged ions to attract?

(A) nuclear

(B) electromagnetic

(C) tension

(D) gravitational

(E) normal

Answers:

(A) is incorrect. The nuclear force holds together the subatomic particles in an atom's nucleus.

(B) is correct. The electromagnetic force is the force between charged particles that causes them to attract or repel each other.

(C) is incorrect. Tension is a force that results from an object being pulled or hung from a rope or chain.

(D) is incorrect. The gravitational force is the attractive force between masses.

(E) is incorrect. The normal force pushes up against an object resting on a surface.

Weight

The gravitational force felt by an object on the surface of the earth is called the object's **WEIGHT**. The acceleration due to gravity on the surface of the earth is $g = 9.8$ m/s^2 and always points toward the center of the earth. Using Newton's second law, the weight W of an object of mass m is: $W = mg$.

You won't need to memorize any specific equations for this subtest, but understanding the mathematical foundation of basic forces and machines can help you answer questions correctly.

Example

The acceleration due to gravity is 9.8 m/s^2 on the surface of the Earth and 1.6 m/s^2 on the moon. How would a person's weight on the Earth compare to their weight on the moon?

(A) The person would weigh more on the Earth than on the moon.

(B) The person would weigh less on the Earth than on the moon.

(C) The person would weigh the same on the Earth and the moon.

(D) The person would have a weight on the Earth but will have no weight on the moon.

(E) There is not enough information to determine the relationship between a person's weight on the Earth and the moon.

Answer:

(A) is correct. Weight is the result of the gravitational pull of a body. Objects experiencing a larger acceleration due to gravity will have a larger weight.

(B) is incorrect. The acceleration due to gravity on the moon is less than that of the Earth, so a person will weigh more on Earth than on the moon.

(C) is incorrect. A person will have different weights on the Earth and moon because the gravitational force on each body is different.

(D) is incorrect. A person will have a weight any time they are close enough to feel the gravitational force of a body.

(E) is incorrect. Because the person's mass is the same, all that's needed to find the person's weight is the acceleration due to gravity.

Tension

A common type of applied force is TENSION, the force applied by a rope or chain as it pulls on an object. In a free-body diagram, the vector for tension always points along the rope away from the object. Tension plays an important role in pulley systems, as shown in Figure 7.2. The tension in the pulley's rope acts against the mass's weight, and the magnitude of the two forces determines whether the mass moves up or down.

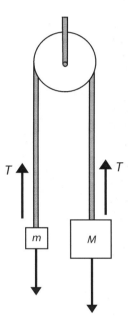

Example

In Figure 7.2, if mass M is much greater than mass m, what direction do both masses move?

(A) Mass M will move down, and mass m will move up.

(B) Mass M will move up, and mass m will move down.

(C) Neither mass will move; the system is in equilibrium.

(D) Both masses will move down.

(E) Both masses will move up.

Figure 7.2. Pulley System

Answers:

(A) is correct. If mass M is larger, then the weight of mass M will produce a larger force than the weight of mass m. The larger force will move mass M down and mass m up.

(B) is incorrect. If mass M is larger, then the weight of mass M will produce a larger force than the weight of mass m. The larger force will move mass M down and mass m up.

(C) is incorrect. The forces are not balanced. Mass M will have a larger weight, so the system is not in equilibrium.

(D) is incorrect. A pulley will not allow the masses to move in this way.

(E) is incorrect. A pulley will not allow the masses to move in this way.

Friction

Microscopically, no surface is perfectly smooth. The irregular shape of the surfaces in contact will lead to interactions that resist movement. The resulting force is FRICTION. Friction opposes motion and describes the resistance of two surfaces in contact as they move across each other. On a free-body diagram, friction always points in the direction opposite the object's motion.

There are two types of friction: static and kinetic. STATIC FRICTION is applicable to an object that is not moving and is always equal to the force applied to the object. In other words, it is the amount of force that needs to be overcome for an object to move. For example, a small force applied to a large rock will not move the rock because static friction will match the applied force in the opposite direction. However, when enough force is applied, static friction can be overcome, and an object will begin moving. When this happens, the moving object experiences KINETIC friction. The size of the friction force increases with an object's weight.

Example

In which of the following situations is an object experiencing static friction?

(A) a rock sliding down a hill

(B) an ice skater skating around a rink

(C) a person in a moving car slamming on the brakes

(D) a refrigerator that slides down a ramp

(E) a person leaning against a car

Answers:

(A) is incorrect. Kinetic friction will be in effect because the rock is moving.

(B) is incorrect. Kinetic friction will be in effect because the ice skater is moving.

(C) is incorrect. Kinetic friction will be in effect because the car is moving.

(D) is incorrect. Kinetic friction will be in effect because the refrigerator is moving.

(E) is correct. The person is applying a force to the car, and static friction is keeping the car from moving.

Buoyant Force

Boats float by using the buoyant force. Ships that hold very large loads need a large buoyant force and so need to displace a large amount of water.

When a boat or object is floating or under water or another liquid, the BUOYANT FORCE pushes vertically against the weight of the object. The magnitude of this force is calculated by considering the volume of the object that is submerged in the fluid. The object displaces a volume of liquid equal to its own volume, and the liquid pushes back by an amount that is exactly equal to the weight of the liquid that would exist in that volume.

Example

Which object will experience the largest buoyant force when fully submerged?

(A) a marble

(B) a golf ball

(C) a baseball

(D) a softball

(E) a basketball

Answers:

(A) is incorrect. Of the five, the marble does not have the largest volume.

(B) is incorrect. Of the five, the golf ball does not have the largest volume.

(C) is incorrect. Of the five, the baseball does not have the largest volume.

(D) is incorrect. Of the five, the softball does not have the largest volume.

(E) is correct. A basketball will have the largest volume and will displace the most water. This will lead to the largest buoyant force of the five.

SIMPLE MACHINES

A simple machine changes the magnitude or direction of an applied force, with the result leading to a MECHANICAL ADVANTAGE for the user. This advantage is the ratio of force that is output from the machine relative to the force input. The equation for mechanical advantage is given by

$$MA = \frac{F_{output}}{F_{input}}$$

A LEVER is a simple machine based on the concept of torque. The axis of rotation and also where the lever rests is called the FULCRUM. Using the figure as a guide, $r_{input} F_{input} = r_{output} F_{output}$. Using the previous definition for mechanical advantages gives

$$MA = \frac{r_{input}}{r_{output}}$$

There are three types of levers. A FIRST-CLASS LEVER has the fulcrum between the input and output forces, and the input force is in the opposite direction of the output force. A SECOND-CLASS LEVER has the input and output forces on one common side of the fulcrum, and both are in the same direction. The output force is closer to the fulcrum than the input force is. Like the second-class lever, a THIRD-CLASS LEVER has the input and output forces on one common side of the fulcrum, and both are in the same direction. The input force is closer to the fulcrum than the output force is.

The idea of simple machines was invented by Archimedes in the third century BCE.

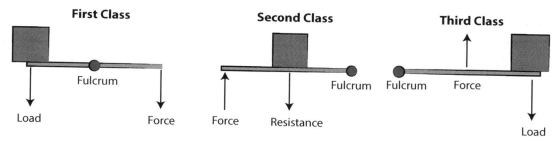

Figure 7.3. Types of Levers

An INCLINED PLANE is a simple machine (a ramp) that reduces the amount of force needed to raise a mass to a certain height. Earlier in this text it was shown that the weight of a mass on an inclined plane has a portion that pushes into the plane. Only a fraction of the weight is in the direction down the plane. This is the operating principle for this simple machine. In terms of work, the input work to move an object up an inclined plane of length L is $W_{in} = F_{input} \times L$. The output work is what is required to lift the object up to a height h, $W_{output} = F_{output} \times h$, where F_{output} is the object's weight. Combining these gives the mechanical advantage

$$MA = \frac{L}{h}$$

where L is the length of the inclined plane and h is the height.

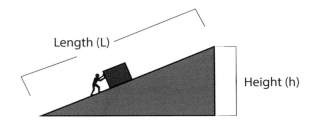

Figure 7.4. An Inclined Plane

A **PULLEY** is a simple machine that redirects force by supporting a rope that can move freely by rotating the pulley. A single pulley lifting a weight will have a mechanical advantage of 1. When a second pulley is added in a block-and-tackle configuration, the input force required to lift the weight is halved, and so the mechanical advantage is 2. Similarly, a three-pulley system will have a mechanical advantage of 3.

$$MA = \text{number of pulleys}$$

A **WEDGE** is a simple machine that converts an input force onto one surface into a force that is perpendicular to its other surfaces. A wedge is often used to separate material; common examples are an ax or knife. Using the same reasoning as used for an inclined plane (a wedge is effectively two inclined planes on top of each other), the mechanical advantage is

$$MA = \frac{L}{W}$$

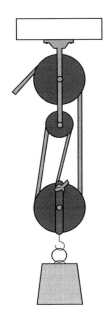

Figure 7.5. A Three-Pulley System

where L is the length of the inclined plane on the wedge, and W is the width (the length of the back edge).

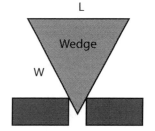

Figure 7.6. A Simple Wedge

A **WHEEL AND AXLE** is a simple machine that has a rotating structure with two different radii. The larger radius is the wheel, and the smaller radius is the axle. It is similar conceptually to a lever, where the different radii convert the torque on the wheel into a torque on the axle (or vice versa). The mechanical advantage is the same as for the lever: $MA = \frac{r_{input}}{r_{output}}$ where r_{input} is the radius of the input, and r_{output} is the radius of the output.

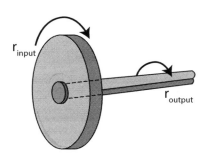

Figure 7.7. A Wheel and Axle

GEARS are simple machines that are circular and have notches or teeth along the outer edge. Several gears in contact form a gear train. Again, the force applied along a gear train is related to the torque, where a large-radius gear will apply a large torque to a smaller gear on the train. The number of teeth on a gear is directly related to the radius of the gear, allowing the mechanical advantage to be written as

$$MA = \frac{\tau_{output}}{\tau_{input}} = \frac{N_{output}}{N_{input}}$$

where τ are the torques from each gear, and N is the number of teeth on each gear.

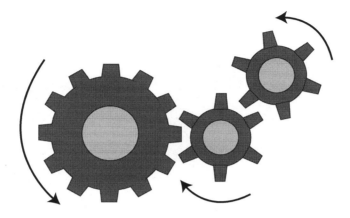

Figure 7.8. A Gear Train

Another concept for a gear train is the **GEAR RATIO**, or speed ratio, which is a ratio of the angular velocity of the input gear to the angular velocity of the output gear. At the point of contact, the linear velocity must be the same, so $v = \omega_{input} \, r_{input} = \omega_{output} \, r_{output}$. So, the gear ratio is

$$\frac{\omega_{input}}{\omega_{output}} = \frac{r_{output}}{r_{input}} = \frac{N_{output}}{N_{input}}$$

A **SCREW** is a simple machine that converts rotational motion into linear motion. In general, a screw is a cylinder with an inclined plane wrapped around it. The wrapped inclined plane is called the thread, while the distance between the planes is called the pitch. The pitch is directed along the length of the screw. Again considering the work done, $W_{input} = F_{input} \, 2\pi r$, where r is the radius of the screw; and $W_{output} = F_{output} \, h$, where h is the pitch. The mechanical advantage then becomes

$$MA = \frac{2\pi r}{h}$$

where r is the radius of the screw, and h is the pitch.

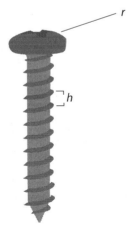

Figure 7.9. A Screw

CONTINUE

Examples

1. Which is an example of a first-class lever?

   (A) crowbar

   (B) wheelbarrow

   (C) scissors

   (D) tweezers

   (E) stapler

   Answers:

   (A) is incorrect. This is a second-class lever.

   (B) is incorrect. This is a second-class lever.

   (C) is correct. This is a first-class lever.

   (D) is incorrect. This is a third-class lever.

   (E) is incorrect. This is a third-class lever.

2. Which mechanical advantage is the best for the user?

   (A) 10

   (B) 5

   (C) 2

   (D) 1

   (E) 0.5

   Answer:

   (A) is correct. The highest mechanical advantage is the best for the user.

PRACTICE TEST

SIMPLE DRAWINGS

2 minutes

This section measures your ability to quickly process visual information. Each question includes five figures. Four of these figures are the same, and one is different. Your task is to identify the figure that is different from the others.

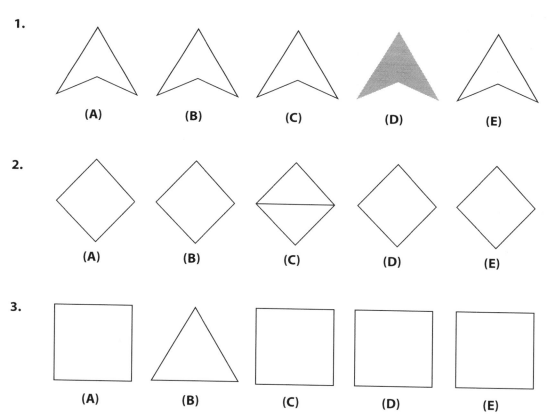

1.

(A)   (B)   (C)   (D)   (E)

2.

(A)   (B)   (C)   (D)   (E)

3.

(A)   (B)   (C)   (D)   (E)

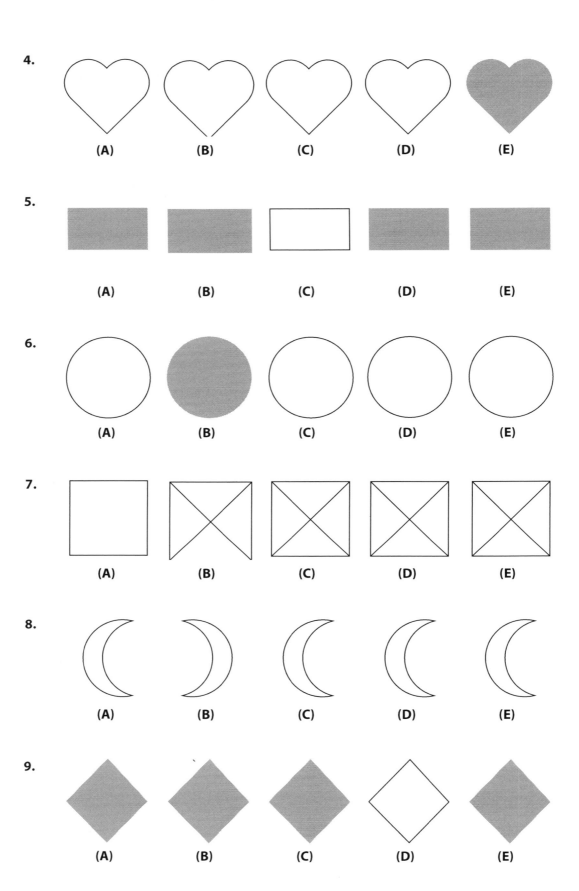

4.

    (A)   (B)   (C)   (D)   (E)

5.

    (A)   (B)   (C)   (D)   (E)

6.

    (A)   (B)   (C)   (D)   (E)

7.

    (A)   (B)   (C)   (D)   (E)

8.

    (A)   (B)   (C)   (D)   (E)

9.

    (A)   (B)   (C)   (D)   (E)

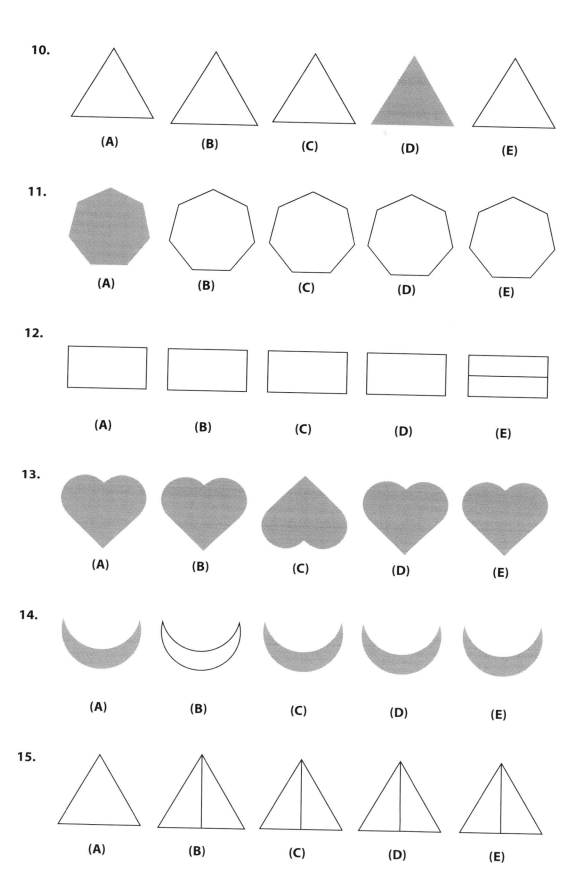

10.

(A)   (B)   (C)   (D)   (E)

11.

(A)   (B)   (C)   (D)   (E)

12.

(A)   (B)   (C)   (D)   (E)

13.

(A)   (B)   (C)   (D)   (E)

14.

(A)   (B)   (C)   (D)   (E)

15.

(A)   (B)   (C)   (D)   (E)

16.

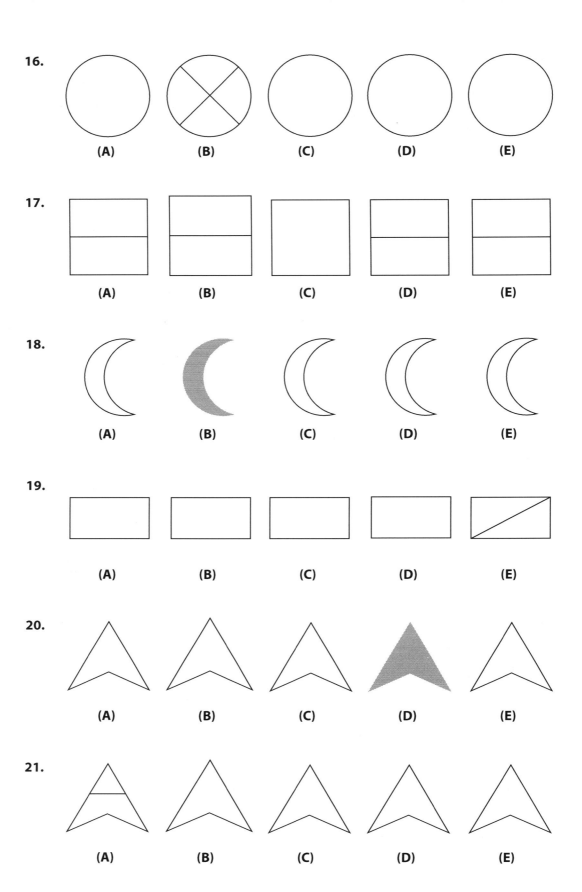

17.

18.

19.

20.

21.

22.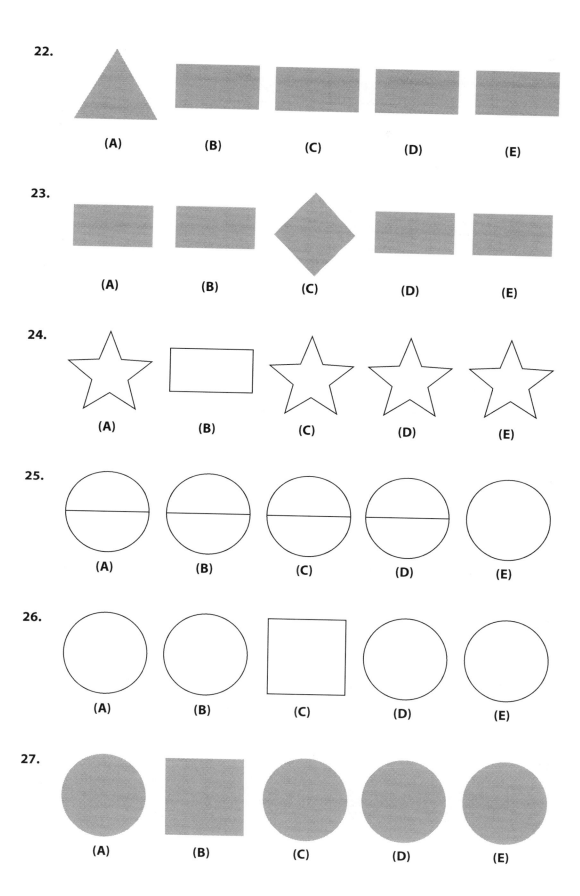

(A)   (B)   (C)   (D)   (E)

23.

(A)   (B)   (C)   (D)   (E)

24.

(A)   (B)   (C)   (D)   (E)

25.

(A)   (B)   (C)   (D)   (E)

26.

(A)   (B)   (C)   (D)   (E)

27.

(A)   (B)   (C)   (D)   (E)

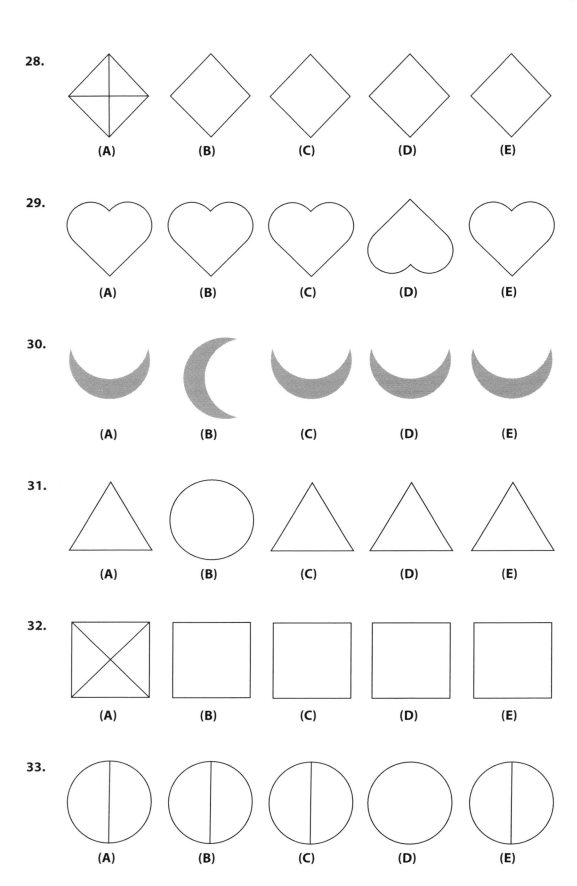

28.   (A)   (B)   (C)   (D)   (E)

29.   (A)   (B)   (C)   (D)   (E)

30.   (A)   (B)   (C)   (D)   (E)

31.   (A)   (B)   (C)   (D)   (E)

32.   (A)   (B)   (C)   (D)   (E)

33.   (A)   (B)   (C)   (D)   (E)

34.

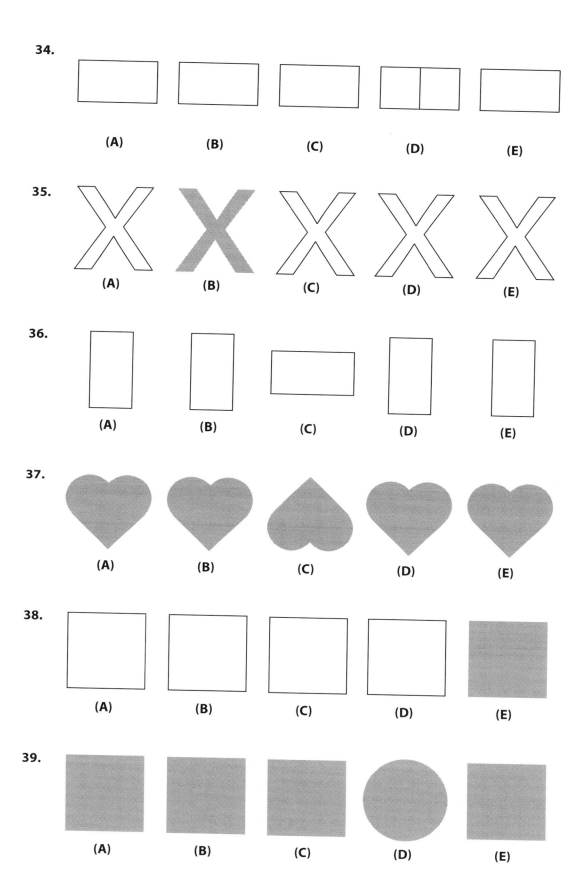

(A) (B) (C) (D) (E)

35.

(A) (B) (C) (D) (E)

36.

(A) (B) (C) (D) (E)

37.

(A) (B) (C) (D) (E)

38.

(A) (B) (C) (D) (E)

39.

(A) (B) (C) (D) (E)

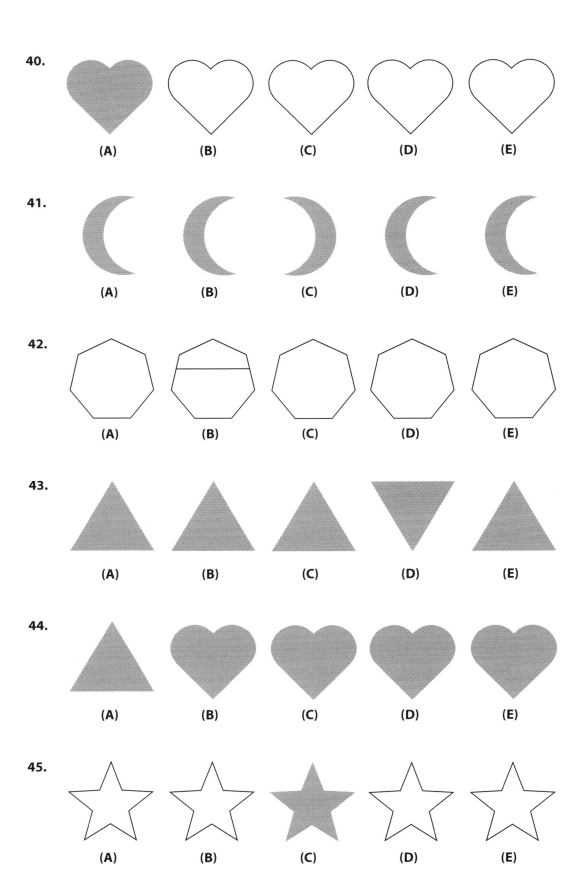

40.   (A)   (B)   (C)   (D)   (E)

41.   (A)   (B)   (C)   (D)   (E)

42.   (A)   (B)   (C)   (D)   (E)

43.   (A)   (B)   (C)   (D)   (E)

44.   (A)   (B)   (C)   (D)   (E)

45.   (A)   (B)   (C)   (D)   (E)

46.

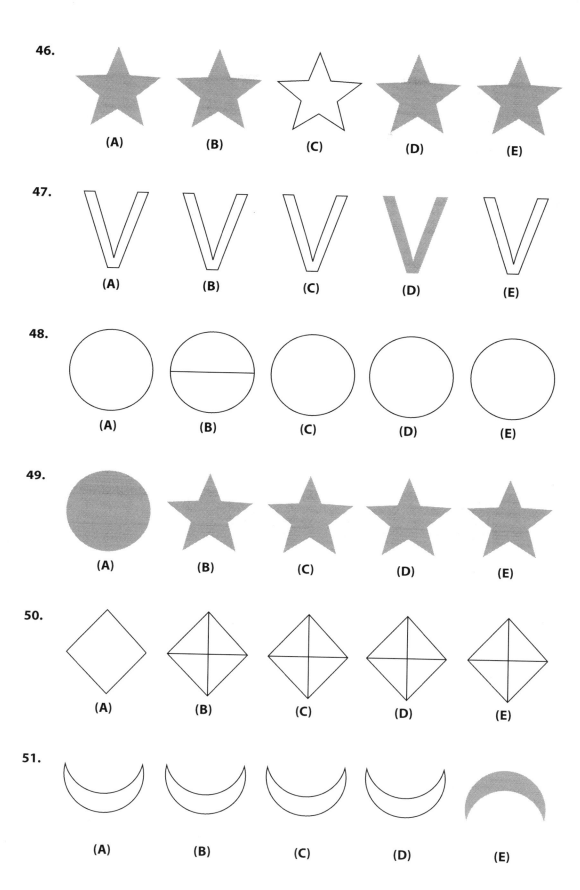

(A)   (B)   (C)   (D)   (E)

47.

(A)   (B)   (C)   (D)   (E)

48.

(A)   (B)   (C)   (D)   (E)

49.

(A)   (B)   (C)   (D)   (E)

50.

(A)   (B)   (C)   (D)   (E)

51.

(A)   (B)   (C)   (D)   (E)

52.

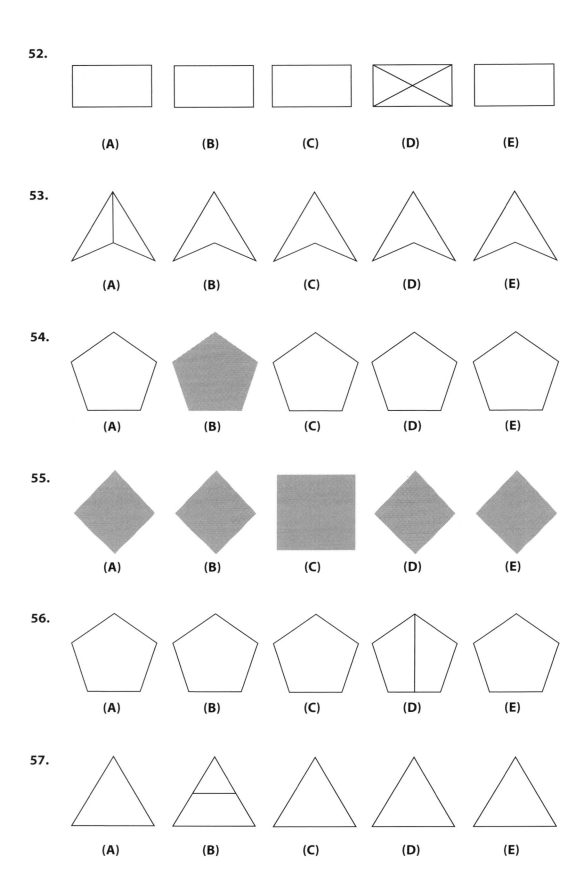

(A)   (B)   (C)   (D)   (E)

53.

(A)   (B)   (C)   (D)   (E)

54.

(A)   (B)   (C)   (D)   (E)

55.

(A)   (B)   (C)   (D)   (E)

56.

(A)   (B)   (C)   (D)   (E)

57.

(A)   (B)   (C)   (D)   (E)

58.

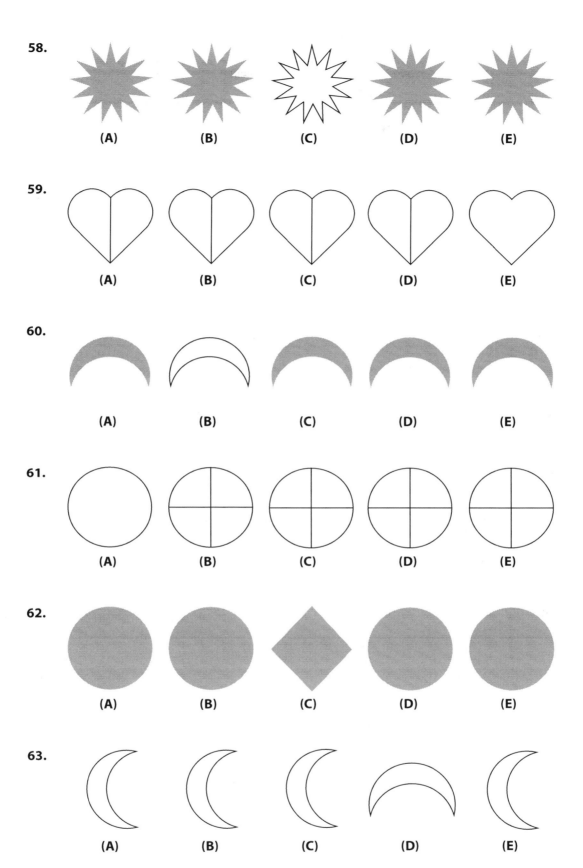

(A)   (B)   (C)   (D)   (E)

59.

(A)   (B)   (C)   (D)   (E)

60.

(A)   (B)   (C)   (D)   (E)

61.

(A)   (B)   (C)   (D)   (E)

62.

(A)   (B)   (C)   (D)   (E)

63.

(A)   (B)   (C)   (D)   (E)

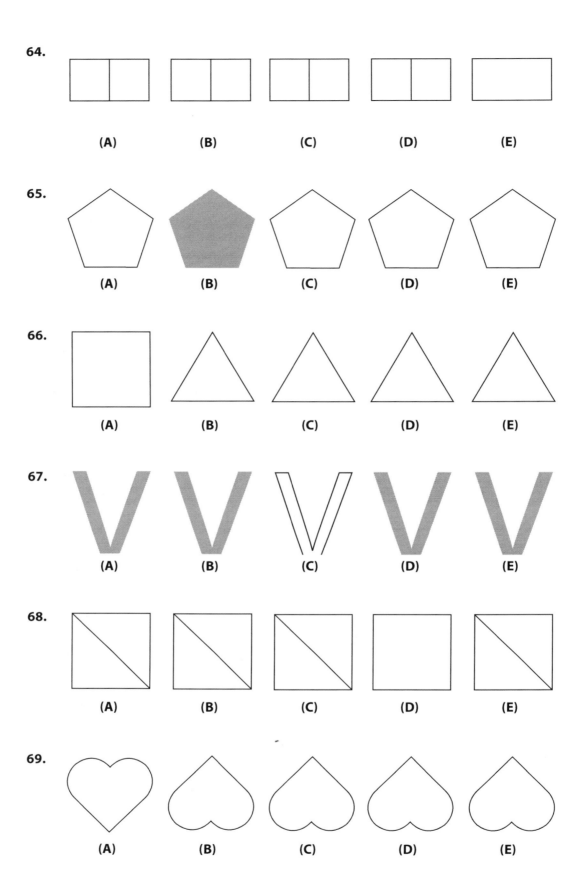

64.

(A)   (B)   (C)   (D)   (E)

65.

(A)   (B)   (C)   (D)   (E)

66.

(A)   (B)   (C)   (D)   (E)

67.

(A)   (B)   (C)   (D)   (E)

68.

(A)   (B)   (C)   (D)   (E)

69.

(A)   (B)   (C)   (D)   (E)

70.

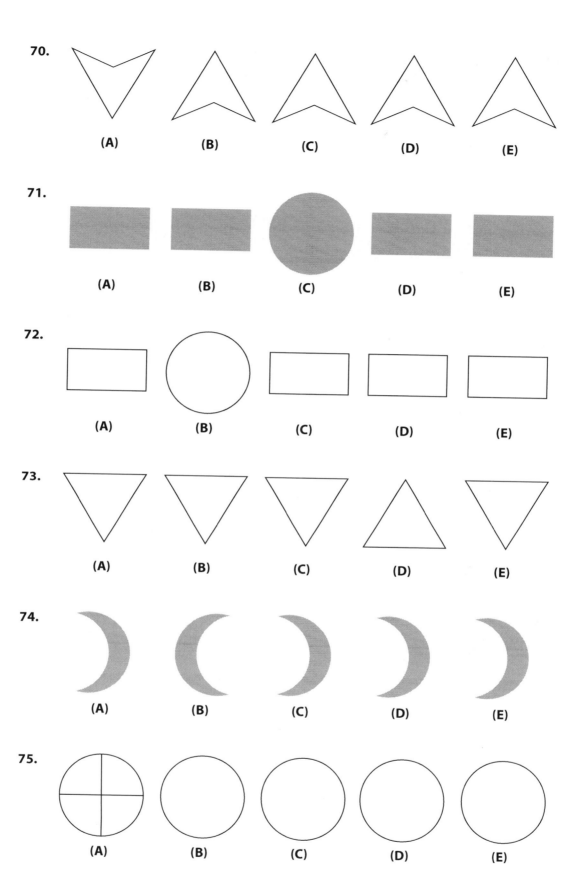

(A)　(B)　(C)　(D)　(E)

71.

(A)　(B)　(C)　(D)　(E)

72.

(A)　(B)　(C)　(D)　(E)

73.

(A)　(B)　(C)　(D)　(E)

74.

(A)　(B)　(C)　(D)　(E)

75.

(A)　(B)　(C)　(D)　(E)

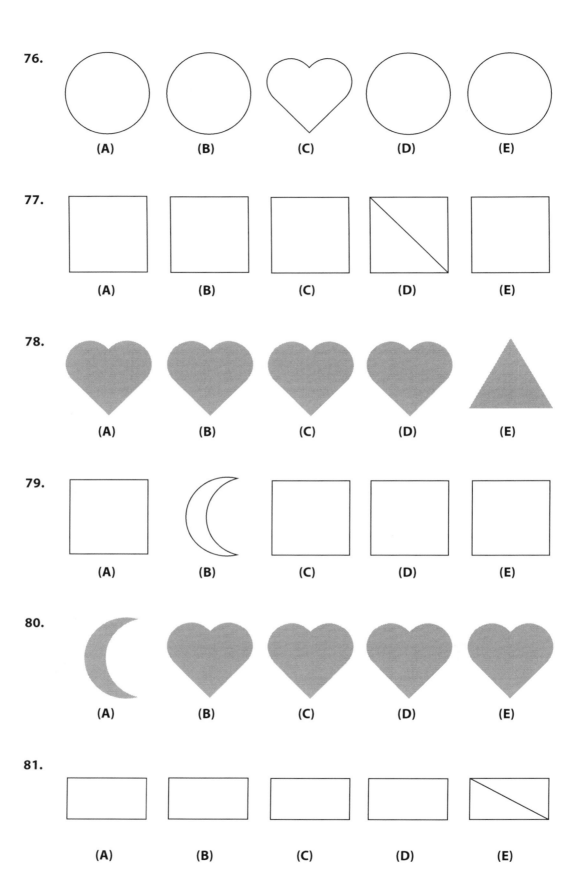

76.
    (A)   (B)   (C)   (D)   (E)

77.
    (A)   (B)   (C)   (D)   (E)

78.
    (A)   (B)   (C)   (D)   (E)

79.
    (A)   (B)   (C)   (D)   (E)

80.
    (A)   (B)   (C)   (D)   (E)

81.
    (A)   (B)   (C)   (D)   (E)

82.

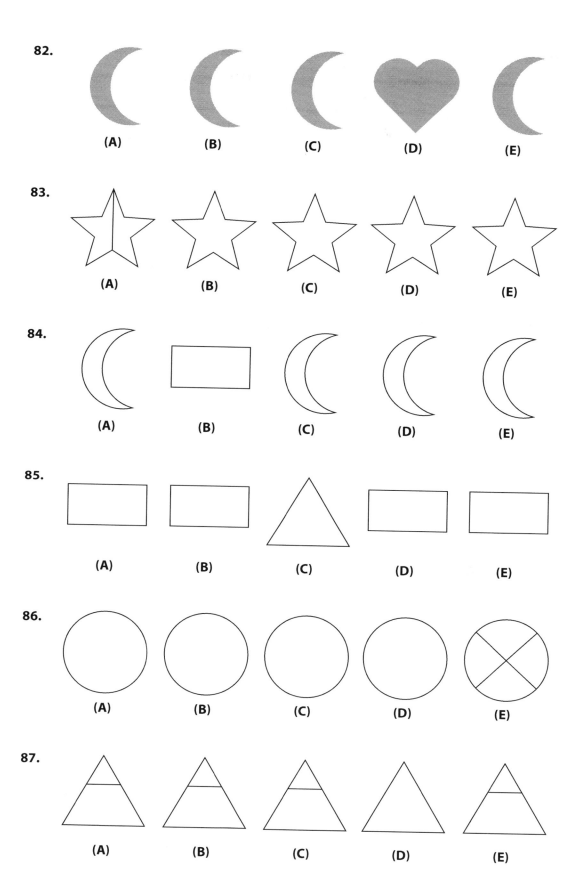

(A)   (B)   (C)   (D)   (E)

83.

(A)   (B)   (C)   (D)   (E)

84.

(A)   (B)   (C)   (D)   (E)

85.

(A)   (B)   (C)   (D)   (E)

86.

(A)   (B)   (C)   (D)   (E)

87.

(A)   (B)   (C)   (D)   (E)

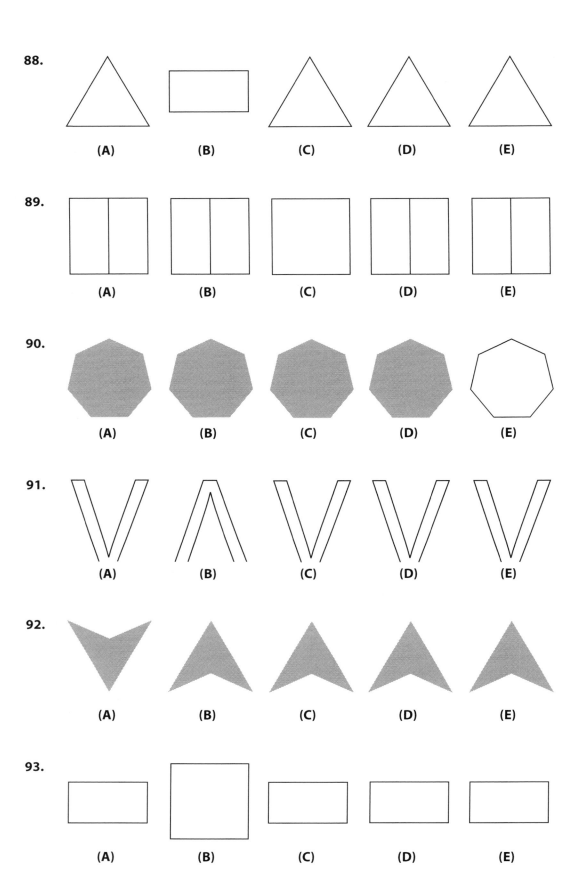

88.

(A)   (B)   (C)   (D)   (E)

89.

(A)   (B)   (C)   (D)   (E)

90.

(A)   (B)   (C)   (D)   (E)

91.

(A)   (B)   (C)   (D)   (E)

92.

(A)   (B)   (C)   (D)   (E)

93.

(A)   (B)   (C)   (D)   (E)

94.

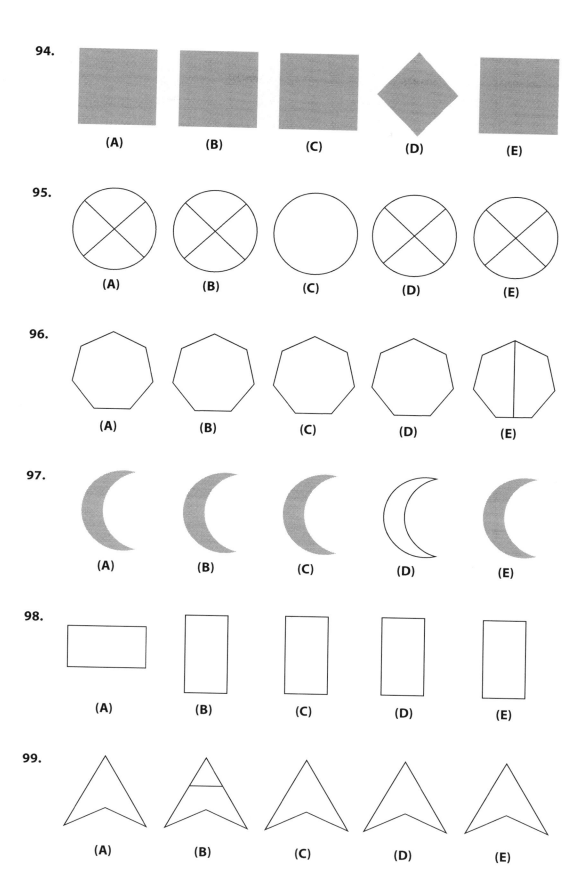

(A) (B) (C) (D) (E)

95.

(A) (B) (C) (D) (E)

96.

(A) (B) (C) (D) (E)

97.

(A) (B) (C) (D) (E)

98.

(A) (B) (C) (D) (E)

99.

(A) (B) (C) (D) (E)

100.

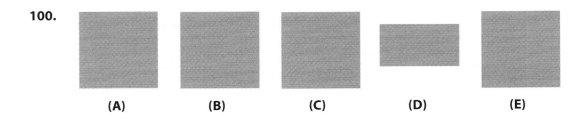

(A)   (B)   (C)   (D)   (E)

HIDDEN FIGURES

5 minutes

This section measures your ability to quickly process visual information. Each question includes a set of five shapes labeled A – E and five numbered drawings. Your task is to identify which of the five shapes can be found within each drawing. Shapes may appear in more than one drawing, or they may not appear at all.

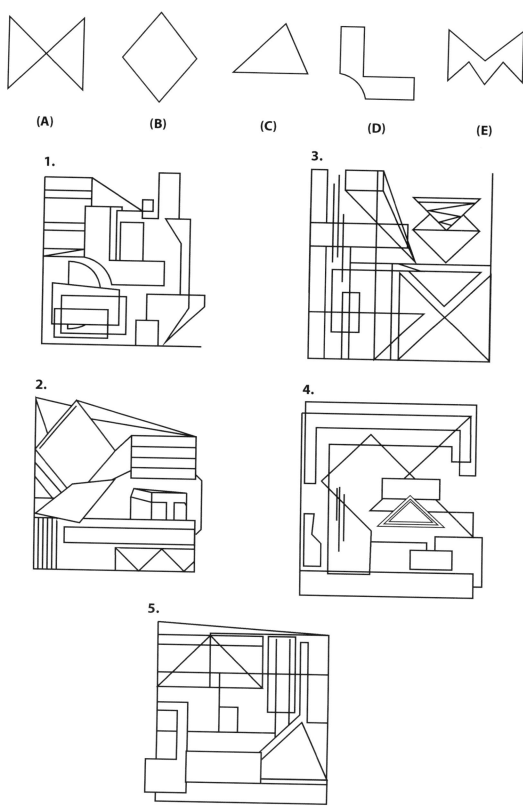

(A)　　　　(B)　　　　(C)　　　　(D)　　　　(E)

1.

2.

3.

4.

5.

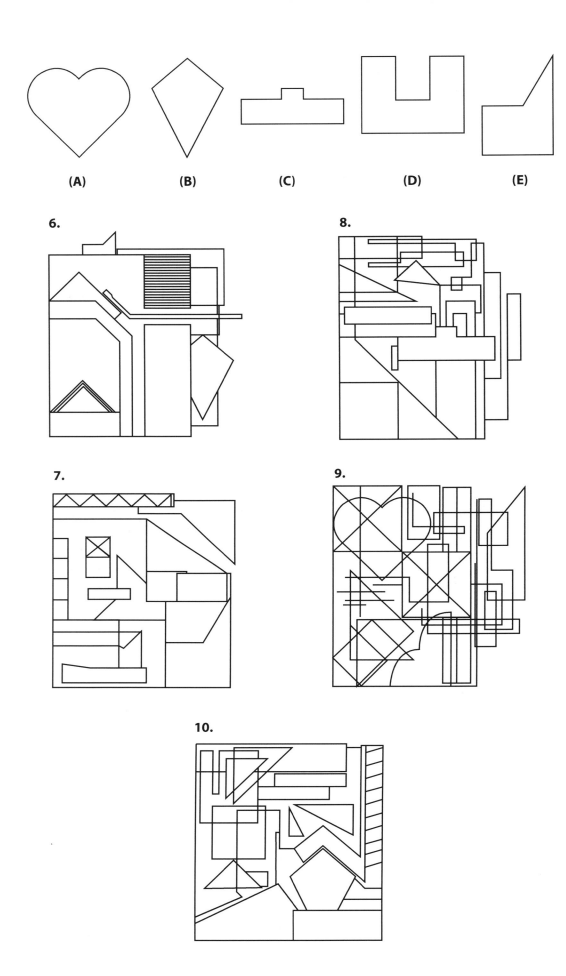

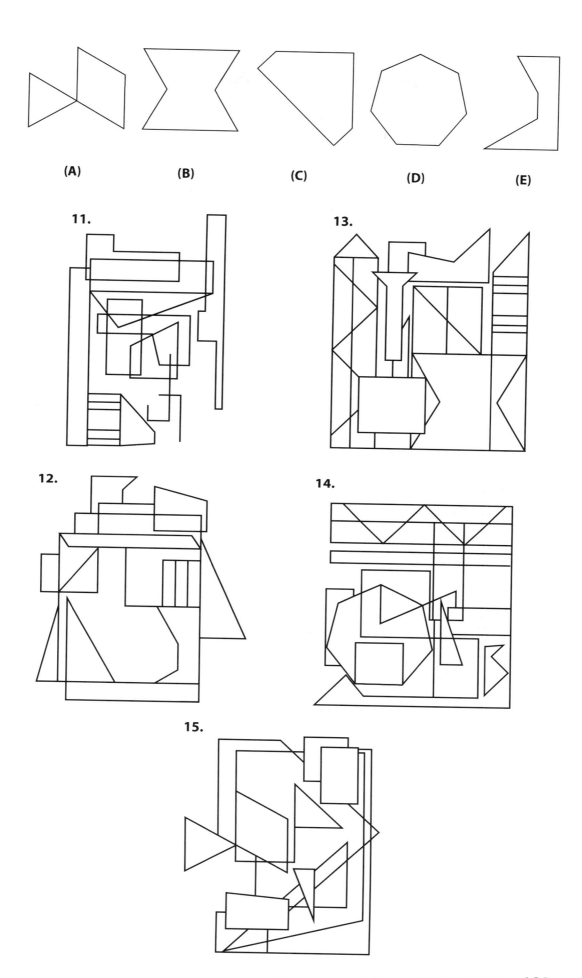

(A)　　　(B)　　　(C)　　　(D)　　　(E)

11.

12.

13.

14.

15.

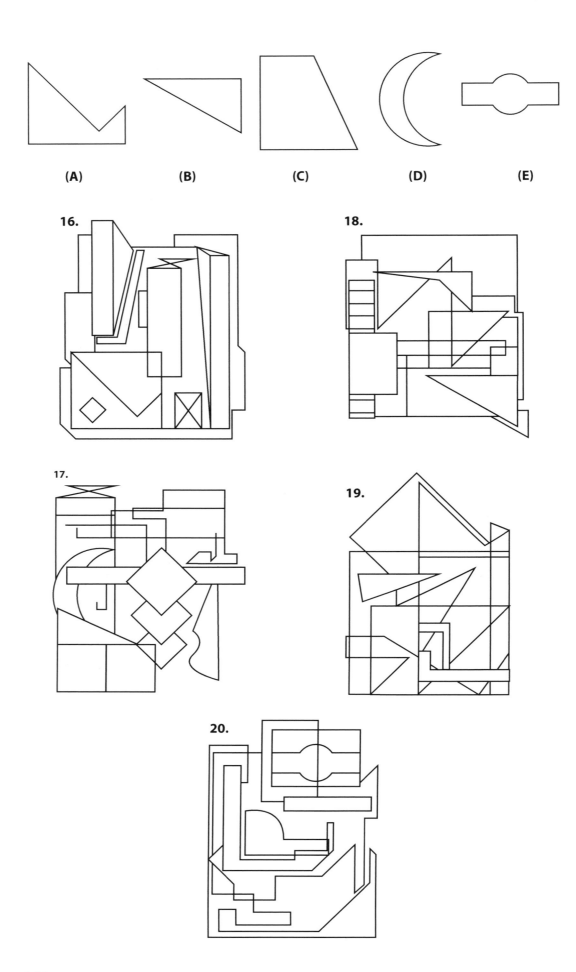

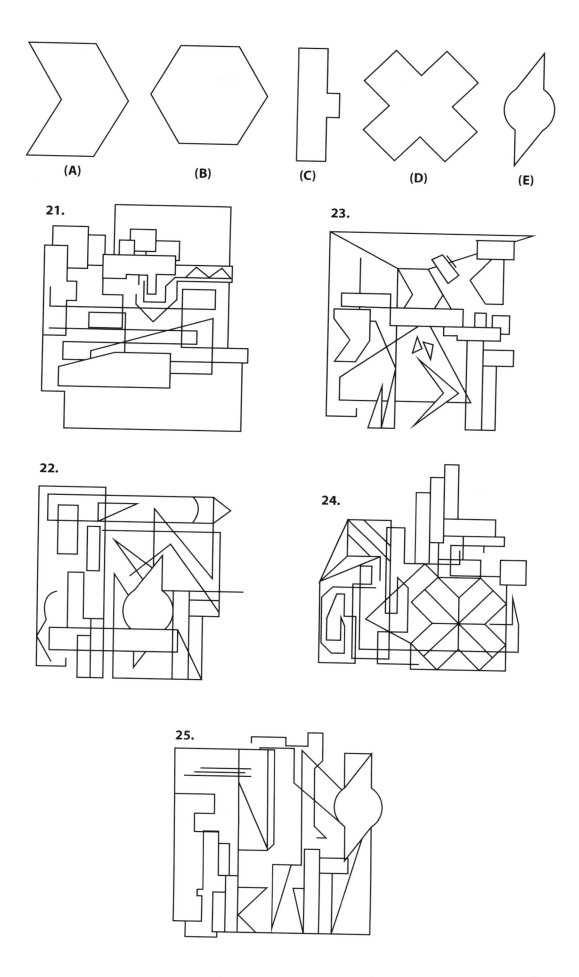

(A)   (B)   (C)   (D)   (E)

21.

22.

23.

24.

25.

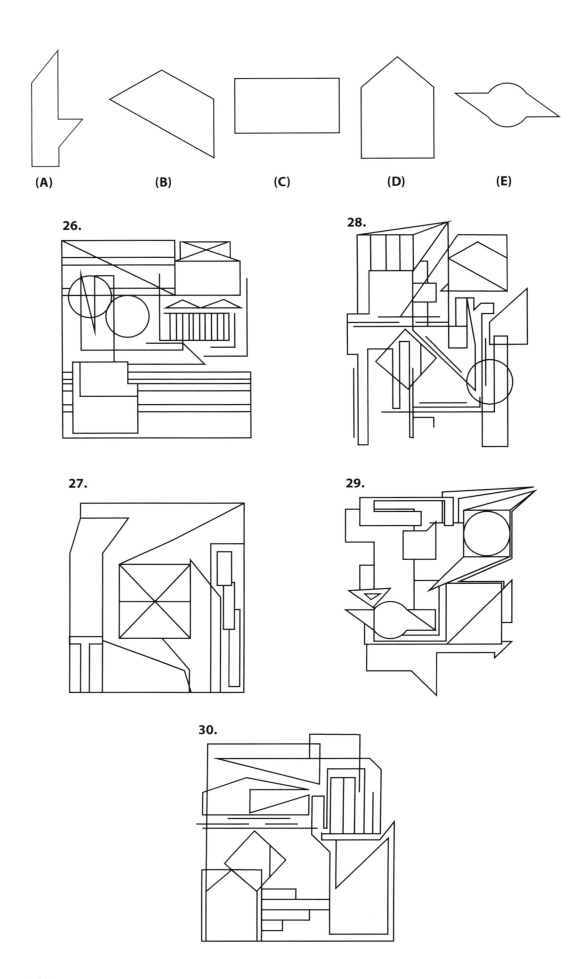

(A) (B) (C) (D) (E)

26.

27.

28.

29.

30.

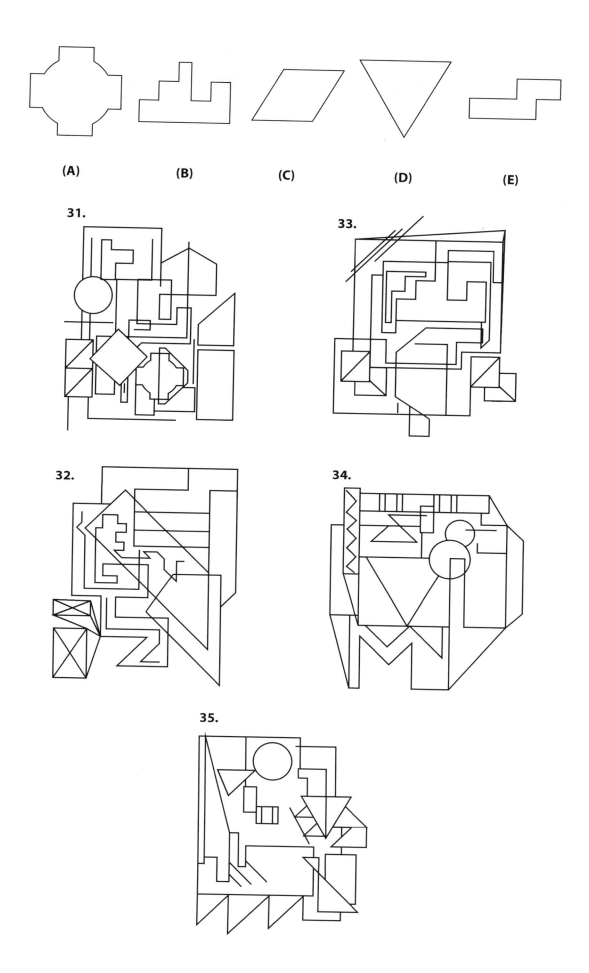

(A) **(B)** **(C)** **(D)** **(E)**

31.

33.

32.

34.

35.

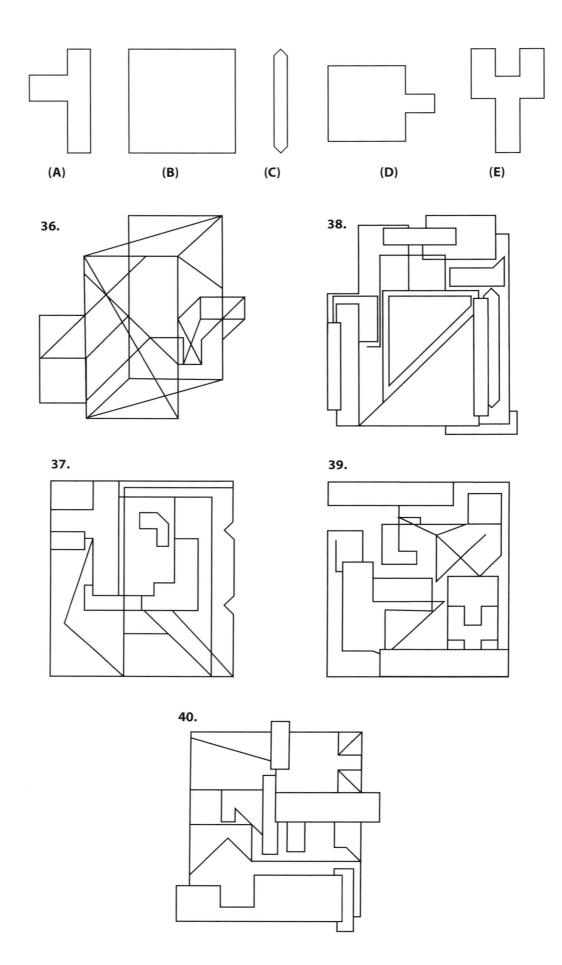

(A) (B) (C) (D) (E)

36.

37.

38.

39.

40.

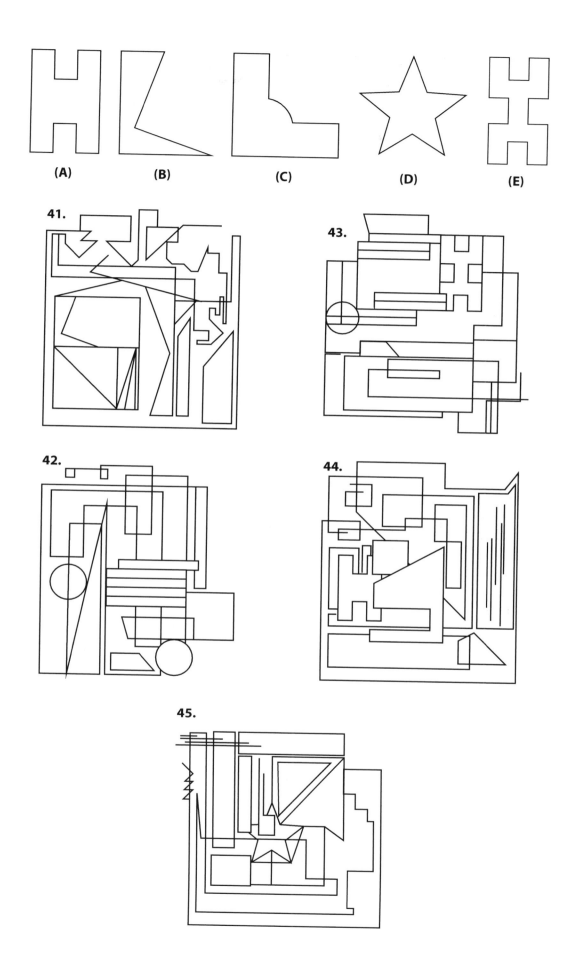

(A) (B) (C) (D) (E)

41.

43.

42.

44.

45.

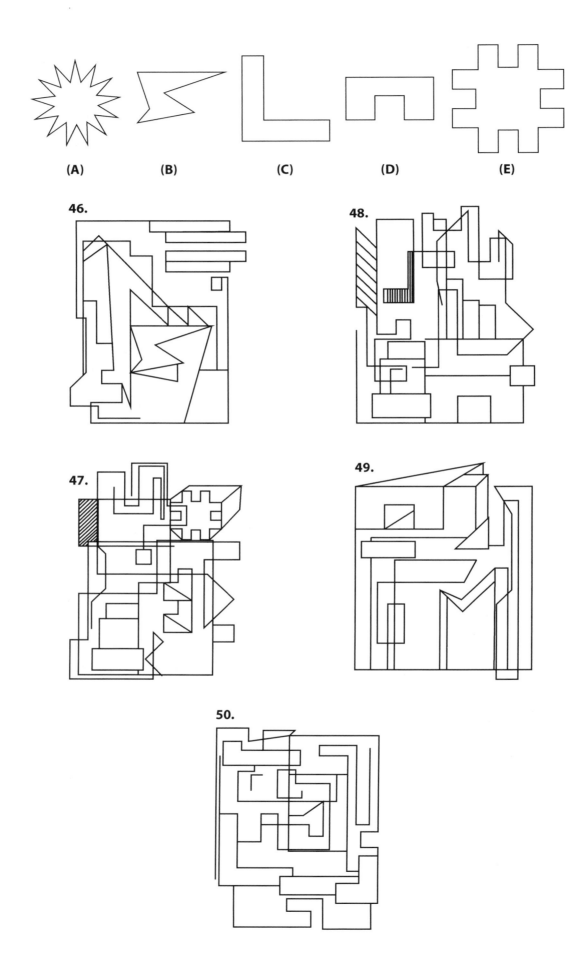

(A)　　　　(B)　　　　(C)　　　　(D)　　　　(E)

46.

48.

47.

49.

50.

ARMY AVIATION INFORMATION

30 minutes

This section measures your knowledge of aviation. Each of the questions or incomplete statements is followed by five choices. You are to decide which one of the choices best answers the question or completes the statement.

1. What part of a rotary-wing aircraft makes directional control possible?

   (A) the teeter hinge

   (B) the swashplate

   (C) the ducted fan

   (D) the tail boom

   (E) the skids

2. Which of these US Army helicopters is classified as tandem rotor?

   (A) LUH-72

   (B) CH-47

   (C) AH-64

   (D) UH-60

   (E) OH-58D

3. What is the preferred method of ground movement for helicopters on airports?

   (A) ground taxi

   (B) air taxi

   (C) taxi

   (D) hover taxi

   (E) progressive taxi

4. Which war became known as the "Helicopter War" because helicopters, in their first large-scale use in combat operations, quickly became a decisive force-multiplier for United States' forces?

   (A) Korean War

   (B) World War II

   (C) Vietnam War

   (D) Operation Desert Storm

   (E) 1967 Arab-Israeli War

5. What type of helicopter design uses a ducted fan in place of a tail rotor to cancel torque effect?

   (A) the coaxial rotor system

   (B) the NOTAR

   (C) the tandem rotor system

   (D) the semi-monocoque

   (E) the skids

6. Which aerodynamic force(s) must a rotary-wing aircraft balance in order to hover?

   (A) weight, lift, thrust, and drag

   (B) translational lift

   (C) dissymmetry of lift

   (D) gyroscopic precession

   (E) autorotation

7. How would a high-density altitude affect the performance of a helicopter?

   (A) Performance would be good due to the high value of the air density.

   (B) Performance may improve or be decreased: the density altitude has to be corrected for nonstandard temperature.

   (C) Engine performance would increase, but rotor performance would decrease.

   (D) Performance would be decreased due to low value of the air density.

   (E) Density altitude is not as important a factor in performance as temperature and humidity.

8. If the airspeed indicator needle is in the yellow and approaching the red line during a maneuver, what would be the correct response?

    (A) change attitude by 90 degrees
    (B) decrease altitude
    (C) decrease airspeed
    (D) increase airspeed
    (E) increase thrust

9. Which pitot-static instrument makes use of both pitot and static pressure?

    (A) vertical speed indicator
    (B) airspeed indicator
    (C) magnetic compass
    (D) altimeter
    (E) vacuum-powered gyro-compass

10. What effect does the cyclic control have on the rotor system?

    (A) It alters the pitch of the main rotor blades equally and simultaneously.
    (B) It increases or decreases the main rotor speed cyclically.
    (C) It alters the pitch of the main rotor blades individually and cyclically.
    (D) It alters the pitch of the tail rotor blades to increase or decrease thrust.
    (E) It tilts the main rotor mast to produce a cyclic change in rotor disk angle.

11. The angle of attack (AOA) is the angle between the

    (A) airfoil chord line and the resultant relative wind.
    (B) fuselage longitudinal axis and the flight path.
    (C) rotor disk and the local horizon.
    (D) airfoil chord line and the rotational relative wind.
    (E) airfoil mean chord line and center of pressure.

12. What item was developed to reduce compass reading errors?

    (A) a heading indicator
    (B) low latitude charts
    (C) a three-pointer compass
    (D) sectional charts
    (E) a vertical card compass

13. What effect is principally used to counteract main rotor torque with the NOTAR system used on the MD-520N and MD-900 helicopters?

    (A) Venturi effect
    (B) Coanda effect
    (C) ground effect
    (D) Doppler effect
    (E) Coriolis effect

14. Which type of drag is caused by production of lift?

    (A) induced drag
    (B) vortex drag
    (C) parasite drag
    (D) aerodynamic drag
    (E) profile drag

15. Risk management is composed of which four risk elements?

    (A) regulatory, technical, personal, and corporate
    (B) pilot, aircraft, weather, and peer pressure
    (C) regulatory, technical, schedule, and external factors
    (D) pilot, aircraft, environment, and external pressures
    (E) mission, aircraft, training, and experience

16. What is the unit of measure for airspeed?

    (A) AOA
    (B) degrees
    (C) knots
    (D) MSL
    (E) rate of climb

17. What is the degree increment between the hash marks on the attitude indicator?

   (A) 10 degrees
   (B) 30 degrees
   (C) 45 degrees
   (D) 90 degrees
   (E) 180 degrees

18. What three conditions are necessary for a helicopter to be in danger of a dynamic rollover?

   (A) high rate of descent, little or no airspeed, and some power applied
   (B) pivot point, sloping ground, and right crosswind
   (C) hard landing on one skid or wheel, defective drag dampers, and defective landing-gear struts
   (D) pivot point, rolling motion, and exceeding critical angle
   (E) high gross weight, high-density altitude, and operating within critical wind azimuth headings

19. What are the three regions of a rotor in autorotation?

   (A) positive lift, positive stall, and reverse flow
   (B) reverse flow, negative stall, and driving
   (C) driven, positive lift, and equilibrium region
   (D) stall, reverse flow, positive lift
   (E) driven, driving, and stall

20. Empennage refers to the
   _____.

   (A) fuselage
   (B) landing gear section
   (C) propellers or rotor blades
   (D) tail section
   (E) wings

21. What is resultant relative wind?

   (A) rotational relative wind modified by induced flow
   (B) the speed and direction of the airfoil passing through the air
   (C) air velocity in the reverse flow region
   (D) the result of the rotation of the rotor blades, flowing opposite the physical path of the airfoil and striking the blade at 90° to the leading edge and parallel to the plane of rotation
   (E) the lifting force on the rotor blades that causes coning

22. The atmospheric pressure on the top surface of an airfoil decreases as the velocity of the air moving past it increases. This is an example of

   (A) Bernoulli's principle.
   (B) Venturi flow.
   (C) laminar flow.
   (D) dynamic pressure.
   (E) transverse flow effect.

23. When entering and exiting Class C controlled airspace, which statement is true regarding airspace clearance?

   (A) The ATC must acknowledge the pilot by responding with the aircraft's call sign for communication to be considered established.
   (B) An ATC response of only "Standby" is enough to establish approval for entry to the controlled airspace.
   (C) No approval for clearance is needed.
   (D) Only jets flying faster than 200 mph need to request or receive approval for clearance.
   (E) A pilot does not need approval to exit Class C airspace.

24. Which is true of helicopter performance in ground effect (IGE)?

(A) Proximity to the ground interferes with the development of a full air circulation pattern and therefore increases the power required to hover.

(B) The increased viscosity of the denser air requires more power to overcome induced drag.

(C) Ground effect is increased over tall grass, bushes, rough terrain, and water.

(D) The rotor system becomes more efficient since the ground interferes with the circulation pattern, and less power is required to hover.

(E) Vortices coming off the main rotor strike the ground unpredictably and make the helicopter difficult to control.

25. Which term is used to describe the weight of an aircraft, including all hydraulic and oil systems, full, trapped and unusable fuel, and all fixed equipment?

(A) *empty weight*

(B) *basic operating weight*

(C) *maximum ramp weight*

(D) *basic weight* or *basic empty weight*

(E) *zero fuel weight*

26. What aerodynamic condition can occur when a helicopter is descending at greater than 300 fpm, has 20 to 100 percent power applied, and an airspeed less than effective translational lift?

(A) steep approach

(B) effective translational lift

(C) transverse flow effect

(D) pinnacle approach

(E) settling with power

27. What one of the acronyms for all-up weight is defined as the total aircraft weight at any given moment during flight?

(A) AGW

(B) MLW

(C) MRW

(D) MTOW

(E) OEW

28. How would a pilot recognize the onset of transverse flow effect?

(A) During takeoff, a vibration and a right rolling motion occurs as the aircraft accelerates through 10 to 20 knots.

(B) During takeoff, as the aircraft accelerates through 16 to 24 knots, the rotor becomes more efficient as airspeed increases until reaching best-rate-of-climb airspeed.

(C) The rate of descent cannot be arrested with increased collective pitch.

(D) At high airspeed, increased vibration and buffeting with an eventual left roll and nose pitching up.

(E) A self-energizing oscillation of the fuselage occurs.

29. If magnetic north is a positive 15-degree variation (west) from true north, to convert true north to magnetic north when flying eastbound, what is the adjustment a pilot must make to the magnetic compass?

(A) add 7.5 degrees

(B) add 15 degrees

(C) add 345 degrees

(D) subtract 15 degrees

(E) subtract 345 degrees

30. As air becomes less dense, it causes the following change in force:

    (A) an increase in altitude
    (B) an increase in altitude and lift
    (C) an increase in lift
    (D) an increase in thrust
    (E) a reduction in power at the engine intakes

31. When an aircraft is approaching to land, the leading and trailing edges of its flaps are extended to create the following force(s).

    (A) a decrease in drag
    (B) a decrease in lift
    (C) an increase in airspeed
    (D) an increase in airspeed and drag
    (E) maximum lift and high drag

32. If there is no increase in thrust, which action would result in an ultimate stall?

    (A) descending to a lower altitude
    (B) decreasing pitch
    (C) extending the ailerons and flaps
    (D) increasing pitch
    (E) turning the rudder to the left or right

33. What causes a rotary-wing aircraft to drift laterally due to tail rotor thrust?

    (A) a coaxial rotor system
    (B) translating tendency
    (C) gyroscopic precession
    (D) the tail rotor
    (E) translational lift

34. Which aircraft component(s) affect yaw?

    (A) the ailerons
    (B) the elevators
    (C) the rudder
    (D) the spoilers
    (E) the wings

35. What flight control maintains the engine within optimal flight parameters?

    (A) the cyclic
    (B) the collective
    (C) the tail rotor pedals
    (D) translating tendency
    (E) the throttle

36. What gives the pilot control over the yaw axis of the aircraft?

    (A) the cyclic
    (B) the collective
    (C) the tail rotor pedals
    (D) translating tendency
    (E) the throttle

37. Which ATC (air traffic control) radio transmission permits entry into Class C airspace for N4227HC?

    (A) "Aircraft calling Providence Approach Control, standby."
    (B) "Helicopter 4227HC, remain outside the Class Charlie airspace and standby."
    (C) "Helicopter 4227HC, standby."
    (D) "Helicopter calling, standby."
    (E) "Helicopter 4277HC, standby."

38. Which instrument indicates if an aircraft is in a climb, in a descent, or in level flight?

    (A) an altimeter
    (B) a heading indicator
    (C) a magnetic compass
    (D) a vertical card compass
    (E) a vertical speed indicator

39. Which type of climb produces the most altitude in a given distance?

    (A) a best angle of climb
    (B) a best rate of climb
    (C) a normal climb
    (D) a shallow climb
    (E) a steep climb

40. When raised elevators push down on the tail of an aircraft, what effect does that have on the aircraft?

   (A) The ailerons automatically extend simultaneously.

   (B) The nose of the aircraft lowers.

   (C) The nose of the aircraft rises.

   (D) The aircraft veers left.

   (E) The aircraft veers right.

SPATIAL APPERCEPTION

10 minutes

This section measures your ability to determine the position of an airplane in flight given the view from the cockpit. Each question shows a coastline as viewed from an aircraft cockpit and five pictures of an aircraft as viewed from outside. Your task is to determine the aircraft's pitch, bank, and heading from the cockpit image. Then, choose which of the following five pictures most closely matches the aircraft's position.

1.

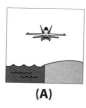   

(A)   (B)   (C)   (D)   (E)

2.

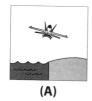  

(A)   (B)   (C)   (D)   (E)

3.

 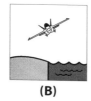   

(A)   (B)   (C)   (D)   (E)

4.

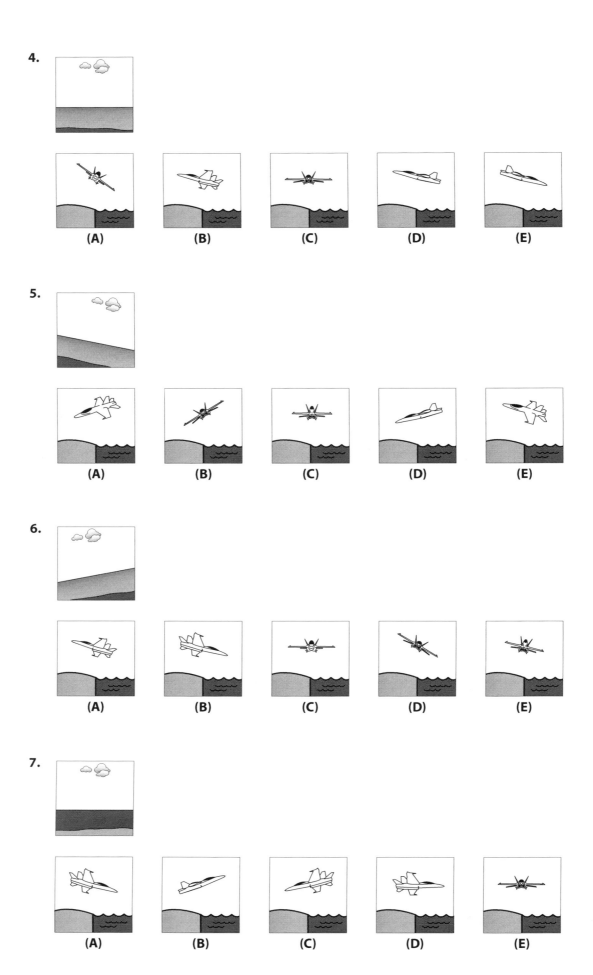

(A)   (B)   (C)   (D)   (E)

5.

(A)   (B)   (C)   (D)   (E)

6.

(A)   (B)   (C)   (D)   (E)

7.

(A)   (B)   (C)   (D)   (E)

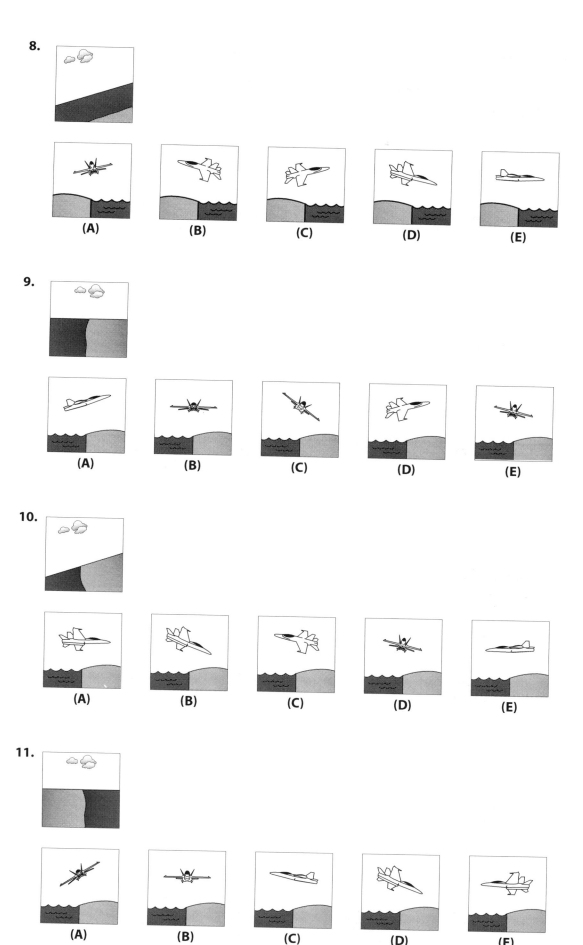

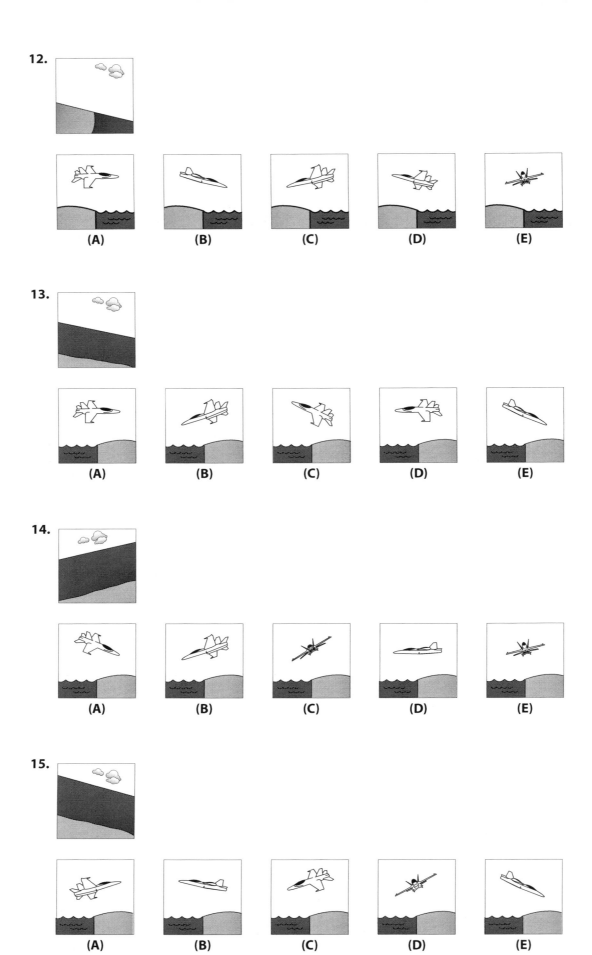

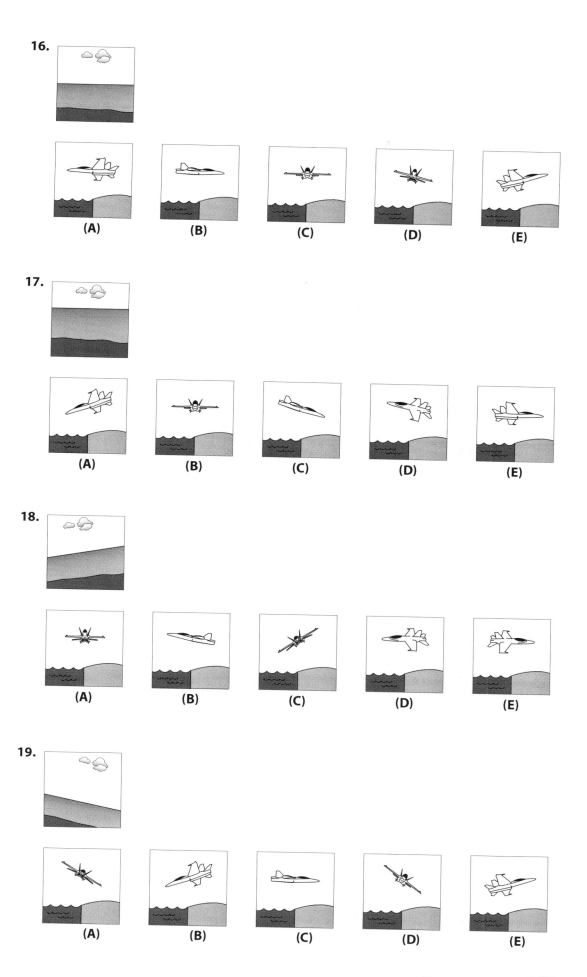

16.

(A) (B) (C) (D) (E)

17.

(A) (B) (C) (D) (E)

18.

(A) (B) (C) (D) (E)

19.

(A) (B) (C) (D) (E)

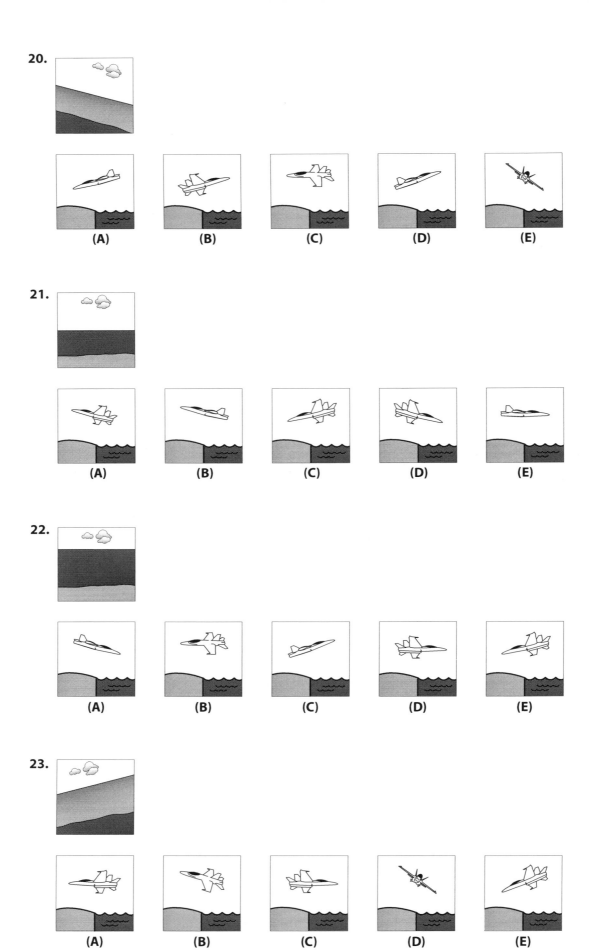

24.

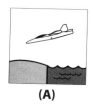 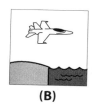 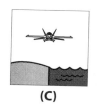  

(A)   (B)   (C)   (D)   (E)

25.

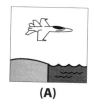    

(A)   (B)   (C)   (D)   (E)

READING COMPREHENSION

30 minutes

This section measures your ability to read and understand written material. Passages are followed by a series of multiple-choice questions. You are to choose the option that best answers the question based on the passage. No additional information or specific knowledge is needed.

The social and political discourse of America continues to be permeated with idealism. An idealistic viewpoint asserts that the ideals of freedom, equality, justice, and human dignity are the truths that Americans must continue to aspire to achieve. Truth is what should be, not necessarily what is. In general, idealists work to improve things and to make them as close to ideal as possible.

1. It can be inferred from the passage that an idealist would agree with which of the following truisms?

    (A) "What goes around, comes around."

    (B) "If you do not know where you are going, you'll end up someplace else."

    (C) "Kindness is all that matters in the end."

    (D) "Knowledge is the lock, and the key is the question."

    (E) "Unhappiness is the denial of the ordinary."

When the Spanish-American War broke out in 1898, the US Army was small and understaffed. President William McKinley called for 1,250 volunteers primarily from the Southwest to serve in the First US Volunteer Calvary. Eager to fight, the ranks were quickly filled by a diverse group of cowboys, gold prospectors, hunters, gamblers, Native Americans, veterans, police officers, and college students looking for an adventure. The officer corps was composed of veterans of the Civil War and the Indian Wars. With more volunteers than it could accept, the army set high standards: all the recruits had to be skilled on horseback and with guns. Consequently, they became known as the Rough Riders.

2. According to the passage, all the recruits were required to

    (A) have previously fought in a war.

    (B) be American citizens.

    (C) live in the Southwest.

    (D) ride a horse well.

    (E) have a college degree.

For an adult person to be unable to swim points to something like criminal negligence; every man, woman and child should learn. A person who cannot swim may not only become a danger to himself, but to someone, and perhaps to several, of his fellow beings. Children as early as the age of four may acquire the art; none are too young, none too old. Doctors recommend swimming as the best all-around exercise. It is especially beneficial to nervous people. Swimming reduces corpulence, improves the figure, expands the lungs, improves the circulation of the blood, builds up general health, increases vitality, gives self-confidence in case of danger, and exercises all the muscles in the body at one time. As an aid to development of the muscular system, it excels other sports. Every muscle is brought into play.

—from *Swimming Scientifically Taught: A Practical Manual for Young and Old* by Frank Eugen Dalton and Louis C. Dalton

3. The primary purpose of the passage is to

    (A) explain the benefits of swimming.

    (B) identify the importance of swimming.

    (C) discuss the reasons people swim.

    (D) persuade people to swim.

    (E) recount the authors' experience with people who could not swim.

The cisco, a foot-long freshwater fish native to the Great Lakes, once thrived throughout the basin but had virtually disappeared by the 1950s. However, today fishermen are pulling them up by the net-load in Lake Michigan and Lake Ontario. It is highly unusual for a native species to revive, and the reason for the cisco's reemergence is even more unlikely. The cisco have an invasive species, quagga mussels, to thank for their return. Quagga mussels depleted nutrients in the lakes, harming other species highly dependent on these nutrients. Cisco, however, thrive in low-nutrient environments. As other species—many invasive—diminished, cisco flourished in their place.

4. It can be inferred from the passage that most invasive species

   (A) support the growth of native species.

   (B) do not impact the development of native species.

   (C) struggle to survive in their new environments.

   (D) cause the decline of native species.

   (E) compete with each other for resources.

Greek mythology provided explanations for the questions of life. One question that is often asked is how human beings became the superior beings of Earth. In Greek mythology, two gods, Epimetheus and Prometheus, were given the work of creating living things. Epimetheus gave good powers to the different animals. To the lion he gave strength; to the bird, swiftness; to the fox, sagacity; and so on. Eventually, all of the good gifts had been bestowed, and there was nothing left for humans. As a result, Prometheus returned to heaven and brought down fire, which he gave to humans. With fire, human beings could protect themselves by making weapons. Over time, humans developed civilization and superiority.

5. The author notes that the good gifts, such as strength and sagacity, were NOT given to humans in order to show

   (A) that humans may be superior, but they are not perfect.

   (B) that humans will not remain superior.

   (C) that living things other than human beings were favored by the gods.

   (D) that fire is dangerous.

   (E) the wisdom of Greek civilization.

In December of 1945, Germany launched its last major offensive campaign of World War II, pushing through the dense forests of the Ardennes region of Belgium, France, and Luxembourg. The attack, designed to block the Allies from the Belgian port of Antwerp and to split their lines, caught the Allied forces by surprise. Due to troop positioning, the Americans bore the brunt of the attack, incurring 100,000 deaths, the highest number of casualties of any battle during the war. However, after a month of grueling fighting in the bitter cold, a lack of fuel and a masterful American military strategy resulted in an Allied victory that sealed Germany's fate.

6. In the last sentence, the word *grueling* most nearly means

   (A) exhausting

   (B) secretive

   (C) costly

   (D) intermittent

   (E) ineffective

At sunset especially did we most enjoy the magnificent sight of the lake, which could be seen from my windows in its whole length. An orange light then stained the west at the place where the mountains of Savoy dip down into the lake. These mountains stood out boldly against the blazing horizon. At the right a purple zone crowned the hills and grew feebler toward the town of Vevey; in the midst of the lake flamed a marvelous fire, while the waters were somber along the area of Villeneuve, of a pallid blue under the area of Veytaux, and of a pearly gray color, cut by red bands, along the shores of Savoy.

—from *The Spell of Switzerland*
by Nathan Haskell Dole

7. Which of the following best describes the organization of the passage?

(A) It explains the reasons the sunsets on Lake Geneva are magnificent.

(B) It mentions the phenomenon of sunsets and presents the details of how water reflects light.

(C) It compares an inland sunset with a sunset on a lake.

(D) It discusses the emotional impact of watching the sun set on a lake.

(E) It presents a spatial description of the light on the mountains, lake, and shore.

In 1953, doctors surgically removed the hippocampus of patient Henry Molaison in an attempt to stop his frequent seizures. Unexpectedly, he lost the ability to form new memories, leading to the biggest breakthrough in the science of memory. Molaison's long-term memory—of events more than a year before his surgery—was unchanged as was his ability to learn physical skills. From this, scientists learned that different types of memory are handled by different parts of the brain, with the hippocampus responsible for *episodic memory*, the short-term recall of events. They have since discovered that some memories are then channeled to the cortex, the outer layers of the brain that handle higher functions, where they are gradually integrated with related information to build lasting knowledge about our world.

8. The main idea of the passage is that

(A) Molaison's surgery posed significant risk to the functioning of his brain.

(B) short-term and long-term memory are stored in different parts of the brain.

(C) long-term memory forms over a longer period than short-term memory.

(D) memories of physical skills are processed differently than memories of events.

(E) the hippocampus stores all memories related to events.

For thirteen years, a spacecraft called *Cassini* has been on an exploratory mission to Saturn. The spacecraft was designed not to return but to end its journey by diving into Saturn's atmosphere. This dramatic ending will provide scientists with unprecedented information about Saturn's atmosphere and its magnetic and gravitational fields. First, however, *Cassini* will pass Saturn's largest moon, Titan, where it will record any changes in Titan's curious methane lakes, gathering information about potential seasons on the planet-sized moon. Then it will pass through the unexplored region between Saturn itself and its famous rings. Scientists hope to learn how old the rings are and to directly examine the particles that make them up. It is likely that the spectacular end to *Cassini* will introduce new questions for future exploration.

9. According to the passage, scientists want to learn more about Titan's

(A) gravity, based on examination of its magnetic field.

(B) rings, based on the particles that compose them.

(C) seasons, based on changes to its lakes.

(D) age, based on analysis of its minerals and gases.

(E) atmosphere, based on measurements of its gravity.

Researchers at the University of California, Berkeley, decided to tackle an age-old problem: why shoelaces come untied. They recorded the shoelaces of a volunteer walking on a treadmill by attaching devices to record the acceleration, or g-force, experienced by the knot. The results were surprising. A shoelace knot experiences more g-force from a person walking than any rollercoaster can generate. However, if the person simply stomped or swung their feet—the two movements that make up a walker's stride—the g-force was not enough to undo the knots. Researchers also found that while the knot loosened slowly at first, once it reached a certain laxness, it simply fell apart.

10. The author includes a comparison to rollercoasters in order to

(A) illustrate the intensity of force experienced by the knots.

(B) describe an experiment undertaken by researchers.

(C) critique a main finding of the experiment.

(D) provide further evidence to support the study's conclusion.

(E) insert humor into the description of the study.

Archaeologists have discovered the oldest known specimens of bedbugs in a cave in Oregon where humans once lived. The three different species date back to between 5,000 and 11,000 years ago. The finding gives scientists a clue as to how bedbugs became human parasites. These bedbugs, like those that plague humans today, originated as bat parasites. Scientists hypothesize that it was the co-habitation of humans and bats in the caves that encouraged the bugs to begin feeding on the humans. The three species found in the Oregon caves are actually still around today, although they continue to prefer bats. Humans only lived seasonally in the Oregon cave system, however, which might explain why these insects did not fully transfer to human hosts like bedbugs elsewhere did.

11. With which of the following claims about bedbugs would the author most likely agree?

(A) Ancient bedbugs did not easily transition to new animal hosts, slowing their evolution.

(B) Modern bedbugs that prefer humans thrive better in areas with extensive light.

(C) Bedbugs are a relatively fragile species that has struggled to survive over time.

(D) The transition to humans significantly accelerated the growth of bedbug populations.

(E) Bedbugs that prefer humans originated in caves that humans occupied year-round.

The Bastille, Paris's famous historical prison, was originally built in 1370 as a fortification, called a *bastide* in Old French, to protect the city from English invasion during the Hundred Years' War. It rose 100 feet into the air, had eight towers, and was surrounded by a moat more than eighty feet wide. In the seventeenth century, the government converted the fortress into an elite prison for upper-class felons, political disruptors, and spies. Residents of the Bastille arrived by direct order of the king and usually were left there to languish without a trial.

12. In the first sentence, the word *fortification* most nearly means

(A) royal castle.

(B) national symbol.

(C) seat of government.

(D) defensive structure.

(E) secret retreat.

The Scream of Nature by Edvard Munch is one of the world's best known and most desirable artworks. While most people think of it as a single painting, the iconic creation actually has four different versions: two paintings and two pastels. In 2012, one of the pastels earned the fourth highest price paid for a painting at auction when it was sold for almost $120 million. The three others are not for sale; the Munch Museum in Oslo holds a painted version and a pastel version, while the National Gallery in Oslo holds the other painting. However, the desire to acquire them has been just as strong: in 1994 the National Gallery's version was stolen, and in 2004 the painting at the Munch Museum was stolen at gunpoint in the middle of the day. Both paintings were eventually recovered.

13. The primary purpose of the passage is to

(A) describe the image depicted in *The Scream in Nature*.

(B) explain the origin of the painting *The Scream in Nature*.

(C) clarify the number of versions of *The Scream in Nature* that exist.

(D) prove the high value of *The Scream in Nature*.

(E) outline the different ownerships of *The Scream in Nature*.

A legendary superstition has furnished materials for many a wild story in that region of shadows; and the specter is known at all the country firesides, by the name of the Headless Horseman of Sleepy Hollow. It is remarkable that the visionary propensity I have mentioned is not confined to the native inhabitants of the valley, but is unconsciously imbibed by everyone who resides there for a time. However wide awake they may have been before they entered that sleepy region, they are sure, in a little time, to inhale the witching influence of the air, and begin to grow imaginative, to dream dreams, and see apparitions.

—from *The Legend of Sleepy Hollow* by Washington Irving

14. It can be inferred that everyone who resides in Sleepy Hollow for a time becomes

(A) a lost soul searching for something unknown.

(B) an individual who prefers to live hidden and alone, in the shadows.

(C) a seer of wild and irregular images.

(D) a person who has lost the ability to reason and behave rationally.

(E) a visionary who is seeking a secure, predictable, and peaceful place to live.

At midnight on Saturday, August 12, 1961, units of the East German army moved into position and began closing the border between East and West Berlin. Destroying streets that ran parallel to the border to make them impassable, they installed ninety-seven miles of barbed wire and fences around West Berlin and another twenty-seven miles along the border between West and East Berlin. By Sunday morning the border was completely shut down. Families woke up that morning suddenly divided, and some East Berliners with jobs in the west were unable to get to work. West Berlin was now an isolated island surrounded by a communist government hostile to its existence.

15. The primary purpose of the passage is to

(A) describe the impact of the closing of the Berlin border.

(B) analyze East Germany's motives for closing the Berlin border.

(C) explain the Western response to the closing of the Berlin border.

(D) inform the reader about the methods used to close the Berlin border.

(E) provide a history of the Berlin border.

In 1989, almost a million Chinese university students descended on central Beijing, protesting for increased democracy and calling for the resignation of Communist Party leaders. For three weeks, they marched, chanted, and held daily vigils in the city's Tiananmen Square. The protests had widespread support in China, particularly among factory workers who cheered them on. For Westerners watching, it seemed to be the beginning of a political revolution in China, so the world was stunned when, on July 4, Chinese troops and security police stormed the square, firing into the crowd. Chaos erupted with some students trying to fight back by throwing stones and setting fire to military vehicles. Tens of thousands more attempted to flee. While official numbers were never given, observers estimated anywhere from 300 to thousands of people were killed, while 10,000 were arrested.

16. It can be inferred from the passage that after July 4

   (A) the protest movement in China gained increasing support.

   (B) Western countries intervened on behalf of the university protestors.

   (C) factory workers took action in defense of the protestors.

   (D) the government implemented significant reforms to military practices.

   (E) the movement for increased democracy in China fell apart.

One of the most dramatic acts of nonviolent resistance in India's movement for independence from Britain came in 1930, when independence leader Mahatma Gandhi organized a 240-mile march to the Arabian Sea. The goal of the march was to make salt from seawater, in defiance of British law. The British prohibited Indians from collecting or selling salt—a vital part of the Indian diet—requiring them instead to buy it from British merchants and pay a heavy salt tax. The crowd of marchers grew along the way to tens of thousands of people. In Dandi, Gandhi picked up a small chunk of salt

and broke British law. Thousands in Dandi followed his lead as did millions of fellow protestors in coastal towns throughout India. In an attempt to quell the civil disobedience, authorities arrested more than 60,000 people across the country, including Gandhi himself.

17. With which of the following claims about civil disobedience would the author most likely agree?

   (A) Civil disobedience is a disorganized form of protest easily quashed by government.

   (B) Civil disobedience requires extreme violations of existing law to be effective.

   (C) Civil disobedience is an effective strategy for effecting political change.

   (D) Civil disobedience is only effective in countries that already have democracy.

   (E) Civil disobedience can only work on a small scale to effect local change.

When a fire destroyed San Francisco's American Indian Center in October of 1969, American Indian groups set their sights on the recently closed island prison of Alcatraz as a site of a new Indian cultural center and school. Ignored by the government, an activist group known as Indians of All Tribes sailed to Alcatraz in the early morning hours with eighty-nine men, women, and children. They landed on Alcatraz, claiming it for all the tribes of North America. Their demands were ignored, and so the group continued to occupy the island for the next nineteen months, its numbers swelling up to 600 as others joined. By January of 1970, many of the original protestors had left, and on June 11, 1971, federal marshals forcibly removed the last residents.

18. The main idea of this passage is that

    (A) the government refused to listen to the demands of American Indians.

    (B) American Indians occupied Alcatraz in protest of government policy.

    (C) few people joined the occupation of Alcatraz, weakening its effectiveness.

    (D) the government took violent action against protestors at Alcatraz.

    (E) American Indians wanted Alcatraz to be a new cultural center.

After World War I, powerful political and social forces pushed for a return to normalcy in the United States. The result was disengagement from the larger world and increased focus on American economic growth and personal enjoyment. Caught in the middle of this was a cache of American writers, raised on the values of the prewar world and frustrated with what they viewed as the superficiality and materialism of postwar American culture. Many of them, like Ernest Hemingway and F. Scott Fitzgerald, fled to Paris, where they became known as the "lost generation," creating a trove of literary works criticizing their home culture and delving into their own feelings of alienation.

19. In the third sentence, the word *cache* most nearly means

    (A) a group of the same type.

    (B) a majority segment.

    (C) an organization.

    (D) a dispersed number.

    (E) a new school.

In an effort to increase women's presence in government, several countries in Latin America, including Argentina, Brazil, and Mexico, have implemented legislated candidate quotas. These quotas require that at least 30 percent of a party's candidate list in any election cycle consists of women who have a legitimate chance at election. As a result, Latin America has the greatest number of female heads of government in the world, and the second highest percentage of female members of parliament after Nordic Europe. However, these trends do not carry over outside of politics. While 25 percent of legislators in Latin America are now women, less than 2 percent of CEOs in the region are female.

20. What is the main idea of the passage?

    (A) Few women in Latin America are selected as CEOs of public companies.

    (B) In Latin America, political parties must nominate women for office.

    (C) Latin America is the region with the greatest gender equality.

    (D) Women in Latin America have greater economic influence than political influence.

    (E) Women have a significant presence in Latin American politics.

MATH SKILLS

40 minutes

This section measures your knowledge of mathematical terms and principles. Each question is followed by five possible answers. You are to decide which one of the five choices is correct.

1. An equilateral triangle is drawn next to a trapezoid as shown in the figure below. What is the approximate area of the new figure?

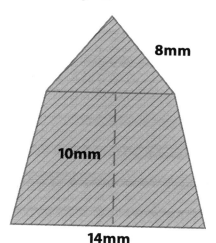

8mm

10mm

14mm

(A) 128.0 mm²

(B) 137.7 mm²

(C) 140.5 mm²

(D) 142.1 mm²

(E) 149.0 mm²

2. If a person reads 40 pages in 45 minutes, approximately how many minutes will it take her to read 265 pages?

(A) 202

(B) 236

(C) 265

(D) 298

(E) 300

3. Simplify: $\sqrt[3]{64} + \sqrt[3]{729}$

(A) 13

(B) 15

(C) 17

(D) 31

(E) 35

4. A high school cross country team sent 25 percent of its runners to a regional competition. Of these, 10 percent won medals. If 2 runners earned medals, how many members does the cross country team have?

(A) 8

(B) 10

(C) 80

(D) 125

(E) 1250

5. If $j = 4$, what is the value of $2(j-4)^4 - j + \frac{1}{2}j$?

(A) 0

(B) −2

(C) 2

(D) 4

(E) 32

6. A company interviewed 21 applicants for a recent opening. Of these applicants, 7 wore blue and 6 wore white, while 5 applicants wore both blue and white. What is the number of applicants who wore neither blue nor white?

(A) 1

(B) 6

(C) 8

(D) 12

(E) 13

7. Which of the following is equivalent to $(5^2 - 2)^2 + 3^3$?

(A) 25

(B) 30

(C) 108

(D) 556

(E) 538

8. Juan plans to spend 25% of his workday writing a report. If he is at work for 9 hours, how many hours will he spend writing the report?

(A) 2.25

(B) 2.50

(C) 2.75

(D) 3.25

(E) 4.00

9. If angles a and b are congruent, what is the measurement of angle c?

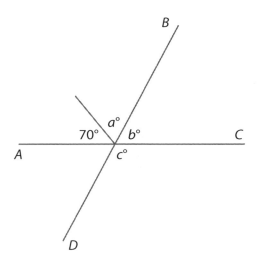

(A) 55°

(B) 70°

(C) 110°

(D) 120°

(E) 125°

10. An ice chest contains 24 sodas, some regular and some diet. The ratio of diet soda to regular soda is 1:3. How many regular sodas are there in the ice chest?

(A) 1

(B) 4

(C) 6

(D) 18

(E) 24

11. Which of the following is equivalent to $z^3(z + 2)^2 - 4z^3 + 2$?

(A) 2

(B) $z^5 + 4z^4 + 4z^3 + 2$

(C) $z^6 + 4z^3 + 2$

(D) $z^5 + 4z^4 + 2$

(E) $z^5 + 4z^3 + 6$

12. Erica is at work for $8\frac{1}{2}$ hours a day. If she takes one 30-minute lunch break and two 15-minute breaks during the day, how many hours does she work?

(A) 6 hours, 30 minutes

(B) 6 hours, 45 minutes

(C) 7 hours, 15 minutes

(D) 7 hours, 30 minutes

(E) 7 hours, 45 minutes

13. Kendrick has $2,386.52 in his checking account. If he pays $792.00 for rent, $84.63 for groceries, and $112.15 for his car insurance, how much money will he have left in his account?

(A) $1,397.74

(B) $1,482.37

(C) $1,509.89

(D) $2,189.22

(E) $3,375.30

14. W, X, Y, and Z lie on a circle with center A. If the diameter of the circle is 75, what is the sum of $\overline{AW}$, $\overline{AX}$, $\overline{AY}$, and $\overline{AZ}$?

(A) 75

(B) 100

(C) 125

(D) 300

(E) 150

15. $(3x + 2)^2 =$

(A) $9x^2 + 4$

(B) $9x^2 + 36$

(C) $9x^2 + 6x + 4$

(D) $9x^2 + 10x + 4$

(E) $9x^2 + 12x + 4$

16. A group of 20 friends is planning a road trip. They have 3 cars that seat 4 people, 3 cars that seat 5 people, and 1 car that seats 6 people. What is the fewest number of cars they can take on the trip if each person needs his or her own seat?

(A) 3 cars

(B) 4 cars

(C) 5 cars

(D) 6 cars

(E) 7 cars

17. Solve for x: $5x - 4 = 3(8 + 3x)$

(A) -7

(B) $-\frac{3}{4}$

(C) $\frac{3}{4}$

(D) 7

(E) 8

18. What is the percent increase in an employee's salary if it is raised from $60,000 to $63,000?

(A) 0.3%

(B) 0.4%

(C) 3%

(D) 4%

(E) 5%

19. A grocery store sold 30% of its pears and had 455 pears remaining. How many pears did the grocery store start with?

(A) 602

(B) 650

(C) 692

(D) 700

(E) 755

20. What is the perimeter of the shape below if each side is congruent?

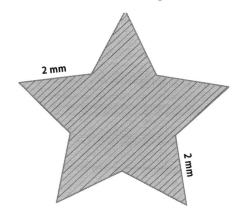

(A) 2 mm

(B) 4 mm

(C) 10 mm

(D) 20 mm

(E) 40 mm

MECHANICAL COMPREHENSION

15 minutes

This section measures your understanding of basic mechanical principles. Each question is followed by five possible answers. You are to decide which one of the five choices is correct.

1.

Pulley B will rotate

(A) in the same direction as Pulley A but opposite of Pulley C.

(B) in the same direction as Pulley C but opposite of Pulley A.

(C) in the same direction as both Pulley A and Pulley C.

(D) in the opposite direction of both Pulley A and Pulley C.

(E) in neither direction because Pulley B cannot move.

2.

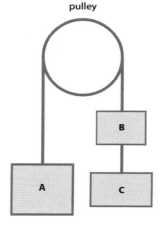

Blocks A, B, and C are hanging from a pulley as shown in the figure. If Block A weighs 70 pounds and Block B weighs 20 pounds, what must the weight of Block C be in order for the blocks to be at rest?

(A) 30 pounds

(B) 35 pounds

(C) 50 pounds

(D) 55 pounds

(E) 60 pounds

3.

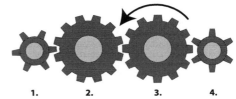

Which of the other gears is moving in the same direction as Gear 3?

(A) Gear 1 only

(B) Gear 2 only

(C) Gear 4 only

(D) Gears 2 and 4 only

(E) Gears 1, 2, and 4

4.

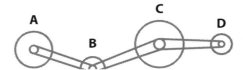

If Pulley B is the driver and turns clockwise, which pulley turns the slowest?

(A) Pulley A turns the slowest.

(B) Pulley C turns the slowest.

(C) Pulley D turns the slowest.

(D) All the pulleys have the same speed.

(E) There is not enough information to determine the answer.

5. Because a pair of tweezers has the effort between the fulcrum and the resistance, it is an example of a

(A) first-class lever.

(B) second-class lever.

(C) third-class lever.

(D) first- and third-class lever.

(E) second- and third-class lever.

6.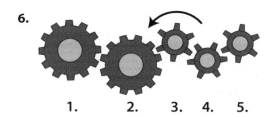

1.   2.   3.   4.   5.

Which of the gears are moving in the opposite direction of Gear 3?

(A) Gear 2 only

(B) Gear 1 and Gear 5 only

(C) Gear 1 and Gear 4 only

(D) Gear 2 and Gear 4 only

(E) Gear 2 and Gear 5 only

7. A single pulley is attached to the ceiling. It is holding a rope that is attached to the floor on one side and a person of weight 100 N on the other. What is the tension in the rope?

(A) 0 N

(B) 50 N

(C) 100 N

(D) 150 N

(E) 200 N

8. A wooden ball and a steel ball are both held at 15°C. Which ball will feel colder and why?

(A) The wooden ball will feel colder because it has a higher density.

(B) The wooden ball will feel colder because it has greater conductivity.

(C) The steel ball will feel colder because it has a higher density.

(D) The steel ball will feel colder because it has greater conductivity.

(E) The objects will feel the same because they have the same temperature.

9.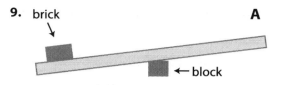

Compared to figure A above, the brick in figure B will

(A) be lifted the same height, and it will take the same amount of effort to do so.

(B) be lifted higher, and it will take more effort to do so.

(C) not be lifted as high, and it will take more effort to do so.

(D) be lifted higher, and it will take less effort to do so.

(E) not be lifted as high, and it will take less effort to do so.

10.

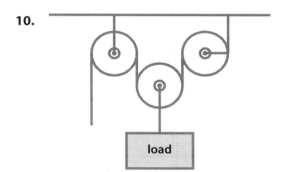

A block is hanging from a pulley system as shown in the figure. The theoretical mechanical advantage of the system is

(A) 1.

(B) 2.

(C) 3.

(D) 4.

(E) 5.

11.

For which value of θ will the box experience the greatest acceleration if the magnitude of the pulling force stays the same?

(A) 0 degrees

(B) 30 degrees

(C) 45 degrees

(D) 60 degrees

(E) 90 degrees

12.

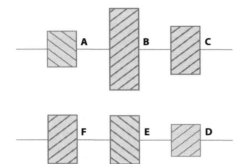

Gear C is intended to mesh with

(A) Gear A only.

(B) Gear B only.

(C) Gear E only.

(D) Gear F only.

(E) Gears E and F.

13. Two ropes are connected on either side of a mass of 100 kg resting on a flat surface. Each rope is pulling on the mass with 50 N of force, parallel to the ground. What can be said about the motion of the mass?

(A) The mass will accelerate to left.

(B) The mass is in equilibrium.

(C) The mass will accelerate to the right.

(D) The mass will be lifted up.

(E) Not enough information is given.

14.

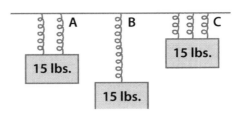

Three 15-pound blocks are attached to the ceiling using identical springs, as shown. If *A*, *B*, and *C* are the forces on their respective springs, which of the following is true?

(A) *B* is greater than *C* but less than *A*.

(B) *B* is greater than *A* but less than *C*.

(C) *C* is greater than *A* but less than *B*.

(D) *C* is greater than *B* but less than *A*.

(E) *A* is greater than *C* but less than *B*.

15.

An object is being carried by three people as shown above. Which person bears the most weight?

(A) A

(B) B

(C) C

(D) B and C

(E) All three bear the same weight.

16.

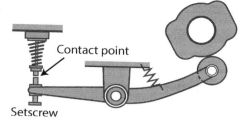

Contact point

Setscrew

As Cam 1 makes two complete turns, how many times does the set screw hit the contact point?

(A) 2

(B) 4

(C) 5

(D) 6

(E) 8

17.

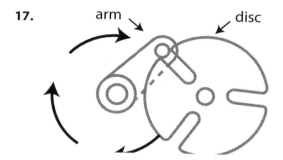

arm   disc

The figure shows a slotted disc turned by a pin on a rotating arm. Three revolutions of the arm turns the disc

(A) $\frac{1}{3}$ turn.

(B) $\frac{2}{3}$ turn.

(C) 1 turn.

(D) $1\frac{1}{3}$ turn.

(E) 3 turns.

18. On Earth, Objects A and B have the same mass and weight. If Object B is moved to the moon, which of the following statements is true?

(A) Object A now has a greater mass and weight.

(B) Object B now has a greater mass and weight.

(C) Both objects have the same mass, but Object A now has the greater weight.

(D) Both objects have the same weight, but Object A now has the greater mass.

(E) Both objects still have the same mass and weight.

19.

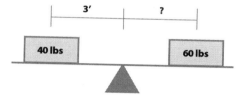

3'   ?

40 lbs   60 lbs

A 40-pound block and a 60-pound block are placed on a uniform board as shown above. How far to the right of the fulcrum must the 60-pound block be placed in order for the board to be balanced?

(A) 1 foot

(B) 2 feet

(C) 4 feet

(D) 5 feet

(E) 6 feet

CONTINUE

20.

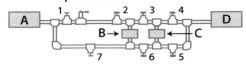

In the figure shown above, assume that all valves are closed. For the air to flow from A to D without flowing through B and C, it is necessary to open valves

(A) 1, 2, and 5.

(B) 2, 3, and 7.

(C) 3, 4, and 5.

(D) 1, 2, 3, and 4.

(E) 5, 6, and 7.

ANSWER KEY

Simple Drawings

1.	(D)	26.	(C)	51.	(E)	76.	(C)
2.	(C)	27.	(B)	52.	(D)	77.	(D)
3.	(B)	28.	(A)	53.	(A)	78.	(E)
4.	(E)	29.	(D)	54.	(B)	79.	(B)
5.	(C)	30.	(B)	55.	(C)	80.	(A)
6.	(B)	31.	(B)	56.	(D)	81.	(E)
7.	(A)	32.	(A)	57.	(B)	82.	(D)
8.	(B)	33.	(D)	58.	(C)	83.	(A)
9.	(D)	34.	(D)	59.	(E)	84.	(B)
10.	(D)	35.	(B)	60.	(B)	85.	(C)
11.	(A)	36.	(C)	61.	(A)	86.	(E)
12.	(E)	37.	(C)	62.	(C)	87.	(D)
13.	(C)	38.	(E)	63.	(D)	88.	(B)
14.	(B)	39.	(D)	64.	(E)	89.	(C)
15.	(A)	40.	(A)	65.	(B)	90.	(E)
16.	(B)	41.	(C)	66.	(A)	91.	(B)
17.	(C)	42.	(B)	67.	(C)	92.	(A)
18.	(B)	43.	(D)	68.	(D)	93.	(B)
19.	(E)	44.	(A)	69.	(A)	94.	(D)
20.	(D)	45.	(C)	70.	(A)	95.	(C)
21.	(A)	46.	(C)	71.	(C)	96.	(E)
22.	(A)	47.	(D)	72.	(B)	97.	(D)
23.	(C)	48.	(B)	73.	(D)	98.	(A)
24.	(B)	49.	(A)	74.	(B)	99.	(B)
25.	(E)	50.	(A)	75.	(A)	100.	(D)

1.	(D)	26.	(C)
2.	(B)	27.	(A)
3.	(A)	28.	(B)
4.	none	29.	(E)
5.	(C)	30.	(D)
6.	(B)	31.	(A)
7.	(E)	32.	(E)
8.	(C)	33.	(B)
9.	(A)	34.	(D)
10.	(B)	35.	(D)
11.	none	36.	(B)
12.	(E)	37.	(A)
13.	(B)	38.	(E)
14.	(D)	39.	(E)
15.	(A)	40.	(D)
16.	(A)	41.	(B)
17.	(D)	42.	none
18.	(B)	43.	(E)
19.	(A)	44.	(A)
20.	(E)	45.	(D)
21.	(C)	46.	(B)
22.	(E)	47.	(E)
23.	(A)	48.	(D)
24.	(D)	49.	(D)
25.	(E)	50.	(C)

ARMY AVIATION INFORMATION

1. (A) Incorrect. The teeter hinge allows the blades to flap.
   (B) Correct. The swashplate allows for directions movement of the aircraft.
   (C) Incorrect. The ducted fan is a component of the NOTAR aircraft design.
   (D) Incorrect. The tail boom is a structural component that supports the tail rotor assembly.
   (E) Incorrect. The skids are used as landing gear for rotary-wing aircraft.

2. **(B) Correct.** The CH-47 Chinook is a tandem rotor helicopter.
   (A), (C), (D), and (E) Incorrect. All are conventional main rotor with tail rotor configurations.

3. (A) Incorrect. This phrase is not in the pilot/controller glossary.
   (B) Correct. Air taxi enables the pilot to proceed at an optimum airspeed/altitude, minimize downwash effect, conserve fuel, and expedite movement from one point to another.
   (C) Incorrect. This phrase implies the pilot will taxi on the airport surface via taxiways or other prescribed routes.
   (D) Incorrect. This phrase implies slow movement, usually below 25' AGL.
   (E) Incorrect. This phrase calls for precise taxi instructions to be given to a pilot unfamiliar with the airport or issued in stages as the aircraft proceeds along the taxi route.

4. (A) Incorrect. The Korean War had increased use of helicopters, most notably the H-13 in the medical evacuation role, but other uses of helicopters were very limited.
   (B) Incorrect. Use of helicopters in WWII was limited to a few very specialized roles. One significant milestone was the first combat rescue and medical evacuation in Burma during 1944 using a Sikorsky R-4.
   (C) Correct. The powerful and lightweight turbine engine paired with the simple, robust, and versatile UH-1 airframe gave the United States unparalleled mobility across previously nearly impassable terrain. Nearly all of the present air assault, attack helicopter, reconnaissance, aerial resupply, and medical evacuation doctrine has its roots in the Vietnam experience.
   (D) Incorrect. Extensive use of helicopters was already established doctrine in the US Army by this time.
   (E) Incorrect. The United States did not participate in combat operations during the 1967 Arab-Israeli War.

5. (A) Incorrect. The coaxial rotor system cancels torque effect by using counter-rotating rotor heads.
   (B) Correct. The NOTAR design uses a ducted fan to vector air out of the tail to cancel torque effect.
   (C) Incorrect. The tandem rotor system cancels torque effect through the use of counter-rotating rotor heads.
   (D) Incorrect. The term *semi-monocoque* refers to a fuselage type that utilizes longitudinal reinforcement to add strength.
   (E) Incorrect. The skids are used as landing gear for rotary-wing aircraft.

6. **(A) Correct.** Weight, lift, thrust, and drag must be in balance in order to hover.
   (B) Incorrect. An effective translational lift results from increased efficiency of the main rotor system as directional flight is established.
   (C) Incorrect. Dissymmetry of lift is the unequal lifting of forces created by the advancing and retreating blades.
   (D) Incorrect. Gyroscopic precession is when a force input is applied yet the

force output is felt 90 degrees later in the plane of rotation.

(E) Incorrect. Autorotation is when the rotor blades are driven by relative wind rather than by the aircraft's powerplant.

7. (A) Incorrect. High-density altitude indicates low-density air, which is typically found at high altitudes and above standard temperatures.

(B) Incorrect. Density altitude is pressure altitude corrected for nonstandard temperature.

(C) Incorrect. A high-density altitude would decrease both engine and rotor performance.

(D) Correct. As air density decreases, engine power output, rotor efficiency, and aerodynamic lift also decrease.

(E) Incorrect. Temperature and humidity are factors in determining density altitude and are therefore not more important to performance, although humidity is difficult to calculate and is rarely included in performance calculations.

8. (A) Incorrect. A change of heading would not reduce airspeed.

(B) Incorrect. Decreasing altitude will result in an initial higher airspeed.

(C) Correct. Approaching the red line means the aircraft is reaching the maximum airspeed for the aircraft.

(D) Incorrect. Increasing airspeed will exceed the maximum airspeed of the aircraft.

(E) Incorrect. Increasing thrust will increase airspeed to an excess level if all other forces remain the same.

9. (A) Incorrect. The vertical speed indicator uses only static pressure.

(B) Correct. The airspeed indicator subtracts the static, or ambient, pressure from the total pressure read at the stagnation point at the tip of the pitot tube to derive the dynamic pressure caused by the pressure of air impacting the pitot tube. This pressure is then presented to the pilot as an equivalent airspeed on the instrument dial.

(C) Incorrect. The magnetic compass is not a pitot-static instrument.

(D) Incorrect. The altimeter uses only static pressure.

(E) Incorrect. The gyro-compass is not a pitot-static instrument.

10. (A) Incorrect. This is the function of the collective pitch control.

(B) Incorrect. No flight control does this.

(C) Correct. The cyclic control alters the pitch of the main rotor blades individually and cyclically so that any blade at a given point in the rotor disk has the same pitch at that point until the cyclic control is moved. This aerodynamically tilts the rotor disk and therefore the thrust vector in the direction of cyclic control movement.

(D) Incorrect. This is the function of the tail rotor pedals.

(E) Incorrect. No flight control does this.

11. **(A) Correct.** The angle of attack is an aerodynamic angle between the airfoil chord line and the resultant relative wind.

(B) Incorrect. This describes the term *deck angle*.

(C) Incorrect. This angle is not relevant.

(D) Incorrect. The angle of incidence— the angle between the chord line and the rotational relative wind—is a mechanical angle set by the flight controls that does not change unless the flight controls position changes.

(E) Incorrect. The center of pressure is a point located on the chord line, so there is no angle between them.

12. (A) Incorrect. Compasses are used when the heading indicator fails.

(B) Incorrect. These do not correct in-flight compass reading errors.

(C) Incorrect. This compass has inherent errors.

(D) Incorrect. These do not correct in-flight compass reading errors.

(E) Correct. This compass was developed to reduce reading errors.

13. (A) Incorrect. This refers to confined fluid flow.

(B) Correct. Pressurized air is expelled from two slots that run the length of the right side of the tail boom. This develops a boundary-layer control called the Coanda effect, which causes the tail boom to effectively become a wing flying in the downwash of the rotor system. This produces about 60 percent of the required anti-torque force. The remainder, plus directional control, is accomplished by the rotating thruster at the end of the tail boom.

(C) Incorrect. Ground effect is the added performance a rotor experiences when close to the ground.

(D) Incorrect. *Doppler effect* refers to changes in wave frequency due to relative motion.

(E) Incorrect. *Coriolis effect* is the result of the law of conservation of angular momentum.

14. **(A) Correct.** The airflow over an airfoil producing lift moves back along the surface and down. Since the total aerodynamic force acts approximately perpendicular to the flow, it is tilted aft. Lift acts vertically opposing gravity, so there is a rearward component remaining of the total aerodynamic force that is designated induced drag.

(B) Incorrect. Vortices are a phenomenon of all drag.

(C) Incorrect. Parasite drag is incurred from form drag, skin friction, and interference drag associated with the fuselage, engine cowlings, mast and hub, landing gear, wing stores, external load, and rough-finish paint.

(D) Incorrect. All drag that is being considered here is aerodynamic.

(E) Incorrect. Profile drag develops from the frictional resistance of the blades passing through the air.

15. (A) Incorrect. Technical risk may be grouped under aircraft. The rest may be considered external pressures.

(B) Incorrect. Weather is one of several considerations that comprise the environment. Peer pressure is one of many factors that comprise external pressures.

(C) Incorrect. These may be all grouped under external factors.

(D) Correct. During each flight, decisions must be made regarding events that involve interactions between the four risk elements: the pilot in command (PIC), the aircraft, the environment, and external pressures such as the purpose of the operation. The decision-making process involves an evaluation of each of these risk elements to achieve an accurate perception of the flight situation.

(E) Incorrect. This list ignores the influence of the environment.

16. (A) Incorrect. AOA is the angle between the direction of the airflow and the chord on a wing—the imaginary reference line that extends from the leading edge to the trailing edge.

(B) Incorrect. A degree is the directional measurement for an aircraft.

(C) Correct. Airspeed is measured in knots.

(D) Incorrect. Mean sea level (MSL) is an altitude measurement.

(E) Incorrect. Rate of climb is a type of climb performed to navigate above obstacles during takeoff.

17. (A) Incorrect. The attitude increment hash marks are not in 10-degree increments.

(B) Correct. The attitude indicator hash marks are in 30-degree increments.

(C) Incorrect. The attitude increment hash marks are not in 45-degree increments.

(D) Incorrect. The attitude increment hash marks are not in 90-degree increments.

(E) Incorrect. The attitude increment hash marks are not in 180-degree increments.

18. (A) Incorrect. This is the definition for settling with power.

(B) Incorrect. Although these conditions increase the danger of dynamic rollover, a normal slope landing is completely achievable with proper technique.

(C) Incorrect. These conditions may lead to ground resonance.

(D) **Correct.** Dynamic rollover begins when the helicopter starts to pivot around its skid, wheel, or any portion of the aircraft in contact with the ground. A rolling motion moves the aircraft toward its critical angle. The rotor system has a maximum angle at which it can deliver lateral thrust. If the fuselage exceeds this angle, thrust cannot be delivered to counteract the rolling motion.

(E) Incorrect. These conditions may contribute to loss of tail rotor effectiveness.

19. (A) Incorrect. These are regions of a rotor in powered flight.

(B) Incorrect. The first two terms are regions of a rotor in powered flight.

(C) Incorrect. Positive lift is a region of a powered rotor.

(D) Incorrect. Reverse flow and positive lift are regions of a powered rotor.

(E) **Correct.** The driven region, where the total aerodynamic force (TAF) vector is tilted aft resulting in an overall drag force, is about the outer 30 percent of the disk radius. Next is the driving region, varying from about 25 percent to 70 percent of the radius, where the TAF vector is tilted forward and accelerates the rotation of the rotor system. The inner stall region, about the inner 25 percent of the blade, is operating beyond its critical AOA and produces drag.

20. (A) Incorrect. The fuselage includes the crew, passenger, and cargo areas.

(B) Incorrect. The tail section is separate from the landing gear section.

(C) Incorrect. These are not part of the tail section, the empennage.

(D) **Correct.** The tail section is known as the empennage.

(E) Incorrect. The wings are not part of the empennage.

21. (A) **Correct.** Resultant relative wind is rotational relative wind modified by induced flow.

(B) Incorrect. This is the definition of flight-path velocity.

(C) Incorrect. Although there are areas of reverse flow in the rotor system, this value does not have a specific term.

(D) Incorrect. This is the definition of rotational relative wind.

(E) Incorrect. This force is simply lift.

22. (A) **Correct.** Bernoulli's principle is a statement of the law of conservation of energy. There is a fixed amount of energy in a volume of air divided between internal fluid pressure, or static pressure, and fluid velocity, or dynamic pressure. If one increases, the other must decrease. Thus if velocity increases, the pressure must decrease.

(B) Incorrect. Venturi flow more properly concerns a confined flow passing through fixed cross-sections.

(C) Incorrect. Laminar flow is the boundary layer flow that is similar to layers or laminations of air sliding smoothly over one another.

(D) Incorrect. Dynamic pressure is the component of total pressure that is the result of movement of the air.

(E) Incorrect. Transverse flow effect is a phenomenon caused by the differences in airflow between the fore and aft portions of a rotor disk.

23. **(A) Correct.** The pilot must be acknowledged with the aircraft call sign to establish communications.

(B) Incorrect. This is true for Class C and D controlled airspaces but not true for Class B airspace.

(C) Incorrect. Approval for clearance is required for Class A through D controlled airspaces.

(D) Incorrect. When aircraft clearances are required, it applies to all types of aircraft.

(E) Incorrect. If clearance is required for entering an airspace, clearance is also required for exiting it.

24. (A) Incorrect. The more vertical inflow of air caused by a full circulation pattern requires an increase in the blade angle of attack, causing an increase in induced drag and power required.

(B) Incorrect. Any increase in viscosity is minute.

(C) Incorrect. Ground effect is actually at a maximum over a smooth, hard surface.

(D) Correct. By interfering with the circulation pattern, ground effect permits the relative wind to be more horizontal, lift vector to be more vertical, and induced drag to be reduced. This allows the rotor to be more efficient and require less power.

(E) Incorrect. These vortices are not a factor in ground effect.

25. (A) Incorrect. This is the weight of the airframe, engines, all permanently installed equipment, and unusable fuel.

(B) Incorrect. This is the empty weight of the aircraft plus the weight of the required crew, their baggage, and other standard items such as meals and potable water.

(C) Incorrect. This is the maximum weight approved for ground maneuver, including the weight of start, taxi, and run-up fuel. This is usually applicable to fixed-wing aircraft.

(D) Correct. The correct term is *basic empty weight* (*HFH*, p. 6-2).

(E) Incorrect. This is the weight of an aircraft without fuel.

26. (A) Incorrect. A steep approach will maintain airspeed above effective translational lift until approximately the last 100 feet.

(B) Incorrect. Effective translational lift is the increased efficiency a rotor system experiences as it gains speed, outruns the recirculation of old vortexes, and begins to work in relatively undisturbed air.

(C) Incorrect. Transverse flow effect is the result of air passing through the rear portion of the rotor disk having a greater downwash angle than air passing through the forward portion. It can be noticed by the pilot as a vibration and right roll as the aircraft accelerates through 10 to 20 knots.

(D) Incorrect. Pinnacle approaches are highly variable and situationally dependent.

(E) Correct. The aerodynamic condition is settling with power. The following combination of conditions is likely to cause settling with power in any helicopter: 1. A vertical or nearly vertical descent of at least 300 fpm (actual critical rate depends on the gross weight, rpm, density altitude, and other pertinent factors). 2. The rotor system must be using some of the available engine power (20 to 100 percent). 3. The airspeed must be slower than effective translational lift.

27. **(A) Correct.** This is the acronym for aircraft gross weight, also known as all-up weight (AUW). This weight changes during the flight due to consumables (i.e., oil and fuel).

(B) Incorrect. This is the acronym for maximum landing weight.

(C) Incorrect. This is maximum ramp weight.

(D) Incorrect. This is maximum takeoff weight.

(E) Incorrect. This is operating empty weight.

28. **(A) Correct.** Air entering the rotor system at the rear has a greater induced flow, causing a reduced angle of attack, less lift, and unequal drag between the fore and aft portions of the disk. The difference in angle of attack causes a right roll due to gyroscopic procession, and a vibration results as the effect moves from front to rear.

(B) Incorrect. This is a description of effective translational lift.

(C) Incorrect. This is a symptom of settling with power.

(D) Incorrect. This is a symptom of retreating blade stall.

(E) Incorrect. This is a symptom of ground resonance.

29. (A) Incorrect. Do not halve the degree of variation.

(B) Correct. "East is least, west is best." The adjustment is a 15-degree west variation.

(C) Incorrect. Do not take the difference from 360 degrees to determine variation.

(D) Incorrect. "East is least, west is best." Subtract for an easterly variation, and add for a westerly variation.

(E) Incorrect. Do not take the difference from 360 degrees to determine variation.

30. (A) Incorrect. Although the aircraft may increase its altitude, less dense air does not cause that effect.

(B) Incorrect. Although the aircraft may increase its altitude and lift, less dense air does not cause that effect.

(C) Incorrect. Although the aircraft may increase its lift, less dense air does not cause that effect.

(D) Incorrect. Although the aircraft may increase its thrust, less dense air does not cause that effect.

(E) Correct. Less dense air reduces the power received by the engine intakes.

31. (A) Incorrect. The airflow over and around the extended wings causes an increase in drag.

(B) Incorrect. On an approach to land, since airspeed is decreased, maximum lift is required to keep the aircraft airborne until touchdown.

(C) Incorrect. An aircraft must decrease airspeed when approaching to land.

(D) Incorrect. Although high drag is created, an increase in airspeed is not created.

(E) Correct. Since airspeed is decreased, maximum lift is required plus high drag to slow the aircraft.

32. (A) Incorrect. This would increase airspeed.

(B) Incorrect. This would increase airspeed.

(C) Incorrect. Extending the ailerons and flaps would decrease thrust, but this is done during landing to slow the aircraft.

(D) Correct. When increasing pitch, thrust must be increased to provide lift and maintain vertical speed or a stall will result.

(E) Incorrect. The rudder has no effect on thrust.

33. (A) Incorrect. A coaxial rotor system cancels torque effect by using counter rotating rotor heads.

(B) Correct. Translating tendency causes a rotary-wing aircraft to drift laterally due to tail rotor thrust.

(C) Incorrect. Gyroscopic precession is when a force input is applied yet the force output is felt 90 degrees later in the plane of rotation.

(D) Incorrect. The tail rotor cancels out the torque effect.

(E) Incorrect. An effective translational lift results from increased efficiency of the main rotor system as directional flight is established.

34. (A) Incorrect. The ailerons affect the longitudinal axis of the aircraft during turns.

(B) Incorrect. The elevators affect pitch.

(C) Correct. The rudder affects yaw; it controls the vertical axis of the aircraft.

(D) Incorrect. The spoilers reduce lift, increase drag, and control speed.

(E) Incorrect. The position of the wings adjusts the airflow pressure, controlling lift and drag.

35. (A) Incorrect. The cyclic controls the pitch and roll axis of the aircraft.

(B) Incorrect. The collective changes the pitch of the blades simultaneously.

(C) Incorrect. The tail rotor pedals control the yaw axis of the aircraft.

(D) Incorrect. Translating tendency causes a rotary-wing aircraft to drift laterally due to tail rotor thrust.

(E) Correct. The throttle maintains the engine within optimal flight parameters.

36. (A) Incorrect. The cyclic controls the pitch and roll axis of the aircraft.

(B) Incorrect. The collective changes the pitch of the blades simultaneously.

(C) Correct. The tail rotor pedals control the yaw axis of the aircraft.

(D) Incorrect. Translating tendency causes a rotary-wing aircraft to drift laterally due to tail rotor thrust.

(E) Incorrect. The throttle maintains the engine within optimal flight parameters.

37. (A) Incorrect. The controller did not use the aircraft call sign.

(B) Incorrect. The controller issued an instruction to remain clear of the Class C airspace.

(C) Correct. If the controller responds with "(Aircraft call sign) standby," radio communications have been established, and the pilot can enter the Class C airspace.

(D) Incorrect. The controller did not use the aircraft call sign.

(E) Incorrect. The controller did not use the correct aircraft call sign. The pilot should inquire if there is an aircraft on the frequency with a similar call sign.

38. (A) Incorrect. This instrument displays the altitude.

(B) Incorrect. This instrument displays the heading (degrees) of the aircraft.

(C) Incorrect. This instrument is used as a backup if the heading indicator fails.

(D) Incorrect. This instrument displays the heading of the aircraft.

(E) Correct. This instrument will indeed display if the aircraft is in a climb, in a descent, or in level flight.

39. **(A) Correct.** This climb is used to clear obstacles that may be in the flight path.

(B) Incorrect. This climb is used to cover the most distance, not the most altitude.

(C) Incorrect. This climb will not produce the greatest altitude.

(D) Incorrect. This is not a type of climb.

(E) Incorrect. This is not a type of climb.

40. (A) Incorrect. Ailerons require pilot input.

(B) Incorrect. The nose of the aircraft rises when the tail is pushed down.

(C) Correct. When the elevators are raised, the tail of the aircraft is pushed down, which increases the pitch and raises the nose of the aircraft.

(D) Incorrect. The elevators do not control left turns.

(E) Incorrect. The elevators do not control right turns.

SPATIAL APPERCEPTION

1. **(A)** climbing, no bank, sea on the left

2. **(C)** level flight, banking left, sea on the right

3. **(B)** level flight, banking right, sea on the left

4. **(D)** climbing, no bank, in to land

5. **(E)** climbing, banking left, in to land

6. **(A)** climbing, banking right, in to land

7. **(B)** climbing, no bank, out to sea

8. **(C)** climbing, banking right, out to sea

9. **(B)** level flight, no bank, sea on the left

10. **(D)** climbing, banking right, sea on the left

11. **(B)** level flight, no bank, sea on the right

12. **(E)** climbing, banking left, sea on the right

13. **(D)** level flight, banking left, out to sea

14. **(B)** descending, banking right, out to sea

15. **(C)** descending, banking left, out to sea

16. **(B)** level flight, no bank, in to land

17. **(C)** descending, no bank, in to land

18. **(E)** level flight, banking right, in to land

19. **(E)** climbing, banking left, in to land

20. **(C)** level flight, banking left, in to land

21. **(E)** level flight, no bank, out to sea

22. **(A)** descending, no bank, out to sea

23. **(E)** descending, banking right, in to land

24. **(D)** descending, banking left, in to land

25. **(A)** level flight, banking right out to sea

READING COMPREHENSION

1. (A) Incorrect. The implication of that statement is that eventually people will pay for their misconduct. It is contrary to idealism, which promotes behaving responsibly and offering to make up for any errors.

   (B) Incorrect. This statement expresses pragmatism, which is practical advice for everyday life. The idea expressed is that it's best to move towards your specific goals.

   (C) Correct. Treating others kindly is an ideal; kindness matters the most because it is an ideal truth.

   (D) Incorrect. This statement is also a practical suggestion that knowledge can be gained by asking questions.

   (E) Incorrect. Paying attention to and accepting the ordinary details of life is a realistic viewpoint.

2. (A) Incorrect. The author writes that the officers, not the volunteers, were veterans.

   (B) Incorrect. The passage does not mention a citizenship requirement.

   (C) Incorrect. While most of the volunteers were indeed from the Southwest, the passage does not say this was a requirement.

   (D) Correct. The author writes, "the army set high standards: all of the recruits had to be skilled on horseback…"

   (E) Incorrect. The author does not describe an education requirement.

3. (A) Incorrect. The passage does this; however, the opening sentence indicates the purpose is primarily persuasive. It says, "For an adult person to be unable to swim points to something like criminal negligence," indicating that the authors want people to learn to swim and are trying to convince readers by sharing the benefits.

   (B) Incorrect. Based on the emphatic tone, the authors are identifying the benefits in order to persuade readers.

   (C) Incorrect. There is no indication that people necessarily swim for the reasons provided.

   (D) Correct. The authors indicate that swimming is imperative for safety and exercise.

   (E) Incorrect. This passage is not a personal narrative. It says nothing about the authors' experience; it is the authors' viewpoint.

4. (A) Incorrect. The author provides no evidence that invasive species typically help native species.

   (B) Incorrect. The author writes that the quagga mussels, an invasive species, harmed native species.

   (C) Incorrect. The author implies that quagga mussels are thriving.

   (D) Correct. The author writes that "the reason for the cisco's reemergence is even more unlikely. The cisco have an invasive species, quagga mussels, to thank for their return."

   (E) Incorrect. While the author does describe how quagga mussels are taking nutrients from other invasive species, there is no evidence that this is common.

5. **(A) Correct.** It is probably safe to say that humans do not make the wisest choices, and many living creatures are stronger and faster than humans.

   (B) Incorrect. Nothing in the text suggests that humans will lose superiority.

   (C) Incorrect. It was only one god who gave all the good gifts to living things other than humans; Prometheus made sure that humans were protected.

   (D) Incorrect. This fact is probably the reason it was not one of the "good" gifts, but it is unrelated to the idea suggested by the passage.

(E)   Incorrect. The passage is not about Greek civilization.

6. **(A) Correct.** The context implies that the fighting was intense and tiring.

(B)   Incorrect. The context does not indicate that the fighting was undercover.

(C)   Incorrect. Nothing in the passage addresses the price of the battle.

(D)   Incorrect. The passage indicates nothing about the pattern of fighting.

(E)   Incorrect. The author states that the fighting ultimately led to a US victory.

7. (A)   Incorrect. Although the author begins with the statement that the sunsets are magnificent, the author goes on to provide descriptive details of the sunset on the mountains and lake without giving any specific reasons it is magnificent.

(B)   Incorrect. The sunset is mentioned, but the reader is not told how water reflects light. Details are also included about the light on the mountains and in the sky around the mountains.

(C)   Incorrect. There is no comparison, only description of the colors of the sky and of the light on the water.

(D)   Incorrect. The word "magnificent" has emotional suggestions, but other than that, there is no mention of the emotional impact of the sunset.

(E)   **Correct.** The details are presented spatially from the western sky to the horizon, from the right side of the hills to the midst of the lake, to the shoreline.

8. (A)   Incorrect. While the author does describe his memory loss, this is not the main idea of the passage.

(B)   **Correct.** The author writes, "From this, scientists learned that different types of memory are handled by different parts of the brain."

(C)   Incorrect. The author does explain the differences in long-term and short-term memory formation, but not until the end of the passage.

(D)   Incorrect. While it is implied that memories of physical skills are processed differently than memories of events, this is not the main idea of the passage.

(E)   Incorrect. The author states, "the hippocampus [is] responsible for *episodic memory*, the short-term recall of events," not all memories related to events.

9. (A)   Incorrect. The author discusses plans to study magnetic and gravitational fields on Saturn, not Titan.

(B)   Incorrect. The author writes, "Then it will pass through the unexplored region between Saturn itself and its famous rings." The passage does not mention any rings on Titan.

(C)   **Correct.** The author writes, "…it will record any changes in Titan's curious methane lakes, providing information about potential seasons on the planet-sized moon."

(D)   Incorrect. The author refers to the rings of Saturn, not to Titan, when stating, "Scientists hope to learn how old the rings are."

(E)   Incorrect. The author writes that *Cassini* "will provide scientists with unprecedented information about Saturn's atmosphere," not Titan's.

10. **(A) Correct.** The author writes, "a shoelace knot experiences greater g-force than any rollercoaster can generate," helping the reader understand the strength of the g-force experienced by the knots.

(B)   Incorrect. The author does not describe any actual experiments involving rollercoasters.

(C)   Incorrect. The author does not assess the findings of the experiment.

(D)   Incorrect. The rollercoaster reference is a comparison, not specific evidence.

(E) Incorrect. The reference to rollercoasters is not part of any kind of joke.

11. (A) Incorrect. The author implies that bedbugs transitioned to humans relatively easily.

(B) Incorrect. The author does not address the impact of light on bedbugs.

(C) Incorrect. The author explains that the three discovered species still exist today.

(D) Incorrect. The author does not address the growth rate of bedbug populations.

(E) Correct. The author writes, "Humans only lived seasonally in the Oregon cave system, however, which might explain why these insects did not fully transfer to human hosts like bedbugs elsewhere did."

12. (A) Incorrect. There is no indication that the Bastille was occupied by royalty.

(B) Incorrect. There is no indication that the structure was intended to represent anything.

(C) Incorrect. There is no indication that the Bastille was used for governing.

(D) Correct. The author writes that the Bastille was originally built "to protect the city from English invasion during the Hundred Years' War."

(E) Incorrect. It is clear from the description of the Bastille that it was not hidden or secretive.

13. (A) Incorrect. The passage does not describe the actual artwork at all.

(B) Incorrect. The author names the artist who made the painting but states nothing else about its origin.

(C) Incorrect. While the author does state that there are four versions of the artwork, this is not the primary purpose of the passage.

(D) Correct. The author writes, "*The Scream of Nature* by Edvard Munch is one of the world's best known and most desirable artworks."

(E) Incorrect. The author does name the owners of each version, but this is not the primary purpose of the passage.

14. (A) Incorrect. The text says that people become imaginative, not lost.

(B) Incorrect. Sleepy Hollow is a "region of shadows" where people "dream dreams, and see apparitions," but that does not mean the people live hidden and alone.

(C) Correct. Legendary superstition led to many stories of the headless horseman, and everyone who lives in Sleepy Hollow eventually sees apparitions.

(D) Incorrect. An imaginative person is not necessarily an irrational person.

(E) Incorrect. Based on the text and mention of the headless horseman's visits, Sleepy Hollow is not predictable or in order.

15. **(A) Correct.** The passage describes how the closing of the border affected the geography of the city and the lives of Berliners.

(B) Incorrect. The author does not explain why the border was closed.

(C) Incorrect. The author does not describe the response to the border closing.

(D) Incorrect. The author explains that the East German army closed off West Berlin using barbed wire and fences, but this is not the primary purpose of the passage.

(E) Incorrect. While the author does explain how the border was closed, there is no further discussion of its history.

16. (A) Incorrect. There is no evidence that the protest movement was successful; in fact, the passage implies the opposite.

(B) Incorrect. While the author states that Western countries observed the events in China, there is no evidence they became involved.

(C) Incorrect. There is no evidence in the passage that factory workers had any involvement beyond "cheering on" the protestors.

(D) Incorrect. There is no evidence the government objected to the military's actions.

(E) Correct. The author writes, "it seemed to be the beginning of a political revolution in China, so the world was stunned when, on July 4, Chinese troops and security police stormed the square," stifling any possibility of democratic revolution.

17. (A) Incorrect. The author writes that the protest spread in spite of government attempts to end it.

(B) Incorrect. The author writes, "In Dandi, Gandhi picked up a small chunk of salt and broke British law." Picking up a piece of salt is not itself an extreme act; Gandhi was able to make a big statement with a small action.

(C) Correct. The author describes a situation in which civil disobedience had an enormous impact.

(D) Incorrect. The action the author describes occurred in India when it was controlled by Britain, a colonial and nondemocratic power.

(E) Incorrect. The author explains that this event challenged national law and involved tens of thousands of people throughout the country.

18. (A) Incorrect. While the author states this, it is not the main idea.

(B) Correct. The author states, "Ignored by the government, an activist group known as Indians of All Tribes sailed to Alcatraz in the early morning hours with eighty-nine men, women, and children." The author goes on to describe the nineteen-month occupation of the island.

(C) Incorrect. The author states that up to 600 people joined the occupation.

(D) Incorrect. The author does not describe any violent action towards protestors.

(E) Incorrect. While the author does state this, it is not the main idea of the passage.

19. **(A) Correct.** The author goes on to describe the shared perspectives of these writers.

(B) Incorrect. The author does not indicate the number of writers.

(C) Incorrect. The author provides no context that implies they were an organized group, simply that they shared certain traits.

(D) Incorrect. The author states that they gathered in one place—Paris.

(E) Incorrect. There is no evidence that this was an educational group.

20. (A) Incorrect. The author states that there are few women CEOs in Latin America in the final sentence of the passage; it is not the main idea.

(B) Incorrect. While this fact is stated in the passage, it is not the main idea.

(C) Incorrect. The author writes, "However, these trends do not carry over outside of politics."

(D) Incorrect. The author explains that women have a large amount of political influence but less economic influence.

(E) Correct. The passage discusses the large number of women in political positions in Latin America.

Math Skills

1. **(B)**

   Add the area of the trapezoid and the area of the triangle.

   trapezoid: $A = \frac{h(b_1 + b_2)}{2} = \frac{10(14 + 8)}{2} = 110 \text{ mm}^2$

   triangle: $A = \frac{1}{2}bh = \frac{1}{2}(8)(4\sqrt{3}) = 16\sqrt{3} \text{ mm}^2$

   $110 + 16\sqrt{3} \approx \mathbf{137.7 \text{ mm}^2}$

2. **(D)**

   Write a proportion and then solve for x.

   $\frac{40}{45} = \frac{265}{x}$

   $40x = 11{,}925$

   $x = 298.125 \approx \mathbf{298}$

3. **(A)**

   Simplify each root and add.

   $\sqrt[3]{64} = 4$

   $\sqrt[3]{729} = 9$

   $4 + 9 = \mathbf{13}$

4. **(C)**

   Work backwards to find the number of runners in the competition (c) and then the number of runners on the team (r).

   $\frac{2}{c} = \frac{10}{100}$

   $c = 20$

   $\frac{20}{r} = \frac{25}{100}$

   $\mathbf{r = 80}$

5. **(B)**

   Plug 4 in for j and simplify.

   $2(j - 4)^4 - j + \frac{1}{2}j$

   $2(4 - 4)^4 - 4 + \frac{1}{2}(4) = \mathbf{-2}$

6. **(E)**

   Set up an equation to find the number of people wearing neither white nor blue. Subtract the number of people wearing both colors so they are not counted twice.

   $21 = 7 + 6 + neither - 5$

   $neither = \mathbf{13}$

7. **(D)**

   Simplify using PEMDAS.

   $(5^2 - 2)^2 + 3^3$

   $(25 - 2)^2 + 3^3$

   $(23)^2 + 3^3$

   $529 + 27 = \mathbf{556}$

8. **(A)**

   Use the equation for percentages.

   $part = whole \times percentage = 9 \times 0.25 = \mathbf{2.25}$

9. **(E)**

   Use the two sets of linear angles to find b and then c.

   $a = b$

   $a + b + 70 = 180$

   $2a + 70 = 180$

   $a = b = 55°$

   $b + c = 180°$

   $55 + c = 180$

   $c = \mathbf{125°}$

10. **(D)**

    One way to find the answer is to draw a picture.

    Put 24 cans into groups of 4. One out of every 4 cans is diet (light gray) so there is 1 light gray can for every 3 dark gray cans. That leaves 18 dark gray cans (regular soda).

    Alternatively, solve the problem using ratios.

    $\frac{Regular}{Total} = \frac{3}{4} = \frac{x}{24}$

    $4x = 72$

    $\mathbf{x = 18}$

11. **(D)**

    Simplify using PEMDAS.

    $z^3(z + 2)^2 - 4z^3 + 2$

    $z^3(z^2 + 4z + 4) - 4z^3 + 2$

$z^5 + 4z^4 + 4z^3 - 4z^3 + 2$

$z^5 + 4z^4 + 2$

12. (D)

Find the time that Erica spends on break and subtract this from her total time at work.

$30 + 2(15) = 1$ hour

$8\frac{1}{2} - 1 = 7\frac{1}{2} =$ **7 hours, 30 minutes**

13. (A)

Subtract the amount of the bills from the amount in the checking account.

$792.00 + 84.63 + 112.15 = 988.78$

$2{,}386.52 - 988.78 =$ **\$1,397.74**

14. (E)

All the points lie on the circle, so each line segment is a radius. The sum of the 4 lines will be 4 times the radius.

$r = \frac{75}{2} = 37.5$

$4r =$ **150**

15. (E)

Use FOIL to solve.

$(3x + 2)(3x + 2) = 9x^2 + 6x + 6x + 4 =$

$9x^2 + 12x + 4$

16. (B)

Add together the seats in the cars until there are 20.

$6 + 5 = 11$

$6 + 5 + 5 = 16$

$6 + 5 + 5 + 5 = 21$

They fewest number of cars that will seat 20 people is **4 cars**.

17. (A)

Isolate the variable x on one side of the equation.

$5x - 4 = 3(8 + 3x)$

$5x - 4 = 24 + 9x$

$-4 - 24 = 9x - 5x$

$-28 = 4x$

$\frac{-28}{4} = \frac{4x}{4}$

$x = -7$

18. (E)

Use the formula for percent increase.

$percent\ increase = \frac{amount\ of\ change}{original\ amount} =$

$\frac{3{,}000}{60{,}000} = 0.05 =$ **5%**

19. (B)

Set up an equation. If p is the original number of pears, the store has sold $0.30p$ pears. The original number minus the number sold will equal 455.

$p - 0.30p = 455$

$p = \frac{455}{0.7} =$ **650 pears**

20. (D)

To find the perimeter, add the length of each side to find the total.

$P = 2(10) =$ **20 mm**

MECHANICAL COMPREHENSION

1. **(D) is correct.** When the ropes in the pulleys are crossed, adjacent pulleys rotate in opposite directions. Pulley B is in the middle, so it will be rotating in the opposite direction of the other two pulleys.

2. **(C) is correct.** The blocks will be at rest when the net force on the system is zero, meaning the total weight on the left side of the pulley must be equal to the weight on the right side. Block C needs to be 50 pounds so that there are 70 pounds on both sides of the pulley.

3. **(A) is correct.** Adjacent gears rotate in the opposite directions. Gears 2 and 4 will move in the same direction, and Gears 1 and 3 will both move in the direction that is opposite to Gears 2 and 4.

4. **(B) is correct.** The larger the radius of a pulley, the slower it will turn. Because Pulley C has the largest radius, it will turn the slowest.

5. **(C) is correct.** When the effort is in the middle, a lever is always considered to be a third-class lever.

6. **(D) is correct.** Adjacent gears rotate in opposite directions, so Gears 2 and 4 will rotate in the opposite direction of Gear 3.

7. **(C) is correct.** The tension will be equal to the weight it supports, or 100 N.

8. **(D) is correct.** Steel is a conductor, and wood is an insulator, so the steel object will feel colder. The transfer of heat that makes the ball feel cold occurs because of conductivity, not because of density.

9. **(B) is correct.** Moving the block farther from the brick changes the location of the fulcrum. The weight of the brick will have more torque since it is farther from the fulcrum; therefore it is going to take more force to lift. The increase in distance also will lift the board higher than before.

10. **(B) is correct.** The theoretical mechanical advantage is the total number of ropes that are in contact with the load, so the advantage is 2.

11. **(A) is correct.** Since the force is constant, the acceleration on the block increases as the horizontal component of the force increases. The force has the greatest horizontal component when the angle is zero degrees.

12. **(C) is correct.** The gear that will mesh with Gear C needs to have the opposite orientation and be similar in size. The only gear that meets these conditions is Gear E.

13. **(B) is correct.** The net force on the object will be zero, so the mass is in equilibrium.

14. **(E) is correct.** The total force on each of the blocks is the same, so the block with the most springs will have the smallest force per spring. Block B's spring will experience the greatest force, then Block A's, and then Block C's.

15. **(A) is correct.** The weight is evenly distributed on both sides of the object. Because B and C are helping each other carry the weight on the right side, A is bearing the most weight.

16. **(B) is correct.** The screw will hit the contact point for each bump in the cam, so the screw will hit the contact point twice per turn. There are two turns, so the screw will hit the contact point a total of four times.

17. **(C) is correct.** Each rotation of the arm rotates the disc to the next slot. This disc rotates a third of a turn for each rotation of the arm. If the arm turns three times, the disc performs one complete turn.

18. **(C) is correct.** The mass of an object is constant. The weight of an object depends on the force of gravity that the object experiences. The gravity of the moon is less than Earth's, so Object B will have the same mass but a smaller weight.

19. **(B) is correct.** The board is balanced when the net torque is zero, meaning the torque from each block is equal.

$$T_1 = T_2$$
$$F_1 l_1 = F_2 l_2$$
$$40(3) = 60 l_2$$
$$l_2 = \frac{120}{60} = \textbf{2 ft.}$$

20. **(E) is correct.** To make air flow in the desired direction, open a valve on the opposite path. This causes a difference in pressure that will keep the air flowing on the desired path. To make the air flow through the top path, open all the valves on the bottom: 5, 6, and 7.

Go to **www.triviumtestprep.com/sift-online-resources** to access your second SIFT practice test and other online study resources.

Made in the USA
Middletown, DE
17 November 2019

78763461R00115